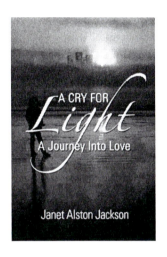

A CRY FOR LIGHT
A Journey Into Love

by

Janet Alston Jackson

A CRY FOR LIGHT
A Journey Into Love

Janet Alston Jackson

A Cry for Light: A Journey into Love may be purchased on the website:

www.JanetAJackson.com

The Library of Congress has catalogued this paperback edition as follows:
Jackson, Janet Alston
A Cry for Light: A Journey into Light / Janet Alston Jackson (paper)
LCCN 2005904441 May 2005
ISBN 0-9634086-1-5

1. parenting
2. adoption
3. African-American
4. memoir

Book design by Cathi Stevenson

THIS BOOK IS DEDICATED *to the thousands*
of foster children and adoptees -- you are indeed special!

To the mental health professionals and child welfare workers
who make a difference in a child's life.

To the foster parents and adoptive parents
who have cried out for light.

Gail,
Keep spreading
your light — you've helped
so many people

ACKNOWLEDGEMENTS

Thank you to my husband Walter for your love, incredible strength, direction, and for always believing in me, and insisting that I follow my dreams. You know you're my hero.

To my children Ryan and Jada for your endless sacrifices, love, and understanding. To my sister Chanetta, and Aunt Queen, for always being there for me. To my brother Geramy for always holding the light. To my mother Evelyn for your love that has always lifted me.

To my son Devon -- For your courage in turning your life around, and for wanting your story to be told to help others.

So many people have been my angels along this journey called life -- too many to mention here. So, I will just name the ones who have walked with me to tell this story.

To my magic eyes whom I met at "The Eye," (CBS Television Network): Dan Bagott, my editor, who spent many painstaking hours hovering with me and this manuscript over a coffee shop table. To Jill Lessard for your proofreading and cheerleading.

To Carolyn Monroe, Claudine Harris, Suzanne Gordon, Velvatine Sykes, Gail White, Kathie Maxwell, Pamelia Davis and Ernie and Carolyn Thornton who have been my sounding boards, and supported me as I vented my frustrations over navigating the system.

To my spiritual teachers Eiko Michi and Pisit, who quietly showed me through example how to stop venting and start meditating.

To the village of professionals who helped me and Walt to guide Devon: The Hathaway outpatient team; The UCLA Ties Adoption team including Evelyn Wright. To our dynamic and fearless educational advocate, Lori Waldinger. To our understanding IEP team John Donato and Dr. Gallinot.

To a super IEP team; John Donato, Department of Mental Health and Debbie J. Gallinot, Ph.D., Los Angeles Unified School District.

To the incredible Devereux Treatment Team who helped our family to heal, and reassured me that I wasn't crazy: Diane Collins, Annie Kissoondath, Michael Berno, Ph.D., Paul Friery, Broderick Frank, Maggie Losoya, Mark Thomas, and Holden James.

To my Higher Power -- my constant companion on this journey. Need I say more?

Janet Alston Jackson
Los Angeles, CA
May 2005

FOREWORD

What a journey!

Janet Jackson drew me into the journey of reading this insightful, painful, and ultimately hopeful book. I found that at times I wanted to read faster so that I could get to the next chapter. "A Cry FOR LIGHT: A Journey into Love" could only have been written by someone intimately familiar with, and living with, a person who had experienced early life trauma which resulted in an impairment in, and a fragmentation of, his capacity to love... to develop trust... to recognize the need for others in his life. As thousands of families attempt to help a child, to build a family, many of them share Jackson's experiences. Many of them would not describe their journey as being one "into love" but rather of being one into pain, conflict, hurt, rejection, frustration, and yes, for some a journey even into hell.

Each day of my life I sit with families struggling to improve the quality of their journeys; many are quite successful, yet others suffer in relative isolation as they continue to ask themselves countless, and sometimes pointless, questions: Why me? Why us? What were we thinking? Should we have known? Why weren't we prepared? These could go on for pages. All express the suffering people experience as they attempt to enter a hurt child's life. What is so beautiful about Jackson's sharing is that while her journey did include stops at horrible rest areas along the road, she finally does reach her destination with the child she loved so much *and* with the child loving her.

Jackson's family endured much pain and suffering, about which she eloquently shares. I do not think that I have ever read a book in which the author shared so much about her reality. I have not met Janet, but I feel that I know her so well. Her pain, her hope, her love, her brilliance, her dark side, her faith, her husband Walt, her children Ryan, Jada and Devon, are all here, so alive. Her gift of writing draws the reader into her experiences, triggering emotions as well as thoughts.

I found that I shared her anger at "the system" as it failed so many; as a parent I shared her hope when mere glimmers of light appeared. As she traipsed through airports, to team meetings, etc., I shared her fatigue. I feel that readers, particularly those in adoptive families and foster families, those who work in child welfare, and other professionals who understand the difficulty of living with severely damaged children, will know that Jackson has taken a journey.

Families need to remember that their child is a work in progress. Readers of this book will find that this progress is not always forward. Progress in human development includes all of the following: forward movement, plateaus, regressions, and forward movement. This pattern goes on throughout the lifespan. Jackson brilliantly integrates these elements in her organization of the book. There are "throw in the towel" chapters; there are "we have finally arrived chapters," and there are "here we go again!" chapters. Much like the life of a child – "he's walking" or "now he's not!" "He's potty trained!" "Oops, another accident!" Human development happens like this, and when families "hang in there" and do what they need to do, they may find that they, like Jackson, reach their destination.

I think that "A CRY FOR LIGHT" will help prepare families who choose to embark on helping hurt children. It will provide a great reality check for those families already in the middle of something they had no idea they would be facing. Professionals who place disturbed children in families will get an inside look as to why so many families adopting children with high levels of disturbance look so crazy AFTER a placement has been made. I've heard so many professionals say, "These people looked great while we were studying their home. I wonder what happened to them?" Well, join Janet, Walt, Ryan, Devon, and Jada on their journey into love. I know that you will wonder no more.

GREGORY C. KECK, Ph.D.
Founder, Director
Attachment and Bonding Center of Ohio
Co-author of *Adopting the Hurt Child &
Parenting the Hurt Child*

AUTHOR'S NOTES

The Los Angeles Department of Children and Family Services has made tremendous strides over the years since our family was first introduced to the agency in the early 1990's when this story begins.

Back then, DCFS, the largest child welfare system in the nation, was an embattled agency, overburdened with 50,000 children who were wards of the court. These children were taken from their homes because of abuse and neglect. Today approximately 26,000 children are in out-of-home placement under DCFS' protective care.

I believe that this significant reduction of children in the system is partly due to the tremendous changes made in DCFS with new policies, leadership, and laws that have helped perfect the department. But especially because of the tireless work of dedicated social workers who have found thousands of children permanent homes and reunited others with their families.

Today, I have tremendous respect and admiration for all of those at the Department of Children and Family Services who are trying to protect children. Back then, I had a very different opinion.

This book was written with the purpose that we must never forget what happens to a child like many across the country, who have been trapped, abused, lost, and forgotten in the child welfare system. It's still happening across the country today.

The names and other identifying characteristics of certain persons depicted in this book have been changed in order to protect their privacy and dignity.

Janet Alston Jackson
Los Angeles, CA

CHAPTER ONE

Driving the steep, winding road into Angeles National Forest was like orbiting into outer space. I was traveling only 25 miles per hour, but my mind raced at rocket speeds. Our green mini-van snaked around the chaparral-covered mountain, passing looming, jagged rock walls that reminded me of the moon. The drive reflected the last 12 years of my life. A lonely, treacherous climb into uncharted territories.

I knew where the road was taking me physically, but not mentally. What would the future hold?

My 14-year-old son, Devon, sitting next to me, was motionless. He stared straight ahead as the pine and fir-covered slopes blurred past our windows. His fate was at hand. He didn't believe that I would follow through. I didn't believe it, either.

The wind buffeted the sides of the car as we passed bright yellow sunflowers waving from their spindly stalks, animating the still life picture around us.

Like a mummy waking from the dead, Devon slowly reached his caramel hand to turn on the radio as if to drown out my avalanche of thoughts. But we were traveling in silence. Neither of us knew what to say.

Ahead, another cluster of mountains came into view. They stood like an ancient ghost family that quietly watched over us as we drove deeper into Los Angeles' 650,000 acre backyard playground.

I caught a glimpse of life on the curving road. A few squirrels scampered among the bushes, a small lizard sunned on a rock, and a hawk glided gracefully above us. The mountains reminded me of the isolation my husband Walter and I had felt for so long. No one else seemed

1

to understand our painful life with Devon. People simply offered empty, impractical advice that even they wouldn't follow.

The hum of the motor was drowned by radio static and snippets of songs that faded in and out as Devon switched stations, determined to find reception. A few irritating minutes later he found a strong signal on his favorite oldies-but-goodies station that played mostly '60s hits. Devon loved that period. He once told me that he should have been born then. But even he was too wild for that rebellious hippie era. Devon never seemed to fit into the world around him. He was years ahead in intellect for his age, but years behind in emotional maturity.

As we continued climbing the narrow roads, an old Marvin Gaye-Tammy Terrell duet wafted from the radio. It was strange that at such a scary time we both hummed a few bars, and softly sang the few words that we knew. Looking back, the music was probably grounding us, keeping our tightly wound nerves from snapping on that drive. We both remembered the chorus and sang it together.

"Ain't no mountain high enough, ain't no river low enough to keep me from getting to you, babe."

"That's dedicated to you, D," I said with tears brimming in my eyes thinking of our past and his fate ahead. I had already climbed too many mountains of despair and swam in too many rivers of tears raising him. He grinned at me with a cynical look, then snapped his head forward, tapping his leg in time to the music, shutting me and my emotions out. I could feel his tension as he softly hummed after the song was over. Music had always been his salvation. It was the only harmony in his life of constant chaos.

I couldn't believe the coincidence. I hadn't heard that song for years but it was the second time that it came on the radio within an hour. Earlier, we heard Diana Ross belting out her rendition as we were finishing last-minute errands before going into the forest. What were the odds of hearing this song twice? But it was symbolic of our life together. I had spent the last 12 years rescuing Devon, going through hell trying to save him from himself, but still I lost him. I had been willing to do whatever it took to help him, including dragging him to 21 different therapists. No treatment worked, which was why we were taking the drive on this day.

Except for his humming, he was silent. Devon knew what was coming. I had warned him, and the day had finally arrived.

We continued ascending, passing jagged cliffs overlooking the valley once roamed by the Gabrielino Indians. I could feel their souls in those mountains. I wished that I could have talked to them -- learned from their ancient wisdom. I was taking Devon into their mountain home. I thought of the sacrifice those Indian families must have made fighting to keep their land. I, too, was going through a family sacrifice to keep my home.

Devon and I never thought this day would come. I had cajoled, threatened, and bribed him to cooperate, to stop defying authority. The emotional ravage he had heaped on the family was devastating. We constantly suffered battle fatigue. It felt like we were sleeping with the enemy. I stayed on my knees praying, begging God to straighten him out. Why couldn't he be like my other two children? Clearly, he was spitefully different. Devon seemed possessed by demons. I didn't believe in them, but still I found myself wondering. Did this child need an exorcist? His mind worked counter clockwise to the universe. His time had run out.

Now on July 3, 2001, after years of being held hostage to Devon's antics, Independence Day had come a day early for me. It was time to break away from him.

We turned off Little Tujunga Road to Gold Creek Road and followed a winding, sharp turn with signs posted. Ten miles per hour. Navigating this narrow passage that overlooked a thousand foot drop, doubts surfaced about the mission that I was on. But I was not going to turn back now. Not now. I couldn't.

It wasn't an easy decision to take this ride. It ripped me apart like paper going through a shedder. I prayed that the result would result in wholeness for our family. I craved to find the part of me that I had left behind years ago. Because of Devon, I had become an uptight bitch who had long ago lost her joy.

Today I was about to start a new chapter in my life. I was giving up trying to find my happiness through an ideal family. I was giving up trying to stay in control. I was giving up battling with Devon, who was even more controlling than I was. I needed to give it all up to God, who had the real control.

3

We passed a dry riverbed with another sign- -"Flooding." Ten minutes later, we had reached the mountaintop, our destination. Suddenly my breathing became shallow and my palms sweaty. Perspiration poured down my back. I wished that my husband, Walter, was with us. But as fate would have it, his mother was desperately sick, and he was 300-plus miles to the north, in Stockton, California, taking care of her. This was something I would have to do alone.

I slid out of the front seat inhaling the pine scents of Christmas on this hot summer day. Each year in these same mountains our family cut down our Christmas tree. The air was thin and still. It was exceptionally quiet like the day after the holy day when everyone is exhausted from shopping and festivities. But this was no holiday.

Devon ambled out of the car and stood next to me as I looked around. He was nearly my height, handsome and slim in his oversized jeans and green plaid shirt. He flashed me his ever-present grin. I never could figure out if that meant he was in pain or happy. I always felt that it was really his mask.

I smiled at him and took a deep breath. A sudden gust of dry California wind ruffled my hair and the bushes surrounding us. I felt it was God's gentle hand pushing me forward as he whispered, "Don't turn back now."

I looked over toward the scattered, pastel one-story structures that seemed oddly out of place. I pointed and led our way toward the two-tone green building with a sign, "Administration."

As we walked, I stole a glance at Devon. I wished that he would register at least some little bit of remorse or grief in his blank, brown eyes.

"How are you feeling?" I asked.

"Fine." I knew that he wasn't, but I had to ask. "Okay" and "fine" were his stock answers. Devon had taught himself long ago not to feel. Not to trust.

I tried swallowing my sadness. My steps became more deliberate, pounding the pavement to suppress my anxiety. I had a mission to do.

When we reached the building, I pushed open the double glass doors holding them for Devon. He walked slowly and solemnly past me into the residential treatment facility.

How could it have come to this? Why?

CHAPTER TWO

For years I held onto Devon like I was dangling with him from the side of a cliff with bloodied fingers, refusing to let him or me slip into the African-American stereotypes: the young boy who won't behave and the mother who doesn't care.

Like most parents, the way I was raising Devon was a reflection of my own childhood. I was also following my inner voice and intuition, which have always fascinated and terrified me.

When I was a little girl, I was amazed when I sensed something wonderful about to happen. Other times, I was terrified of the heavy feeling that began like a slithering eel in the depths of my stomach, forewarning of a cursed future.

As a child, I couldn't make out the lingering prophesies of gloom. But these premonitions always made me nauseous as they escalated. Waves of darkness haunted me and warned that something ominous was about to happen, and it always did.

I was often plagued by these sensations as an only child growing up in the 1950's on the South Side of Chicago. This was the time the Windy City's black population was 22,000 and growing. Thousands of African-Americans were moving to the city every week.

The South Side had become the capital of Black America as the Harlem Renaissance was fading. Droves of blacks from the Mississippi Delta were migrating into Chi Town, looking for better economic opportunities in defense factories and meat packing plants. With them, they brought the blues. Muddy Waters, who moved to Chicago in 1943, and other great artists were part of the Chicago Blues sound that was a style unique with horns and electric guitars. I have always hated the blues. Maybe it was because my premonitions and the events that followed kept me blue enough.

In October, 1955, my Uncle Bill bought a two-story home with his wife, Queen. Bill, who stood five feet, six inches with cocoa skin, was a concerned and caring man who was always trying to help someone. It was his life's mission. Queen, an ebony beauty, personified her name, which she vehemently disliked.

The mid-'50s was the time the Chicago Housing Authority was constantly trying to integrate blacks into white neighborhoods. Many, if not all, of the CHA efforts were met by strong opposition, such as riots by prejudiced whites, which my family knew about first hand.

Bill and Queen Davis had just moved with their six-year-old daughter, Adrienne, into their new home when they were terrorized by firecrackers constantly exploding in their front and back yards. It was the acts of hostile whites living in the apartment house next door. They were enraged that the Davises dared to integrate the neighborhood, plus they were bitter with envy. How could a black family afford a large, two-story home when they were still renting?

The Davises were also harassed by reports made to the authorities: "Five families have moved into the house," which, of course, was not true. "They're adding on to the house without building permits." That wasn't true either. Undaunted by the torment, my uncle, a hard-working maintenance man for an elementary school, and Queen, a secretary for the federal government, refused to move. They had spent too many years scrimping and saving to get the house of their dreams. Their sacrifice was not going to be in vain.

Uncle and Auntie knew what they were up against even before they moved in. A few blocks away, on 75th Street, whites were burning black homes. In the other direction, another integrating black couple was beaten and their house burned.

Before they bought, Auntie had a talk with the seller, an elderly white widow.

"I hope that's not what is going to happen to us if we buy this house," said Queen, trying to feel the woman out.

"Oh no. We took a vote in the neighborhood," the white-haired woman replied.

"We all agreed to sell out to you people."

I was three -years-old when mom and dad moved us into the Davis's second story, which had been converted into a spacious two-bedroom apartment. It was just months after Uncle and Auntie settled in and, fortunately, I was sheltered from the prejudice, which soon afflicted our neighborhood with massive white flight. We lived in the Chatham section, which quickly morphed into a black middle-class neighborhood. It reflected the hopes of many African-Americans in those days. Chicago was the land of opportunity.

I often heard my mother, Evelyn Alston, a slim, attractive, copper-toned woman, bragging to her visiting friends about our black professional neighbors.

"We've got two doctors, a policeman, several teachers, and a fireman living on our block," she said, beaming. "Mahalia Jackson lives just a few blocks away." Jackson, then the most celebrated gospel singer in the world, lived in a large, corner ranch-style home. Often I would fly by her house on my bike to see if I could get a peek at her, only to meet someone's loose mean collie, who patrolled the streets chasing us kids away.

Chicago in the '50s was a city where a black person could prosper and be somebody. Joe Louis, the heavyweight-boxing champion of the world and the most famous black man in America, and William Dawson, the only black member of Congress, both called Chicago home during that time. The Defender, the most prominent black newspaper in the country, and the ground breaking magazines Negro Digest and Ebony- -"The magazine by us for us"-- were all published in Chicago. At the same time, Olivet Baptist Church, the largest black congregation in the country, was vying for souls in the Windy City along with the Black Muslims, who had recently moved their headquarters from Detroit.

The South Side had a half-dozen shopping districts. The grandest was 47th Street, filled with department stores, banks, nightclubs, and movie houses. It was in this part of town where such nationally known black institutions as the Regal Theater, the Savoy Ballroom, and the Hotel Grand were located.

Almost every Saturday, Mom took me to enjoy the latest feature film and a top stage show at the Regal or the Tivoli Theater. For 50 cents, we could both get in to see a blockbuster movie and a music great such as Ella Fitzgerald, Ray Charles, Duke Ellington, Sarah Vaughn, Lionel Hampton, Dinah Washington, and my favorite, Pearl Bailey, performing live. Looking back, these Saturday afternoon shows were probably the reason why I later gravitated to a career in show business.

Living and growing up in this progressive Chicago neighborhood gave me a sense of black pride and values that I would later try to instill in Devon and my other children. I didn't want them thinking our history consisted only of being slave descendants and the targets of beatings in the Civil Rights Era, or that we are just the relentless images of angry black men arrested on the 6 O'clock news.

I grew up surrounded by progressive black role models who gave me a spiritual sense of knowing that I, too, am somebody. I would later use that pride to transcend any labels society tried to put on me and any opportunities that I may have been denied because of my color. I knew the truth and I wanted my children to know it too. We were much more than the media images depicting us as shiftless, lazy "niggers" who kill one another.

My Chicago roots molded me with rigid, unwavering values that would not allow me to accept anything less from my children or me. I developed a strong ego that became my two-headed dragon. The Midwestern hard work ethic coupled with racial pride would navigate me through career obstacles. But my ego was also self-righteous, filled with false perceptions. It was the runaway horse that dragged me behind it. Throughout life, I sometimes was the fallen rider who refused to let go of the ego reins. I had yet to learn the spiritual lesson that the ego and its attachments work counterproductive to one's higher power.

I guess as a child I felt the anger that would sometimes sweep over me when I was busy communing with nature. I even tried outrunning that feeling. I flew down our long driveway and raced the wind on my shiny sky-blue-and-silver Monarch bike. I often imagined that I had become the bike's brand name, flying down the middle of the residential streets like a real butterfly. Still there was no escape. The anxiety would persist intermittently for a couple of days until the news matched my unease: "Uncle Fred died today," "Uncle Jerome didn't make it," "Janet, your grandmother is gone," or "Aunt Sis has gone to heaven," "Aunt Ethel passed." A lot of deaths occurred in my family when I was young. I felt frightened, but it would be years before I learned that I was going through feelings of abandonment and suppressed grief.

The grief I felt often was overpowered by the scary feeling of having known something that even the adults didn't know. When I was told someone had passed away, and I reflected on the feeling that came weeks before, it felt like I was running happily in a meadow chasing butterflies when suddenly I encountered a cliff, nearly falling off. As a child, I felt that death meant falling off the earth.

Looking back on all those premonitions, I now see that the great outdoors gave me balance. The baby squirrels, the new blossoms, and buds represented birth, new life, which I needed to keep me from drowning in morbid thoughts of death.

I never told anyone about those premonitions, especially not Mom. She didn't need any more bad news. She had too much pressure and worry over my dad, who had diabetes and constant, near-fatal asthma attacks. It was during these times I felt most lonely. Now I realize that I was trying to suppress my rage.

"How could anyone be so sick and look so good?"

Those were the sentiments echoing among our family and friends about Daddy. The one word I heard most to describe Hurley Alston was jolly. His boisterous laugh could lift a crowded room and often did. He was a large, handsome man with café latte skin, dancing eyes, and dancing feet. One of his favorite pastimes was twirling my mom and other women around on the dance floor at one of the many parties the Davis and Alston clans hosted in our large basement.

Some of my favorite moments with him at these parties were when I would step up on Dad's big brown shoes, holding his strong legs tightly to keep from falling. Gently he would take my hands, balancing me. Once I was stabilized and smiling up at him, Daddy would then move us gingerly around the dance floor in time to the music as everyone smiled at us and clapped. It was the attention and the wonderful feeling of gliding with Daddy as he laughed and danced that gave me joy. I felt secure and so happy. I felt like I was dancing with God.

The Davis-Alston parties were the happening place, and often the entire block attended these soirees that were thrown for no particular occasion. Dazzling female guests arrived in a rainbow of different colored satin and lace evening dresses with taffeta linings, sexy fitted bodices, and strapped stiletto pointed-toe shoes. I marveled at these glamorous women, especially my mother, who twirled their foot-long cigarette holders like movie stars. Mom, whom I thought was the prettiest woman in the world, had a black and silver one which I secretly played with when she was away at work as an underwriter for Great American Insurance Company.

The men arriving at the parties, dressed in earth-tone suits, were impressive in their matching wool fedora hats, which they handed to me since I was the pretend hatcheck girl, even getting tips. Often I would carefully try on their hats, remembering the warnings as I gently laid them aside from the coats to keep them from being crushed.

Everyone was dressed up compared to the casual block parties that were organized each year on our street. The neighbors would get the city to block off the 7900 block of Indiana, and there would be about 20 card tables filled with food, stretching nearly a half block.

Daddy loved cooking for these get-togethers almost as much as he loved cracking jokes and dancing. But once the parties in our basement were in full swing, he would quietly slip away to bed. In a few hours, he would rise in the wee hours of the morning, dressed in his whites, to take two buses and the El train north to the swank Peach Tree restaurant where he worked as the head chef.

He made good money, although he had very few days off in the year, and the hours were long and grueling. His commute was especially difficult in the dead of cold Chicago winters. "The Hawk got me today, baby," he would say to me with his rosy cheeks looking like they were on fire.

I loved being the center of my father's attention. Often when I returned home from school, he would sneak a nondescript brown bag on top of my bed. Delighted, I would open it up to find some small toy. On his days off, he would cook me my favorite breakfast, French toast sprinkled with powdered sugar. It seemed that Doris Day's hit song, "Que Sera Sera," was always playing on the radio. It was hokey but better than the blues. I hummed along as my eyes were glued to Daddy as he moved gracefully around the kitchen like a Tai Chi master. He mesmerized me. Nothing pleased me more than to hear his nickname for me. "Here you are, Angel Cake," he would say, smiling as he placed the seductive smelling French toast in front of me with a glass of milk.

Aside from the deaths and the premonitions, I was a happy child, living a care-free life until one day in the winter of 1962 when my world crashed. I was 10 years old, trudging through calf-high snow coming home from school alone. I remember turning onto our street and seeing a crowd and an ambulance with rotating red, flashing lights in front of our tan bungalow. As I got closer, two men in white were wheeling daddy into the ambulance. The adult neighbors and kids snapped their heads, looking so strangely at me when I approached the crowd. They were eerily quiet. I can remember for some odd reason being embarrassed. There had never been anything like this happening on our block before, and I didn't know how to react. "Your dad fell out on the sidewalk," said Adrienne, her dark eyes wide behind her cat-eyed, black-rimmed glasses.

In the days ahead, I felt like I was swimming through sludge, trying to understand the gloomy feeling that engulfed me. Daddy was still in the hospital when my mother and I sat on our green sofa, talking about our future. My skin crawled. Suddenly she pointed her sharp Cherokee nose upward, a trait from her Native American grandmother, as she tried fruitlessly blinking back tears.

"We're moving to Los Angeles."

Los Angeles? I had been there twice on family vacations and had fallen in love with the palm trees and bright, pastel-colored buildings. They were a stark contrast to the dark old brick buildings in Chi-Town that looked dirty in comparison. But I wasn't sure about moving to L.A. forever, even for Disneyland. I would have to leave the Davises and all of my friends. But, we had no choice. Doctors said that Daddy's latest severe asthma attack meant he wouldn't last another winter in the freezing Chicago weather.

I sat there flashing on a few weeks earlier going Christmas shopping with Daddy downtown. Light, fluttering snowflakes fell on my nose, tickling it as we trudged through the snow, chattering about what to buy Mom. I held Daddy's third finger since I had always found it hard to entirely grip his big hand. All of a sudden, he stopped walking and talking. I looked up at his face as he pulled away his hand, which flew to his chest. His ever-present rosy checks were drained to gray-blue and his brown eyes were filled with panic. His head flew backward and dropped forward as he gasped for air.

"Daddy, what's wrong?"

He couldn't talk as he stumbled backward into the doorway of a closed flower shop.

"I'll get help," I said, turning to call someone, but he grabbed my coat pulling me back toward him, shaking his head no. He leaned against the door gasping. I was terrified as he fumbled in his beige coat pocket for his nebulizer, the lifesaver. So many times in our apartment, I had to run into his bedroom to get that little contraption and bring it to him so that he could get air. But he was never so desperate as I saw him this day.

Quickly he jammed the glass tube into his mouth, sucking on it violently as he pumped the gray rubber bulb on the other end. After a few minutes of wheezing his breathing slowly changed from labored to long, deep breaths. Eventually the color returned to his strained face. His frown that was foreign to me now disappeared. It seemed hundreds of busy Christmas shoppers rushed by as he struggled to breathe, but no one seemed to notice -- or they chose not to get involved. We never did finish our shopping that day. We took the El train home, riding all the long way in silence.

A few years later, after we moved to Los Angeles to be in the climate most conducive to Dad's ailments, he died from another asthma attack.

Now, when I look back on that shopping trip and the ambulance, I realize that was the beginning of my emotional growth, the end of my innocence. The emerging caretaker and the woman-child within would take over in the days ahead. All the while, I would wish that I could have back the childhood that I left behind. But the laughter, the joys of the early carefree childhood years, would be locked away in the vault of my mind, almost unreachable.

Leaving Chicago would be the beginning of a journey inside myself searching for the lost joy from the family life that I left behind in the

Windy City. That quest, that yearning to fill the family gap, would lead me into a tumultuous venture ahead, hoping for my own family one day. It would take me decades to realize that what I was searching for was not so much people but God's loving energy that was channeled through them. It was that love of my eternal father/mother God that was always inside of me, which I thought I had lost as a child. I didn't know that the years ahead, raising my own family, would be a painful, treacherous journey toward this revelation.

CHAPTER THREE

All of the abandonment and demons from my childhood that I had tried to suppress growing up would again surface to be healed when I first met Devon in 1990. Little did I know then that I had some deep issues to clean up in my life. I also had no clue that Devon would be my mirror and become the instrument for my healing, my greatest teacher.

Like many other middle-class blacks, my husband Walter and I had moved from the city of Los Angeles to the suburbs in 1986, leaving neighborhoods like South Central, which were quickly being integrated by young Latino immigrants. The population then in South Central was dramatically swinging from black to brown.

In 1980, there were 30,000 gang members in Los Angeles County and by 1998, there would be an estimated 150,000. Gangs had started dealing heavily in narcotics in 1983, two years before our oldest son Ryan was born. Crack cocaine was the new drug, and the gangs -- black, Asian, and Latino -- were reaping thousands of dollars literally overnight.

The drug problem in South Central was growing fast in 1996. I had no idea that the effects of drugs were about to seep into our suburban home 30 miles away.

Walt and I seemed to be living the American Dream in the suburbs with our four-year-old son, Ryan. The only thing we didn't have was the white picket fence. Back then, I was working as a publicist for the ABC Television Network after having been with CBS for 14 years. Walt was a realtor then and Ryan was a happy, rambunctious preschooler. His feet never hit the floor except to change directions. We were the picture of the typical All-American middle-class family, sitting in our two-story house with two cars parked out front.

I'd like to think that since we moved into our home on February 14th it was Walt's Valentine gift to me. But actually, it was his peace offering to save our marriage. After several years of begging and pleading with him to find us a home and being jealous of his clients that he put in their new homes, I had had enough. I was still on maternity leave from CBS when I packed my bags and took Ryan to San Diego while Walt was at work.

For days, Walt didn't know where we were hiding out. I was contemplating leaving him for good. Tensions had been running high. The stress of a colicky newborn and postpartum blues was holding me hostage. I felt imprisoned in our cramped, one-bedroom that was located on a busy, noisy corner. Some evenings it was like trying to sleep at the side of a freeway.

Evidently my stand worked. Walt later told me that he was going crazy with the thought of losing his family. While we were gone, he cruised in his car for hours praying for directions to find some affordable house when he came upon a tract of new homes. He found the perfect place for us in picturesque Sylmar, a Los Angeles suburb nestled in the foothills. It's called horse country because it has the largest equestrian population in the Los Angeles area.

The new homes were being built over wild strawberry fields, although the
development project was abandoned several times by the builders because of so many rattlesnakes. The homes were a few months from being finished, but the entire tract had been sold when Walt found the project. God had answered his prayers. One of the houses had just fallen out of escrow so Walt quickly made a down payment. Communicating through my mother, he convinced me to come back to him and to see our new home. Satisfied that my point was made and that things between us had changed, I returned. When Walt took me to see the house, I didn't even have to look inside; instantly I was home.

The peace and the quiet of the house's location was the main attraction for me. The neighborhood was extremely peaceful. There were no screeching brakes or honking horns, just the rustling of leaves from soft winds and chirping birds. Our friends who came to visit from fast-paced L.A. said they felt like they were on vacation visiting us, or they had stepped back in time.

Our community was a United Nations. Blacks, whites, Latinos and Asians lived cohesively side by side. Horseback riders in cowboy hats and boots waited patiently for a streetlight to change. Screeching peacocks strutted slowly across the roads, holding up cars. At night, coyotes and possums strayed from their hillside homes in the Angeles Forest, a half a block away, to raid our trash cans. And then there was the neighborhood's old owl who frequently sat on people's warmed chimneys, hooting a lullaby into the night sky that was sometimes streaked with a shooting star.

Back then, we didn't have a clue that the contentment we were feeling would be short-lived. No one could have told us that we wouldn't enjoy true tranquility in our home again for at least another 12 years.

It all began on a brisk Sunday in January 1990, when an invisible force brought Devon into our lives. I called that force my higher power, but years later, as things got worse in our house, I doubted that a loving God could have brought us together.

I remember sitting with Walt on our beige flowered sofa, one of the nicest pieces of furniture we owned, but totally impractical with Ryan, a pre schooler with jelly fingers, around. We were contently watching the evening news, being the news junkies that we are, feeling secure and happy about life. Through that little box, we watched the world spin in turmoil.

Homicides dominated the airwaves that night. Murders had been increasing steadily in Los Angeles since 1985 because of the drug traffic. But between the commercials for the best whitener for your clothes and the best whitener for your teeth, a public service announcement sponsored by Department of Children and Family Services (DCFS) flashed on television. Little did we know that city life, and the effects of drugs that we saw on the evening news, was about to catch up to us.

Singer Marilyn McCoo, then ranked as one of the top 10 black female vocalists on the pop charts, was asking families to adopt the cute little sad faces that flashed on the screen. She seemed to be talking directly to me. At first, I thought it was because we knew one another. I

17

had been the publicist on her CBS television mid-season variety series, "The Marilyn McCoo and Billy Davis Show." But I know now that it was because my spiritual fate was beckoning me through Marilyn's closing words, "and you, too, can adopt."

As I look back on that day, something went off inside of us. We were being lured into the dark underworld of abused and abandoned children, many who would come from South Central, fugitives of the drug epidemic.

The next day we called DCFS, high with hopes of adding a new family member to our home. But within weeks, we felt like we were walking in Antarctica's waist-deep snow. The agonizing, slow steps through the frigid-cold world of the county's processing system was enough to freeze anyone's efforts. Still we were undaunted. Our perseverance was rewarded when we were sent an invitation from DCFS to an adoption party. I was floating on a cloud.

I have a vivid memory of that party on February 11, 1990. Miraculously, everything huge for us always seemed to happen in February, our power month. Walt and I met in February, we moved into our house in February, we bought a car in February, and now we were looking for a second child in February.

We just knew our lives were going to change that day. We were excited having decided to look for a demure three-year-old girl, which was Walt's suggestion. She would balance out our family, especially Ryan, who never sat still. I swore that he had a fire in his little buns. A three-year-old girl would be in the natural order. A year younger than Ryan and a hell of a lot more calm.

Outside our window, it was the kind of day where you could almost see into other dimensions. A tantalizing light breeze and crystal, aquamarine sky. I could almost hear the Universal Presence quietly birthing life. Inside our home that Sunday, we were riding waves of joy. I smiled, hearing tiny footsteps pattering toward our bedroom where I was dressing, followed by the sound of a small fist beating on the closed door.

"Hurry up, Mommy! Daddy says we're going to be late to go get my sister."

Hearing Ryan's sweet, high-pitched voice always melted me. I once thought I would never hear it when he almost died at birth.

"I'm coming, baby."

"Okay, Mommy." I giggled listening to his happy feet scamper away. My smile faded when I remembered the days I thought I would never hear them.

The doctors said it was a mystery to them why Ryan had stopped breathing. But I held onto my dark, guilty secret, feeling the blame. During my labor, I visualized myself dilating like an open flower to give birth trying to avoid painful contractions. I had been reading a yoga book on the mind-body relationship and was taking similar classes in the ministry at night with Walt to deepen our faith. We both wanted a closer relationship with God and Sunday morning services just weren't enough.

Walt checked me into the hospital after an onslaught of contractions. The nurses didn't believe that I would be giving birth any time soon and neither did my doctor, who took his time coming to the hospital. But in my head, I saw a fast delivery. I kept replaying the picture while I was placed in a room.

What I didn't picture was the consequences. The maternity team raced me on a gurney into the delivery room hours earlier than they anticipated. Nor did I foresee that my doctor would arrive just in time to catch Ryan, who flew out of me as if he had wings. Holding Ryan in his hands, the doctor looked like an NFL rookie astonished to catch the ball during the last seconds of the fourth quarter.

It was the perfect delivery I had visualized, fast and swift. I was amazed that Ryan came out looking exactly like Walt, chocolate brown and with identical features. I kept thinking that I went through all of this pain and discomfort for nine months and my baby didn't look anything like me. People would constantly remind me of this for years to come when they would tell me that they didn't think Ryan was mine because of my light skin color. People can be so rude. But I often thought that since Ryan looked so much like Walt, I should have charged them both transportation and carrying charges.

Just when I was first caught up in these superficial thoughts and the nurse was about to place him on my chest, Ryan suddenly stopped breathing. My outstretched, empty arms flopped down to my sides. All

I could do was stare mutely into Walt's eyes to gather strength while the delivery team worked frantically to save our baby. They almost lost him again before discovering that a vital air hose had a hole in it. I couldn't believe that Cedars Sinai, hospital to the stars with state-of-the-art equipment, had a faulty air tube. I kept wondering, was my baby going to die, too, like so many other of my relatives before him? Was I cursed? Suddenly it didn't matter that he didn't look like me. I just wanted my baby to live.

After being resuscitated twice, Ryan was breathing again through a tiny oxygen mask, but while they were rushing him into Intensive Care, his breathing stopped again in the hall. Fortunately, he survived, but we faced a week of critical hours when the doctors told us not to expect him to live. It seemed all of Ryan's vital functions, from kidneys to lungs, stopped functioning properly.

The specialists summoned said that they thought it was all due to Ryan's coming out so fast.

"He didn't have time to convert from breathing in the womb to breathing outside of the womb," one said. Secretly I harbored the guilt of having visualized him coming out so fast. It was a powerful tool, I discovered.

Two weeks later, Ryan was stabilized and had drastically improved. Fortunately, after he came home from the hospital, he never had another health problem.

Spiritually I have always thought that when he stopped breathing his soul saw the work ahead of him in the world and vacillated about coming into this existence. Regardless, after that I became careful of how and what I visualized.

We never considered Ryan's near-death experience as a possible reason why we wanted safely to adopt instead of having more kids, by birth, which we could easily do. Nonetheless, I suspect it may have been our subconscious motivation.

"Jan! What's taking you so long?"

Walter had appeared in the open doorway, gripping the doorknob. His forehead creased with a frown.

"We're going to be late for the adoption party." We have opposite internal clocks. He's always early, and I seemed to always run late.

"I'm getting dressed," I said, struggling to pull my green pants over my hips.

He sighed, and checked his watch. I held my breath and sucked in my stomach, hoping that I could shorten the two-inch gap keeping my zipper from closing. I needed liposuction for that to happen.

"I'm hurrying," I said, puffing and tugging at the pants. "I just want to make sure I have on the right outfit. I was thinking pants would make me seem cool to a kid, but probably a dress would be better. What do you think?"

"I think you should hurry up," he snapped.

"I am. Will you be patient?" Walt stood in the doorway, handsome with his thick brush mustache, rolling his dark alluring eyes that attracted me to him seven years earlier. But at this moment, I tried ignoring them.

"Kids like bright colors. But some of the things I want to wear I can't get into."

The clothes drama didn't sit well with the always impeccably dressed Mr. Physical Fitness, who runs at least five miles a day. Exercise was his daily ritual because sports had saved his life as a teen. A fateful car accident left his best friend dead and Walt clinging to life in a coma with multiple broken bones. But his stamina, developed from sports as a four-star celebrated athlete, helped overturn doctors' prediction that he wouldn't live. His determination and discipline helped him learn how to walk again.

Walt gave me the "you-should-exercise look" for the millionth time in our marriage and turned to leave. I wanted to kick him.

"If we don't get to this party we won't get our daughter," he barked over his shoulder as he stepped into the hall. "Just put on something. Kids don't care."

I kicked the door, slamming it behind him and catching my reflection in the mirror. I did a double take, horrified as I moved closer to look at myself. A pimple sat prominently on my nose. They came like enemy soldiers whenever I was excited. My God, the kid will think I'm a witch. I am too old to be going though puberty.

I wiggled like a reptile shedding skin, shimmying out of the pants. I threw them on the mountain of rejected clothes on the bed. The weight battle was a lifetime war.

Twenty minutes later I sat uncomfortably in our gold Volvo, stuffed into a tight, bright yellow dress with a long black jacket, which I hoped was minimizing my protruding butt. My body felt heavy, like a grounded bumblebee, but my head was buzzing with excitement. We were on our way to pick out our child at the black adoptions pre-Valentine's party, which was a new event for DCFS. The events were conceived because so many African-American children are trapped in the system.

In the county's adoption process, an orphan's social worker and the prospective adoptive family's social worker try to match their clients. When they think they have a match, the social workers enters both parties' data into a computer to see if technology agrees with their choice. I never thought that a computer could do God's work, so when Barbara Darling, our social worker, called to invite us to the DCFS adoption party, I calmly said "yes." When I hung up, I screamed at the top of my lungs for joy.

"When we get her can you take us to the show tonight to see the Ninja Turtle movie, Daddy?" Ryan was in the back of the car hanging out of his child's seat, stretching to roll his tiny toy truck on the window. He was nearly twice the size of an average child his age, having made up for his uncertain start in life by constantly eating.

"Your new sister isn't coming home today, Ryan," said Walt.

"Why not?"

"Remember I told you the Department of Children's Services has to make sure whoever we pick is right for us."

"How will they know who's right? They don't know us, do they?"

"Good question, Ryan," Walt said, smiling. "That's a mystery to both of us, too. No, they don't know us." He went on for ten minutes, patiently explaining the process to Ryan.

Walt is the kind of father who would answer any and every question Ryan could throw at him and sit there explaining it as long as it took for Ryan to understand. In contrast, I often felt like walking off the back of a ship from hearing Ryan ask me "Why?" a zillion times a day. But Walt didn't mind. He also was the one who stayed up nights rocking Ryan on his shoulder when he was a colicky infant. He was my relief since I was ready to jump out the window from the relentless wailing. Mine and Ryan's.

Fatherhood was important to Walt, who didn't have a close relationship or much communication with his parents. He grew up in Stockton, California, an agriculture city 90 miles inland from San Francisco that began as a muddy-street gold rush camp. Gold seekers from Asia, Africa, Australia, Europe, the Pacific Islands, Mexico, and Canada all converged into a great melting pot. In modern times, the area has been the backdrop to many movies and television shows because of its scenic beauty, with five major rivers including the Sacramento River and the San Joaquin River, and its rural charm. But there weren't many opportunities for African-Americans at the nearby prison and the local cannery was just about the only employment blacks could find.

Walt's father, Walter Sr., was a building construction supervisor for the City of Stockton and his mother, Dorothy, a domestic at a local hospital. Before moving into their house, they lived in a government housing project with Walt's younger brother and older sister. The household was one of only a few in the project where both parents lived at home, although they fought constantly. Much to Walt's embarrassment, he often heard people gossiping about his parents, saying they fought like "cats and dogs."

One day, Walt told me the pain he went through growing up.

"I was ashamed because it seemed that all my friends in the projects knew about our family fighting. I tried to justify my feelings, telling myself that at least I had two parents living at home," said Walt. "But I carried a tremendous amount of anger and fear. I didn't understand why."

Those feelings confused Walt about himself and life. The only time that he felt good about himself was on the basketball court, the track, or the football field. He was a four-star athlete, written up constantly in the papers.

"Sports were how I channeled my anger."

Walter Sr. was a very quiet person who also kept his anger bottled up inside and would seldom talk. Possibly that was because he felt unloved, growing up when both of his parents died before he was six. His mother died while giving birth to his younger sister and his father, a construction worker on a bridge, was killed when a pillar collapsed on him. After their deaths, Walter Sr. and his siblings were sent to live with different relatives. He moved in with an aunt who clearly didn't like him.

Walt says his father never knew how to communicate with him, and he never saw his parents discussing their problems. They would simply argue.

"It seemed that arguments and physical fights were the only ways my parents could deal with their differences. I know that I would have turned out just like them if it wasn't for sports that taught me team work and how to work out problems with other people."

One summer Walter Sr.'s brother, Charles Jackson, a career army staff sergeant who had been stationed in Germany and was now stationed in San Francisco, came to visit. The brothers hadn't seen one another in eight years.

"I felt my father's excitement," Walt recalls. "He very seldom showed any type of emotion, but I could sense his happiness this day. I was on the basketball court at school when my father picked up Uncle Charles at the Greyhound bus station. After a good practice, I headed for home. As I walked along, I felt good, I felt talented and special, full of confidence to tackle life's challenges. Sports made me feel that way.

"When I got home Uncle Charles was sitting on the couch in the living room. He hugged me and we sat down to talk about things that I was interested in. Sports. I remember thinking that I would have liked to have had this affection from my parents, but it never happened."

Walter remembers when the next evening Charles and his father, who had gone out together to a bar, came home. Walt's father frequented bars to unwind, but it was unfortunately, where he met other women. It wasn't surprising that Walt's mother had her suspicions that night. When the two men returned home, she seemed to have an even bigger chip on her shoulder than she normally carried, according to Walt.

"Just as Dad and Uncle Charles stepped in the door an argument broke out between my parents. The moment I heard Mom and Dad raising their voices, I got scared. I jumped out of bed and put on my clothes and Converse sneakers, as I had done so many times before, because I just knew I might have to break up another fight… again."

Walter remembers kneeling on the floor, begging God to take his parent's anger away before he went into the kitchen where they were arguing. But all seemed to subside when his father was then talking to Charles, who had taken on Walt and his sister's role calming Dorothy.

Little did anyone know that even though Dorothy was quiet, she was still seething inside, like some witch's brew. She calmly stepped over to the sink, put some water and sugar in a pot, and placed it on a burner. No one thought anything of the fact that she was boiling water. Suddenly, she took the pot from the stove, turned to Walter Sr., who had his back to her, and with an ice-cold expression, threw the boiling water on him.

"He jumped up and ripped off his shirt. And when he did, my father's skin came off with the shirt. All hell broke loose then," said Walt, shaking his head. "I have never understood why my mother ran into the bathroom and locked the door when she could have run through the kitchen and out the front door. It was as though she had a death wish because she knew my father was going to kick her ass."

It didn't take long. With a surge of rage he kicked open the bathroom door.

"Mom was curled up on the floor under the sink. But before Dad could put his hands on her, Uncle Charles and I grabbed him. I tried to take a kitchen knife from him, but he had such a strong grip that when I tried to pull the knife from his hand my fingers went across the blade, cutting me."

Walt bled profusely and immediately all of the attention was shifted to him. Once again, Dorothy would survive another "barn burner." But the rage would continue to burn in Walt for years to come.

It were these types of experiences that made Walter not only want to be a good father and husband, but want to communicate effectively with his family, as well. He would later write a book about that life and give workshops and speeches on overcoming anger. It was also probably another reason why he wanted to adopt. Many kids in the system are orphans because of violence in their homes.

It was 1:00 p.m. when we pulled up to an old gray church in South Los Angeles for the adoption party. I looked around at the well-kept, single-family homes with perfectly manicured lawns thinking that you never see these homes on the 6 o'clock news. The media preferred to report that all of South Los Angeles was one run-down, rat-infested, gang-teeming ghetto when, in actuality, there were plenty of large, attractive homes in tree-lined blocks like this one that could rival any home in the best white sections of town.

We got out of the car and walked past hedges of sweet smelling Jasmin. In front of us was a hastily written sign, "DCFS Valentine's party," with an arrow pointing to the old church's basement entrance at the side of the building.

Carefully I walked down the cracked cement steps, balancing on my black high heels, trying to avoid falling on my face and ripping my dress, which could easily have popped open with just a deep inhalation.

"Are we in the right place?" I asked Walt, who was leading. He stopped halfway down the mildew-smelling stairwell that didn't seem like it had been used for years.

"I think so."

"I don't hear any kids, mommy."

Ryan was right. Usually the squealing and laughing from children's parties can be heard a half block away.

Walt continued down the stairs as we followed. He pushed open a warped door, and we stepped into another world. Inside the big shadowy basement lit by windows near the ceiling, pitiful little red hearts were slapped haphazardly on the walls. A few balloons were stuck on pillars. And then we saw them.

Silhouettes of about 30 children of all ages walked around quietly with big tags strung from their necks with string. I flashed on slavery times. About half of the children looked toward us as we timidly entered the room. I had heard there were approximately 50,000 abused and neglected children who were wards of the court in Los Angeles County, but seeing some of them for the first time this day was heartbreaking. Fifty thousand is an entire city. A city of lost children within a city.

One of them was going to be ours.

CHAPTER FOUR

"Mr. and Mrs. Jackson, I'm so glad you came. You're early."

The friendly voice broke our trance. I shot Walt one of those "you-rushed-me-for-nothing looks." The bright, smiling lady stepping toward us was Barbara Darling, our social worker and a designated greeter for the adoption party.

Ryan shot across the room to play with the kids as we shook hands. Barbara -- bronze skin, classy and slender in Kelly green -- looked like she belonged on a fashion runway or on some millionaire's arm. She was the opposite of our first social worker, whom I nicknamed Mr. Smug. At first, his charming, Jamaican accent lifted me back to my single days of free-spirited Caribbean cruises. But then his arrogance made me uneasy, like sailing into the Bermuda Triangle at midnight. I wanted him to disappear, and through some phone calls, he did.

Mr. Smug had made it clear that he had the power to give us any child we wanted and that angered me to no end. I imagined that he could easily be bribed. He complained to us about having to constantly drive 45 minutes to our house when he had to interview us to see if we were mentally sound for adoption and weren't perverts. I suspected from his wolf expression that he got some type of demented glee from asking us sexual questions. I wondered who gave Mr. Smug his psych test? Since his whole damned attitude sucked, we asked for another social worker and got Ms. Darling.

Later we learned many people are afraid to ask for another social worker fearing it would hurt their chances of adopting. Our confidence stemmed from the fact that we could still have natural children and weren't desperate.

"The kids are so quiet," I said to Barbara as we watched the children, who seemed lost, wandering aimlessly around the room.

"That's because they don't know what to expect. Some of the foster parents didn't properly explain to them about today," she said as she unpacked DCFS adoption brochures from a box. Sad little faces like the ones we saw on the public service announcement were printed on them.

"So they don't know they're here to get adopted?"

"Some think they are, but they also think they'll go home with their new parents from the party today." I walked with her as she flipped on some lights, which didn't brighten up the room as much as they spotlighted the pitiful expressions on some of the kids' faces. They ranged from four years old to teenagers.

"Others have been to these parties many times before, and no one seems interested in them. Still the kids keep hoping."

Barbara seemed aloof as she looked around at them. I sensed that she had put up some type of protection around her heart. It was the only way to survive in her field.

"The older kids, huh?"

She nodded yes. "It's hard for those over three to get adopted, especially our African-American boys."

"Teenagers must really have a hard time."

"Uh huh. What's even tougher for them is seeing the younger foster kids, who they lived with in their foster homes, getting adopted while they get left behind."

Barbara began stacking forms on the check-in table.

"Why don't you sign in and look around for your little girl," she said with a

smile. The thought of finding my daughter lifted me out of the shock of seeing so many children without parents.

"More kids are still on their way," Barbara said handing me a paper. "Take this form. When you find a child that you like, write down her name, and when they are freed."

"Freed?" The "Roots" theme song danced in my head.

"Right. Freed. On the tags, each is wearing her name, her social worker's name, and a date. That's the date they are freed -- eligible to be adopted. Some of the kids are still going through court procedures."

"Really?" I felt bad for them.

"A parent could be in jail or in a rehab center or on the streets. They have until their freed date to get their life in order and claim their child."

Before I could ask another question, she turned to greet a couple at the door. Behind them, other prospective parents were lining up to come to the party.

"So these are the throwaway kids," whispered Walt, surveying the children. He gestured for Ryan to come back over to us as the crowd swelled.

"I guess so," I said slowly, shaking my head.

They're called throwaway children not only because many are unwanted but also because they travel so much between placements. A child can be watching television in his foster home when his social worker suddenly shows up to move him to a new placement. The kid's belongings are quickly thrown into a black plastic trash bag. Many of his personal belongings, especially pictures and documents, are lost during these hasty moves. I can understand why. Some children move into 15 to 37 different homes. It's called foster-care-drift. These kids are constantly moved for a variety of reasons ranging from behavior problems to the unthinkable -- a social worker may feel that they are becoming too attached to a foster family.

"Well, what should we do?" I asked Walt.

He didn't say it, but I knew that he was as overwhelmed as I was. I struggled with a weird stop-and-go feeling inside of me. I wanted to move forward to find a child, but I was momentarily paralyzed, like the times I lay in bed awake, but in a slight dream state, and can't move.

"I don't know. I guess we start talking to them." I needed to push myself into action. "We can start on this side of the room and work across."

As we passed groups of kids and adults, we spotted a little girl about three years old in a robin's-egg-blue dress. She was engrossed in stacking blocks as we approached her. When we got closer, I stooped down and read her name on the tag. Elizabeth. I worried if by just talking to the child it would mislead her into thinking I wanted to be her new mommy even though I was just shopping. After a few awkward minutes of chatting with the expressionless Elizabeth, I felt strange. I stood up, telling her goodbye. She didn't look up.

The whole process seemed so cold and superficial. But how do you pick out a child that you only speak to or interact with a few minutes? By looks? Like buying a new puppy? It seemed so shallow. Besides, what could we tell from the package? Walt scribbled down Elizabeth's name and we moved on.

The next ten minutes we wandered around, probably looking like the children. Lost. The room was getting packed with prospective parents, and I was feeling nauseous from the clashing perfumes the well-dressed women wore who were coming from church. I glanced at the clock. About a half-hour left. My competitive spirit I developed in the entertainment industry suddenly surfaced. I revived myself, bared out my claws, and got focused. Fast. I reminded myself that if we didn't find a child, strangers and a computer would pick our daughter for us.

We pushed politely through the crowds, which were clumped in various circles. Looking over people's shoulders, we could see some small child standing in the middle, looking confused at these gushing adults. It was like trying to see a hot act on a boardwalk with tourists crowding the performer.

Walt was leading Ryan by the hand and we were moving through a maze of people when two women stopped us.

"Hello there, big guy." The heavier woman, dressed in a tan pantsuit, was smiling at Ryan. She then looked at me. "He's sooo cute." She looked back at Ryan.

"What's your name?"

"Ryan" he blurted out with a grin. I smiled, realizing that they assumed he was up for adoption. A while back, the thought crossed my mind briefly when Ryan had a tantrum in the middle of a busy supermarket. I had never been so embarrassed. I wanted to leave him right there.

"Oh… no, he's not up for adoption. He's ours." I smiled, grabbing his hand, pulling him close to me.

"Really?" said the shorter woman in a reddish wig eyeing me suspiciously. Since only foster kids were invited to the party she probably thought I was another possessive hopeful who was trying to adopt him myself. But we had ignored the asterisk line on the invitation requesting that we not bring our own kids. Still we felt it was important that Ryan was a part of the process. Whomever we chose would be his sister for life.

Continuing our search around the room, in a far corner of the basement we saw one woman shamelessly monopolizing a little girl, swinging her around as the child giggled. A few other prospective parents stood by watching. I knew they hoped to interact with the airborne toddler. The possessive woman ticked me off because she may not have been fully approved by DCFS, or she could get disqualified after a completed background check. We had passed the preliminary tests, but Barbara said many parents invited to the party were not fully processed and approved.

The woman was actually holding the girl hostage before our eyes. Her obvious plan was to keep the girl airborne so that no one could read her tag or interact. Sadly, some people wouldn't even try to adopt her since Ms. Kidnapper was hogging the child. The problem would be if the woman didn't qualify. Those who were eligible at the party wouldn't ask for the girl because they would assume Ms. Kidnapper would adopt her. If she didn't, the child would stay in the system and age out at 18, when she would be kicked out of foster care and stripped of health care benefits, given $150, and told to "go find a life."

"Why don't we split up," I said to Walt. "It's getting late and maybe we can cover the room better. We can compare notes in a little while." I looked around at other couples examining children, scribbling their choices on their forms. I kept flashing on slave owners looking for the new best "buck" or "wench" to take back to the plantation.

"All right, I'll take Ryan," said Walt.

I was working my way to one corner of the room where I saw a couple talking to a small girl. When I stopped for a closer look at the child, lightening bolts seemed to crackle out of the woman's eyes. I pretended that I wasn't intimidated and focused on Alicia, the little girl, who was playing with a doll. After a couple of minutes admiring her, I scribbled down Alicia's name and moved on.

The party was almost over when I met up with Walt and Ryan, who were now sitting on brown folding chairs wolfing down hot dogs. I sat down heavily next to Walt, growing more anxious.

"Did you see any other girls you like?" I asked.

"Not really."

I wanted to scream, "Then why don't you keep looking instead of eating?" Instead, I held my tongue and tried using reverse psychology. "Well, I don't want to waste time sitting here. The party is almost over."

Walt kept chewing nonchalantly. Didn't he want a daughter just as much as I did? Wasn't it he who specifically suggested a girl, saying it would balance our home? He was right. Our house was definitely tilting with testosterone. Besides Walt and Ryan, we had Prana, a male German shepherd dog, Chakra, our male cat, and even a tank filled with male Koi fish.

Just when I was about to leave them, three pre-teen boys sat down on both sides of us. The one closest to me, in a sea-moss green shirt, spoke first.

"Hi, I'm Jerome. What's your name?" His bright eyes danced to his smile.

"Mrs. Jackson." I pointed. "… And this is Mr. Jackson and that's Ryan."

"Nice meeting you." He reached to shake my hand. I was moved by this ten-year old charmer who then pointed to the other two grinning boys.

"That's Raymond and Timmy." They nodded to us and then looked back at their leader obviously waiting for him to make the next move.

"He your kid?" asked Jerome eyeing Ryan who was munching on a hot dog. His stuffed jaws reminded me of a squirrel carrying nuts.

"Yes."

"You're here looking for another kid?" his voice lilted with surprise.

"Yes, we are."

"Whatcha looking for?" His eyes widened, he crossed his arms leaning into us, grinning.

"A little girl. Three-years-old." The boy's face suddenly dimmed as fast as it had lit up. He sat back in his chair, and my body tightened when I realized that I had crushed his hopes. I wasn't even thinking when he asked. The boys weren't just trying to be friendly. They apparently had been watching us from across the room. They came over to audition, hoping they would be adopted. At least Jerome did.

I tried changing the subject. "So who did you come with?"

"My social worker over there." A now somber Jerome half-heartedly pointed into a crowd with a limp finger.

"You enter into any of the contests they're having?" asked Walt, trying to lift his spirits. "Looks like fun."

"Yeah… but it's boring," he said, tapping his black tennis shoes on the brown painted cement floor. They play them every time they have these parties."

"So you've been to these before?"

"Coupla times… but everyone's like you," his voice drifted off. "They all want little kids."

I wanted to hold him.

"Hey Jerome, let's go," said Timmy, who was missing a front tooth. "Everybody's in line for the basketball-shooting contest."

"I'm-a win that thing this time," said Jerome, suddenly recharged, and jumping up. "Well… gotta go." We waved goodbye and watched the boys line up to get the ball.

"That's sad, huh?" I said, feeling nauseous again.

"Yep."

"They just want a home."

"Yeah," said Walt, drinking his Coke, turning away.

Maybe I was being oversensitive but my husband seemed insensitive. Was it a male thing? Was Walt just hiding his feelings or was he simply not affected?

"Well, it's almost over." I stood up. "I'm going to go look one more time. Are you coming?"

"No… I'm going to get some cake. Ryan! You want some cake?"

Still chomping on his hot dog, Ryan nodded vigorously. They headed for the refreshment table and I stormed off in the other direction, cursing Walt under my breath.

When I was halfway across the room, I heard him almost shouting.

"Jan… Jan."

I snapped my head in his direction, along with a few other perplexed people. What has gotten into him? When we locked eyes over people's heads, Walt waved frantically for me to come over to him. Managing to squeeze past the crowds, I saw his eyes glowing with excitement.

"Did you see him?" He was electrified. "… you see him?"

"Who? See who?" What person did we know at the party?

"Come on. Follow me." Walt was dragging Ryan, who was licking icing off his fingers. I was always amazed at how much my child could eat. I worried if we could afford him as a teenager.

Walt stopped at the refreshment table covered with half-filled mismatched bowls of chips and various kinds of cookies, many of them picked over and broken.

"There he is."

I spotted a diminutive, sweet-faced little boy dressed in a bright canary yellow sweater and clutching an Asian woman's hand. She had to be his social worker. We stood a short distance away, watching him as he soaked in the activities on the stage. A tall woman was raffling off a truck and a doll.

"I see him. He's cute. Now what about our daughter?"

"Come on," said Walt his eyes glued on the boy. "Let's go talk to him."

"Hey... didn't we agree on a girl?"

"Yeah... but let's just say hello."

"Wal -- " I tried to object in the name of time, but he was in front of them before I could finish. Grudgingly, I followed.

"Hi," said Walt, grinning at the social worker. He didn't wait for her response before he began gushing over the little boy. The child craned his neck back to look up at the giant man hovering over him.

I stood back. Something within me did not want to be involved with this child, even though he was absolutely adorable. I thought then it was because my heart was set on a girl. Looking back on that moment, my soul instantly sensed that, besides joy, this little boy would bring me to near suicide. Something inside must have told me that adopting him would be like jumping off a cliff. Only God could save me.

"Hello," said the petite social worker, her eyes lighting up. "We just got here. I was afraid the party would be over. I'm Valerie Wong, his social worker."

"I'm Walter Jackson." He pointed to Ryan and me. "This is my wife Janet and my son Ryan." We all shook hands.

"I had to drive out to his foster mom's home to get him," Valerie said. "It's an hour there and an hour back. She was supposed to bring him."

Valerie spilled information out so fast that I stepped back. She was like a vacuum cleaner salesperson at my door. But Walt was listening intently, filling in all of her pauses with "Really?" and "Uh huh."

"I want him to have a family. I was so afraid no one would get to see him. I don't think the foster mother wanted me to bring him."

We had heard that some foster parents don't want their foster kids adopted because they grow fond of them. Unfortunately, others will just miss the monthly county paycheck.

Walt was now bending down to eye level with the preschooler.

"What's your name?"

The social worker gingerly pried the boy's hand from hers and pushed him gently toward Walt. He stood stiffly like a toy soldier staring at my gushing husband.

"His name is Devon," said Valerie.

"Hello, Devon. My name is Walter," he said in a high-pitched, Romper Rom voice that I hadn't heard him use before. It's amazing that you can live with someone for years and still not know him.

"Devon," called out Ryan tossing up a balloon that had fallen off the wall.

"Come play with me."

"You want to play with Ryan, Devon?"

The boy, with his little arms pinned to his side looked back at his social worker, who was smiling, nodding her head yes. Devon took small steps toward Ryan, who was now running in circles after the red balloon.

Valerie became animated. "I'm so glad someone is interested in him. He's a great kid." She stepped closer to us. Her face grew dark as she lowered her voice slightly above a whisper. "I know the foster mother is not treating him right. I've got to get him out of that home," she said desperately. "I can't prove it, but I think she is abusing him. That's why I'm so anxious for him to get adopted."

"Oh, God," I gasped. "How do you know?"

"We got tips from the neighbors. Police have been to their house several times."

"What's his background?" Walt took control.

"Well, he's three, and… " she paused, biting her lip, looking around the room.

"I'm not suppose to leave him alone…" She then studied us carefully, "… but let me run to my car to get his file. Would you watch him for me?" Walt nodded eagerly. "Please, don't go anywhere with him."

"We'll be right here when you get back," said Walt, his eyes still glued on Devon.

Valerie hesitated, looked at me, and then looked at Devon, whose eyes were riveted on Ryan. She obviously felt he was safer with us strangers than with an abusive foster mother.

"Devon, I'll be right back," Valerie said to the boy. "Stay here with the nice people." He held out his little hand for her to take him along too, but Walt distracted him and led him over to Ryan. Devon looked back over his shoulder, watching Valerie snake her way through the crowd toward the door.

Ryan quickly grew frustrated with Devon, who wouldn't play. Finally, he gave up and began the impossible task of trying to dribble the balloon with Devon's eyes glued to his every move. The boy reminded me of a little bird with broken wings who couldn't fly. I would learn later that abused kids typically are emotionally and physically withdrawn like Devon.

"Walt. Are you sure you haven't changed your mind about a girl?" I whispered anxiously in his ear. "You know we agreed on a girl."

"I know, I know." Trying to escape me, he quickly moved toward Devon. A few minutes later, Valerie reappeared with the files. Excitedly she leafed through the thick folder. Finding the page, she read Devon's background as Walt hung on every word.

"His mother was a drug addict and his father was unknown. His birthday is in August. He's not in preschool yet."

Devon walked back to hold Valerie's hand.

"Devon, can I pick you up?" asked Walt. The boy looked up at Valerie who was nodding yes. He then looked back at Walt and timidly nodded. Walt bent down and gingerly picked up the toddler, whose little arms stayed pinned to his side.

"Daddy, can we take Devon home?" asked Ryan. "I want him to be my brother."

"Remember what I told you in the car about the steps it takes to adopt?"

"Oh, yeah," said Ryan trying to throw the balloon against the wall. "Forgot," he smacked his head and grinned.

Walt turned Devon around to Ryan.

"Devon, let's see how high Ryan can throw the balloon." The boy would not take his eyes off Walt's face despite how hard my husband cajoled him to watch Ryan. I had never seen a kid stare so intently.

I walked up next to them, examining Devon closer, when my mouth fell open. I spotted a tiny pimple on Devon's nose in the exact spot and side where mine had popped up earlier that morning. Typically, kids that young don't have blemishes, so I knew it was a definite sign. Over the years, I learned to pay attention to life's signs no matter how small or bizarre they may be.

"All right, big fella… I'm going to put you down, but before I do, can I have a hug?" Instantly Devon came alive. He put his tiny arms around Walt's neck and hugged him. And then there was that magical moment. To our amazement, the boy kissed Walt on his cheek.

That kiss sealed Devon's fate. I can't explain what came over me; it must have been fairy dust, but I forgot we were looking for a girl. From the look on Walt's face, I knew he had found another son. We exchanged the knowing husband-wife silent glances of approval. We both now knew that Devon was the reason we were led to the party.

When we told Valerie that we were interested in adopting Devon, she was ecstatic. Eagerly she instructed us on what to write on the adoption request form just as the woman on the stage announced that the party was over.

Ten minutes later, we were in the crowd slowly filing out of the room with Devon and Valerie walking ahead of us. When a couple walking close to us stopped Valerie to inquire about Devon, I felt myself morph into the people whom I had loathed earlier. I held my breath, puffed up, and pierced them with an eagle stare. I was so grateful that the adoption request forms had already been collected and packed up. It was too late for someone else to put in a request.

The crowd behind us was now swarming past us and by osmosis, we were being pushed out of the door. Once outside I saw the same couple standing by a pink rosebush. The woman was biting her lip, hesitating as she watched Devon. He was holding Valerie's hand, taking in all of the people milling outside the church as Valerie chatted with another social worker.

The man was talking to her but the woman's eyes were drinking in Devon. I knew she was trying to decide whether or not to pursue him. Meanwhile I was willing her away from him with all my might. Please, lady, leave. Leave. He's my son now. Valerie was now talking to Walt, oblivious to the interplay. Suddenly the woman turned to her husband and they said something before they walked away. The adrenaline subsided in my body like a pot of boiling water taken off a burner.

After exchanging a few more goodbyes with Devon and Valerie, we headed to our car. Walt and Ryan walked ahead of me. I lingered, watching Devon walk with Valerie. I couldn't take my eyes off the boy. When they stopped at a blue compact, Devon looked over at me. We locked eyes as Valerie leaned inside the car, preparing his toddler car seat. I waved goodbye to Devon but the solemn little boy didn't respond. He simply stared, emotionless, exactly as he had been doing most of the time we were with him.

I stopped to watch Devon climb into the car when suddenly he looked back at me. And then it happened. He lit up like a Fourth of July sparkler, smiling angelically at me. I was breathless. That smile would freeze in my brain for years to come. I snapped my head around to see if Walt had seen the phenomenon, but he was already in our car with his back to us. No one else had seen Devon's light. It was my special blessing. A gift. I then knew the answer to the question that I had asked myself earlier. How do you pick out a child? You fall in love. That love then chooses you.

Now there were absolutely no doubts in my mind. Devon was our son and we were going to do everything that we could to bring him home. I didn't have a clue that we were going to have to fight the system.

CHAPTER FIVE

In the days ahead Devon's sweet, innocent face loomed before me like a rising morning sun lighting up my life. He was a magnetic force pulling me toward his mysterious vortex of energy. I became crazed to adopt him and yet baffled by this strange feeling galvanizing my mind and soul. What was this electrifying force pulling at my insides and where did it come from? I couldn't explain it. It was beyond reason, beyond wanting the love of a child, and deeper than wanting to be someone's mother. I was possessed and obsessed. Why?

Looking back, I now realize that he was my spiritual fate beckoning me to follow what I would soon discover to be a painful, rocky road to higher consciousness.

"I don't know why," I said to Walt one evening. "His smile is in my head when I drive to work. When I do the dishes. When I get into bed... brushing my teeth. I can't get him out of my mind. I'm constantly wondering what he's doing?" My voice dropped, "... and if he's being abused."

"Yeah. I know," said Walt, rolling sky-blue paint on the wall of our spare bedroom. He was following a lesson that we learned from our four years in the ministry. When you desire something, act as if you already have it. Even though we had just met Devon a few weeks earlier, Walt was preparing the room for his arrival.

I loved his motivated energy, which he dismissed as simply a street sense. No one could tell him that Devon was not our son. Whether it was intuition, which I called it, or street sense, as he preferred to say it was, Walt seemed to always be right about people. There were times that we conflicted on people judgment. Sometimes he would sense something wrong about a person that I liked, and he would want me to stay away from them. I, on the other hand, needed concrete reasons why I should break off a friendship. Since Walt couldn't give me those reasons we would both be frustrated and end up arguing with one another.

When I maintained a friendship that Walt questioned, he made sure not to be around that person. If he couldn't avoid them he was totally aloof, and this angered me even more. To my amazement, eventually he would turn out to be right about the person. Inevitably something would happen involving these people proving Walt right even as much as a year later.

It would take me years to trust my own instinct. I had to learn to scrutinize real friends from acquaintances bearing gifts who wanted my television connections. Intuition would be a necessary survival tool in the years ahead dealing with Devon and trying to find him help.

"I see his face, too, Jan."

"You do? I thought it was just me. I don't know why I'm nuts over this kid, especially since we were set on a girl," I said, picking up a small sable paintbrush. Kneeling, I began dabbing the baby-blue paint on the white wall molding. The rooms smelled fresh and clean from the toxic paint fumes. It was another one of life's ironies.

"I called Barbara today," Walt said, bending next to me. He picked up another brush. "Here use this. It's easier to get into the crevices."

"You did? I thought she said to give her a couple of weeks before checking." I look at him, puzzled.

"It's been three weeks. They should know if they agree with our match by now."

"And... ? What did she say?"

"She said they're still processing his paper work and that we should make a scrapbook of our family and give it to them." He started climbing a ladder, balancing a roller in one hand and the paint pan in the other.

"Why? Whom are they showing it to?" I held the ladder for him. "It's not like we've got to convince the mother we're the right family. She lost her rights because she's on drugs," I said, frowning. "From what Valerie says, she has no intention of trying to get off that stuff, or wanting Devon back."

"I don't know." He began rolling vigorously. "I'm just repeating what Barbara told us to do. I guess in case it doesn't work out with Devon, maybe they're thinking about another kid."

"Are there any more families asking for him?" I felt my face twitch.

"No. We're the only ones. Guess cause Devon came to the adoption party so late."

"Thank God." I was now dabbing paint on the baseboard again. "Then it should work out for us to get him. Did she say how long it's going to take?"

"She says she's doing everything she can to make it go fast. I don't think she even knows."

"Did you mention that Devon's social worker thinks he's being abused in the foster home?"

"She knows that. Like Valerie says, they don't have any evidence."

"Even though the neighbors keep calling the abuse hotline on the foster mom?" I shrieked. Walt just shook his head in disgust.

"Check out the article over there." He pointed to the *Los Angeles Times* lying on a paint-splattered stepladder. "I just happened to see it when I was spreading out the paper to paint. Almost threw it away."

I picked up the Times dated March 8, 1990. Walt had placed an X next to a front-page story. I began reading it aloud. "'County Accused of Letting Foster Children Suffer Abuse; California's Chief of Social Services Says L.A. Agency has failed to protect its Wards and Report Problems Promptly.'" I sat down heavily on the floor, "Oh my God, Walt."

It was the first of many articles that we would read about the state threatening to take over foster care licensing from the county. Linda McMahon, head of state social services, was accusing Los Angeles County officials of repeatedly failing promptly to report deaths, abuse and overcrowded conditions in foster homes to state officials.

"Go on," said Walt. Frost dripped from his words.

I read McMahon's quote as blood pounded in my throat. "'The majority of the revocation cases sent to us from Los Angeles County involve sexual molestation, physical abuse or death of children in the care of foster parents.'" I continued reading about the 10 children who slept on the floor of a foster home garage and about ten more young-sters who were living in one bedroom. Six months had passed before referral for legal action had occurred. The *Times* quoted Ms. McMahon saying, "'This is an unacceptable delay.'"

"No wonder Devon is still in that home if DCFS let this happen," I squealed.

Walt's mouth grew taut as he pushed and pulled the roller across the wall, painting over what I knew was his rising anger. Obviously he was feeling as helpless as I was. Terrible things could be happening to Devon, but the county wasn't moving fast enough to prevent it and here was printed proof.

After reading the entire article, we finished painting in silence, immersed in our own thoughts, but our frustration filled the room along with the rhythmic sound of my swishing paintbrush and Walt's groaning roller. No matter how hard I tried I couldn't stop thinking that Devon was in serious trouble.

It was painful waiting for Devon to come to us. I knew it was just as hard for Walt to sit idly. He's a natural go-getter who had once owned a painting company, worked as a realtor, wrote a book, and founded Self Expansion, our motivational speaking company. For years he sold real estate and spoke to many audiences about how to empower their lives by taking control. Now we both found ourselves without control or power as we waited at the mercy of DCFS.

During the long days ahead I vacillated between joy and depression. I was moving daily at lightning speed, working on shows at the network while my personal life was at a dead standstill.

My hands were tied with DCFS and I was going nuts. Back then I didn't know spiritual peace. I numbed myself to make it through the day by eating. It was the only way I knew to endure the wait. I would pig out like some people get drunk. It was the same old dance. I would get a quick Serotonin high, and then my blood sugar would drop, leaving me feeling listless and lethargic. The focus would now be on me. Guilt for over-eating. Then once again I would vow to swear off sugar. It was a sick cycle to avoid my problems, not unlike the alcoholism that I saw in my family background.

As the days passed, I felt like a ghostly, lost soul, floating between two worlds of opposites -- the fastest business in the world, entertainment, and what seemed like the slowest in the world, the social service system. It was getting to the point where I couldn't identify with either one. Journaling and eating were my salvation. I kept copious notes on every conversation that I had with Barbara, even documenting the time of day. It was journaling that helped me to vent my feelings. I had learned well from Shinzen Young and Eiko Michi who taught Walt and me meditation and mindfulness techniques. I wasn't disciplined to keep up the meditations on my own then. It would take me years of agony living with Devon before I would regularly practice them out of desperation. Mindful living and belief in my higher power would be my only salvation. I needed them both to endure my work, which seemed to grow increasingly superficial.

"How's the adoption going?"

Shelia, my perky coworker at the ABC Television Network was poking her precision haircut in my office. She lived for designer clothes and lived in high tech beauty salons. I was talking with Beth, another fellow publicist, who thought more of the horse she owned than of people.

"I don't know. I'm so disgusted." I waved her in. "I was telling Beth that the county keeps losing our documents. It's one delay after another for this adoption."

"You're kidding!" she said, her shiny brown hair bobbing as she plopped on the armrest of my tan sofa. It was the only place for anyone to sit. My office was a sea of scripts and photo proof sheets.

"They even lost a copy of our wedding certificate," I sighed. "I had to send it to them again, which meant another delay. To top it off, our social worker leaves out of town for training. You know, nothing still was done on our case."

"That's ridiculous," said Beth, crossing her arms.

"To top it off still more, her supervisor then goes on vacation for two weeks.

She has to approve everything, so everything stops." I twiddled a pencil in my fingers. "Every time you turn around, something is holding up the process."

Shelia was looking at me blankly with her big sea-green eyes. I realized that she probably expected me to say the adoption was going fine so she could change the subject. How many times do we ask people how they're doing but we really don't want to know?

"How long has it been?" asked Shelia, examining her manicure.

"It's been a couple of months."

"That's not long for adoption," said Beth, flipping her shoulder length blonde tresses back. "Some people wait years."

"Yeah, but that's for Caucasian babies." Both of my white coworkers now locked their eyes on me. "It shouldn't take that long for black baby boys. They're the last ones people adopt." My voice was cracking. "The county should be flying this kid into our home since they suspect he's been abused."

"Someone's abusing him?" asked Shelia, her voice rising like a stage actress. She moved a pile of scripts on the sofa and sat down, swinging her legs up on the oak coffee table as if she was about to watch a television show.

"We think so." They shot one another a mutual I-wouldn't-touch-that-kid-with-a- ten-foot-pole look. But then again, they wouldn't touch any kid. Period. They were like many entertainment people. No families of their own. Living free and uncommitted in a fast-paced party town leaves little room for domestic responsibilities or meaningful relationships. I liked my coworkers, but they were as shallow as a kiddie pool. Looking back, I had once been, too.

"Do you know anything about his background?" Beth asked.

"Just that his mother was on drugs."

"He's a drug baby, too?" Beth shrieked. This time she didn't try to hide her repulsion. The news was filled with stories about drug babies, and rising fear that these kids would tax the American system with their obvious problems. An army of these children would be flowing into the classroom in the next couple of years with their attention deficit problems and no one knew how to handle them. The teachers certainly didn't have the training.

I shrugged slightly and looked away. I knew she was thinking that drug babies were a black issue. I ached to dialogue on the cocaine epidemic that was sweeping the country in the middle '80s, when Devon was born. I wanted to talk to them about the issues that haunted me. Blacks were 20 times as likely as whites to be incarcerated for drug offenses. Studies proved that black babies were more likely than white babies to be taken from their mothers and placed in foster care because of drug exposure. I knew better.

I had tried to have these conversations before with my other white friends, but in return I got blank stares and "uh huhs." They probably felt that they would be stepping on a minefield if they gave it any energy. But I didn't want to get into a racial debate, just a conversation about what was happening with kids. I was the only black in the office and I just hungered to process the horror of these issues. I didn't care if my coworkers had purple stripes. Instead, they always changed the subject and I got no feedback. I became more frustrated, isolated, and angry.

"I would be too afraid to adopt," said Shelia, now examining her split ends.

"The kid's parents could be murderers or something." One thing about superficial Shelia -- she spoke her mind.

This time I changed the subject and asked how the shows they were working on were doing. It's a show business fact. Show business people love talking about one thing -- show business. I could have cared less about the programs or the star gossip, but I needed to change the subject because deep down I wanted their support---and I wasn't -- going to get it.

In the following months my isolation grew. No one else in the office wanted to talk to me about my adoption. It was a contrast to when I was pregnant at CBS with Ryan. Everyone in my office, and crewmembers on the shows I worked, all wanted to give me baby advice. My coworkers threw me an elaborate baby shower and pampered me to no end. There hadn't been a new baby in that publicity office for 20 years and I was drinking up the attention. I never felt so loved.

Sadly, I found that people's response to our adopting a child was drastically different than our telling people I was pregnant. The joy and support were absent. Maybe the difference is because everyone loves babies, and people are more skeptical about an adopted child and his background.

In defense of my ABC coworkers' aloofness, they knew that I was frustrated and that it wouldn't take much for me to get on my soapbox and rant about poor drug babies. They certainly didn't want to hear me talk about the drugs being flown into the country and that black people didn't have the planes, but a large portion of the drugs managed to find their way into the ghetto.

If people in my office were recoiling when I came around, then I was withdrawing from them, too. My job and the entertainment conversations were not so important to me anymore. And getting publicity for shows was beginning to become a painful task compared to the fun that I use to have helping actors and their shows become famous.

Entertainment suddenly seemed so insignificant to the real world. I even began resenting the family shows I was assigned to promote -- "Growing Pains," "The Wonder Years," and "Full House." How could I care about shows with mindless storylines knowing the weighty problems of children in the system? Besides, the kids on those shows were privileged and well cared for both on and off the screen. They even had two families. Their biological parents and their on-screen parents. The abused and neglected kids in the system, who were wards of the court, didn't have anyone. I was growing increasingly manic.

In the days ahead I found myself losing patience working with stars who complained about anything and everything, including the wind is blowing the wrong way. At that time I was working on "Roseanne," another family show. This was during the height of Roseanne Barr's fame, when she had sent ABC ratings through the roof and was warring with her writers and producers. Some she fired, and she constantly insulted the network executives through the press. I liked Roseanne. She was always nice to me. But whether she was right or wrong, I couldn't help thinking, "What could a wealthy, famous star possibly have to complain about compared to the kids drifting in the foster care system?"

I found myself with tunnel vision, measuring everyone's problems against the children trapped in the system.

It's a strange thing about becoming aware of the world around you. Once you have an awakening, it's difficult to go back to sleep. It was like I was living the tale of two cities. Rich, glamorous Hollywood, and the social service world filled with abused and neglected children. My life in Hollywood now seemed like one of the sitcoms that I promoted. Scripted, empty, and fake. But in the days ahead I would start waking up increasingly to the real world, filled with plenty of drama.

CHAPTER SIX

While waiting idly for our adoption to be finalized, I felt paralyzed. It was like watching a forest fire burning toward Devon while my hands were being tied. Hot rage was growing inside of me over his abuse and against the system. How could they expect us to do nothing to help him?

Patience is an important Eastern spiritual principle that I've always admired, but at that time it was too passive for me. I was still steeped in the Western "go-get-èm" mentality. Waiting patiently felt like I was wasting time. For years I had meditated, which gave me some peace, but I hadn't been able to consistently maintain that balance.

In the meantime I was still working in the entertainment industry physically but not emotionally or mentally. My mind and my heart were with Devon. When I did force myself to stay present, I found myself recoiling. Even though I loved working in the industry, it seemed that this was the first time I really saw some people in that world worshiping fame, glamour, and wealth, and I was repulsed. They were reflecting back to me a part of myself that had also been caught up in that game. I didn't want the fame, but I certainly wanted to live a glamorous and wealthy life. I remember when I first got into show business at age 22, I was filled with such envy and jealousy over the actors my age that I promoted. Some didn't have the talent but got rich fast from simply being "discovered."

Back then I was constantly on the move, trying to make things happen. I was the perfect candidate for a 12-step program for compulsive controllers. But I didn't feel it was negative. Controlling was a survival skill. It helped me to endure the mania in Hollywood and to constantly put out fires. I needed to be in control, and control had been my survival tool growing up. When my father passed, my mother married a wonderful, hard-working man who was also a raging, weekend alcoholic.

It was just as important for me to be in control of my career as of my home life, so it was natural for me to gravitate to television, an industry filled with controllers who were speeding through life just like me. I was at home at the networks, where I was given show assignments and the freedom to handle publicity on those programs as I saw fit. I loved the freedom. But the child welfare system was about to show me that the only real control that I had in my world was through my higher power. All else was self-delusion.

I'll never forget the day that I was on my way to work when I was stuck in traffic as usual on the San Diego freeway. I was like a cater-pillar, inching along with other cars. Impatiently I flipped through radio stations: commercial, commercial, rock music, heavy metal, commercial, commercial, news, another person murdered. Click. I turned it off and sighed. Rolling down the window, I plopped my elbow on the door arm rest and drummed my fingers on the steering wheel, fearing I was going to be late.

Suddenly I saw Devon's face loom before me. Was he Ok? What was he doing? No, Janet, stop thinking about him. The inner battle was erupting. I fought hard to force him out of my mind, but in a few seconds thoughts of him returned. It was becoming a sad ritual. Sitting in traffic daily, I would work myself into a frenzy worrying about him, and when I arrived at the office I would be an exhausted witch, ready to curse anyone who dared to cross me.

As I crept along the freeway, I indulged in a lot of self-talk.

"This has to stop. I'm a professional. I have to leave my problems at home." I thought of the upcoming ABC press junket. I needed to focus on my shows. My mind drifted to my position. A year earlier I had been promoted into management, complete with a large office. I was grateful, but I couldn't fully appreciate it since Devon came into our lives. My mind was filled with society's injustices toward homeless children.

I gritted my teeth as I whipped into the fast lane, which meant in the morning rush hour I was crawling about 10 miles an hour. Now the cars ahead of me were completely stopped, and the lane I had left started moving. Great. Cars were going by too fast for me to switch back over. Along with my car's exhaust, anger fumes were coming out of my ears. It was taking me nearly an hour and 15 minutes in rush hour to make the same trip in 35 minutes without traffic.

The Brentwood exit was coming up and I could feel the wealth in the air. Above me, multi-million dollar mansions hung on the hillsides. A tan van pulled up next to me and we inched along together when, suddenly, my eyes casually drifted to the black lettering painted on the side of the vehicle. I came unglued. The Department of Children and Family Services.

All morning I was suppressing my hysteria about Devon, but this was it. I couldn't hang on any longer. Tears streamed down my face, making tracks through my make-up. I had an uncontrollable urge to scream at the innocent driver, staring straight ahead and apparently lost in thought.

The van suddenly shot past me and for the next few minutes I was a babbling idiot, cursing DCFS, shaking my head in a fury behind my rolled-up windows. A couple of drivers gawked at me but snapped their gaze away when we made eye contact. By the time I straggled into work exhausted, I looked as I felt -- a beat-up mess.

Immediately I punched in Barbara's number on my phone to find out the status of our adoption. She wasn't in. Walt had been calling her a couple of times a week, alternating with my calls. We didn't know it, but Barbara said we often phoned her within the same hour. Still she was always polite, even though I knew she wished we would stop calling. That wasn't going to happen. We believed in the cliché, "the squeaking wheels get the grease,' although I felt increasingly like I had rolled into a ditch.

I continued being obsessed with adopting Devon, fearing that we must save him from evil. The fact that the system demanded us to just wait infuriated me. Walt and I both had issues with authority. Pure rebellion. I knew the concept of "let go and let God," but I was not ready to surrender, despite having trained in the ministry. Instead I rationalized that God gave us the impatience and courage to fight against wrongs. I was like many people who take religion classes and attend church every Sunday. We pick and choose the spiritual teachings that are most convenient. I chose the ones that didn't require me to move too far out of my comfort zone.

In the days ahead, I found some of our friends and family members less than supportive of our adoption. So, like the spiritual teachings on patience and understanding that I wasn't ready to follow, we ignored these dear ones.

There was one neighbor who, I thought, was my friend. We had asked her to fill out the adoption reference sheet. I had no idea that secretly she didn't approve. She took her time returning the form, despite knowing that we were up against a deadline to adopt Devon. She became passive-aggressive, giving us excuse after excuse as to why she did not complete the paperwork. When we realized what she was doing, we excused her from our lives.

There were others who questioned why we were adopting since we could have more birth children. One friend was blatant. "Why do you want to adopt someone else's problems?" I was appalled.

I could not find it in my heart to forgive these people. Yes, we were driven by a mission that even we didn't understand, but Lord help anyone who got in our way. Forgiveness was another spiritual principal that I wasn't prepared to use. It was much easier to fume at people and the system. We didn't need their support. We would get Devon despite them.

We found light as well as resistance. Jessie and Teresa, other neighbors whom we had also asked to give us an adoption recommendation, got the forms back to DCFS immediately. I had no idea then that in the coming days Jessie would play a crucial part in our adoption process.

In the meanwhile, I was humiliated having to depend on family and friends for recommendations for this phase of the adoption, which we found invasive. But we were not going to drop out of the process like many blacks, who resented the screenings, fearing Big Brother - - whom they didn't trust -- was watching.

One afternoon we were attending a birthday party in the park for Jessie and Teresa's five-year-old son, Joseph. Teresa had festively decorated the benches and trees with multi-colored balloons and streamers. Barbecuing hot dogs and hamburgers cooked on the grill smoked the air. A half-eaten Ninja Turtle birthday cake, empty soda cups, and used paper plates were left on the now-deserted picnic table as the kids were running amok, fueled with sugar.

Ryan and Joseph streaked past us playing tag, ducking behind our legs and taunting one another as the other party children climbed the trees and playground equipment like picnic ants. Weary parents watched vigilantly like police on tactical alert, fearing a late afternoon visit to the hospital.

"How's the adoption going, Jan?" asked Teresa, a bronze beauty with braids. She was a stay-at-home mom, who represented the dream for us crazed, working mothers. She kept herself in great shape. Her hair was always perfectly styled, makeup artistically applied, and her clothes were carefully coordinated. I always envied how she seemed so calm and relaxed. Teresa appeared to breeze through motherhood like she was riding on a sailboat. In contrast, I grunted and grinned my way through each day. I dreamed of having, like her, the time to give to myself. Running after our rambunctious four-year-old, the long commute to work, and babysitting spoiled actors who acted like four year olds left little time for me. I always felt sloppily thrown together standing next to her.

"What part of the nightmare do you want to hear about the system?" I said.

At that time Jessie and Walt, who had been talking sports, joined our conversation.

"What do you mean?" asked Jessie, his eyes narrowed. I could almost see his news antenna going up. Jessie was producer of KABC, Eyewitness News, on channel 7, the local ABC Television news program, and he was good at his power job. We were proud of his being an African-American surviving years in a cutthroat environment that demanded quick thinking and sound judgment.

For the next 15 minutes Walt and I kept the couple spellbound as we walked them through the world of children trapped in the system. Jessie's eyes widened with shock as he hung on our every word. I could see him picking it up on his newsman's internal radar screen.

"Listen, it sounds like a good story. Would you be willing to come forward to talk about it?" asked Jessie.

"Well…ah yes. I guess so," said Walt, looking over at me as if he had won something. "But, let me get back to you on that." We were reading one another's thoughts. How would DCFS react?

"Okay. There could be other families dropping out of the process since it takes so long." I could see Jessie's mind rolling. "Those kids deserve homes."

That night Walt and I discussed Jessie's interest in a news story as we got into bed. It gave us support and a surge of hope. But at the same time we knew that media exposure could short out our fuse with DCFS. They could find ways of dumping us from the screening process even though we had passed the preliminary steps. Devon would then remain trapped in the system. Still, we held onto Jessie's offer like a trump card in a high stakes card game.

About a week later I awakened to the loud squawking of blackbirds feasting on the mulberry tree outside our bedroom window, which made me flash on Alfred Hitchcock's famous horror movie, "The Birds." Bleary-eyed, I turned on the television and flipped through the channels to see what actors were on the early morning news shows as I got dressed for work. Most likely I'd find one of our ABC stars on a segment. ABC was on the top of the ratings. I knew my boss in the staff meeting would ask who had seen a certain interview. I think it was his way of measuring sharp publicists who were motivated.

I don't remember what news program I had turned to, but I caught a segment featuring Taurean Blacque, who starred on the hit series "Hill Street Blues." His show then was one of the hottest drama series on the air and had swept the Emmy Awards. The unmarried actor, known for his spirituality, was being interviewed on why he chose to adopt nine children from the county's foster care system by himself. He definitely would need God to raise all of those kids alone.

A couple of hours later I was in the office on the phone, trying to track the actor down through my studio contacts. Maybe he could give me advice on how we could speed up the adoption process or, better yet, maybe he had a DCFS connection that I could use. He didn't know me, but I was sure that with ABC behind my name he would talk to me -- and I was right. The next day when I came back from lunch, I found a message that the actor had called.

The commanding, calm baritone voice on the other end of the phone was receptive, especially when I spoke about our commonality adopting through DCFS. The actor didn't have the special connections to fly Devon into our home, but he did have a lead. He had just finished taping a public service television spot for an adoption and foster care agency. He gave me the phone number. Maybe the person in charge could help.

A few days later Walter and I were keeping an appointment to see Gonzalo Medina, Director of a Latino Adoption agency, the actor's contact.

When we walked into a brand new office located in East Los Angeles, the fresh smell of processed wood wrapped around me like a forest wind. Vibrations of rebirth were in the newly constructed walls and in the staff. They seemed giddy with excitement as they rushed past us smiling, carrying objects and settling into their new offices like ants storing food in their nests.

We continued past a pile of new oak furniture that was stacked against a wall, covered with plastic sheets and waiting to be distributed. Pictures of smiling children graced the walls. Sitting behind a rounded desk, a smiling, perky receptionist wearing a bright floral dress, asked how she could help us. The energy and the people in this agency were light years from the heaviness that permeated the DCFS offices where we attended the adoption orientation. I'll never forget our first day visiting DCFS. Walt and I walked through the bleak, dark hallways leading to the orientation room, which was just as gloomy. I could feel the souls of the abused and neglected children crying out in those halls.

Five minutes later we were walking into 36 modest office filled with files stacked on the floor. A tall, attractive man dressed in a dark blue suit stood up from his desk, greeting us with a wide smile as if we were old friends. He looked more like a stockbroker than a children's worker as he jabbed his hand toward us to shake.

Photos of two little girls were on his desk in a wooden frame and, in another, Gonzalo was pictured smiling with an attractive woman I guessed was his wife. Children's drawings, the kind only parents could love, were tacked on a bulletin board behind his desk.

The sunlight bathing his office was like a spiritual sign that this man definitely carried the light. Gonzalo was a former county social worker who had become frustrated with the system and opened up his own non-profit adoption and foster care agency. He had no idea that the agency would become so successful. In 15 months his agency placed 60 children in adoptive homes, more than five of the Los Angeles County agencies together had placed during that period. Soon he was getting speaking engagements and requests to consult with other agencies around the country. They all wanted his advice on how to implement rapid adoption placements. He was an authority on placing children in homes and quoted in Time and Newsweek magazines.

Gonzalo also made appearances on national morning talk shows and even sat on a panel with former First Lady Barbara Bush. The Institute was booming with clients, which was the reason why they had just moved into a bigger space. Satellite offices were soon to open in several other Los Angeles counties. Some of Gonzalo's staff, former county social workers, had defected to his side, having grown weary of the system.

We sipped coffee as we told Gonzalo about our problems adopting Devon, and I was surprised that he wasn't surprised. "This is common," he deadpanned. "That's why I founded the agency."

An intercom buzz interrupted us. Gonzalo held up his finger to us as if to say one minute and picked up the phone. "Ah huh…okay, yeah, you're right. Oh that's great. Happy to hear it. Okay, I'll sign them. Bring them in." He hung up the phone, smiling broadly, leaning back in his chair and folding his hands across his stomach as if he had just eaten a satisfying meal.

"Sorry for the interruption," Gonzalo said. "I have some adoption papers to sign. It will be just a moment. Another child is being placed in a home." He was grinning like a proud papa. He stood up and took off his jacket, draping it across the back of his black leather chair. "I love it when these finalize."

A few seconds later an attractive woman in her 30s carrying a stack of papers appeared, smiling warmly. I have always found that people outside of the entertainment industry who readily smile are often light bearers. In Tinsel Town it was hard for me to tell the light bearers from the cutthroats. Everybody seemed to smile.

"Mr. and Mrs. Jackson, this is Celia Lopez, my associate."

"Nice meeting you," she said warmly, shaking our hands. Celia was a former county social worker, like Gonzalo, who operated the Institute with him. The full-figured woman, dressed smartly in a gray pants suit and black heels, wore her hair pulled back into a bun, showcasing her tan, heart-shaped face. Obviously detail oriented, Celia stood next to Gonzalo behind his desk, vigilantly watching him sign, making sure she hadn't missed any blank spaces in the stack of papers she had given him.

"Celia, the Jacksons are adopting through the County. I don't have to tell you, they're running up against problems." She looked up at us with an animated grimace. "I was telling them that's why we started the agency."

"We have a much higher placement rate than the county," said Celia proudly.

"Yeah, we heard," said Walt. "I wish we had known about this place before we went through the county."

"We're trying to get the word out," said Gonzalo.

"You know, Janet is a publicist for ABC," said Walt. "Maybe she could help you get more actors." I usually cringe and burn inside when Walt offers my services without checking with me first. I was constantly on guard like celebrities, worrying if people were using my friendship to get close to the limelight of television. But this time I didn't mind it since I would be helping children find homes.

"Yeah, I'd be glad to help," I said. "Actors are always looking for causes to promote. I have to warn you, though. For some it's a way to truly give back for all of their blessings. For others it's just another form of publicity to keep their names out there. You want someone who is truly behind your purpose. I'll keep an eye out."

"Hey, we'd like that. Thanks," said Gonzalo, shooting Celia a thumbs-up glance. After listing for us celebrities they had lined up for their public service announcements on radio and TV, the conversation shifted to our adoption. Sadly, when we learned there was nothing more that anyone could do to speed up the process, I deflated like a balloon.

"Actually, you're way ahead of the game compared to other perspective parents who have been eliminated from the county adoption process," said Gonzalo. "Many of the families who have signed up with the institute say they were turned down by the county for a variety of stupid reasons."

"One couple told us that they were rejected because the social worker said they were too happily married," said Celia. "Probably thought they were putting on an act."

"You've got to be kidding," I said.

"Another of our clients who went through the county said she was turned down because her crystal collection was not child-proofed."

"But that's something she could easily fix. Right? Just get a case for it?" I was naive.

"You would think so," said Gonzalo dryly.

"We had a couple who came to us after they said the county rejected them because a light bulb was not at the top of a dark staircase. Another applicant said she was turned down because she was overweight and had hypertension," said Celia.

"That's half of the population," I snapped.

"One of our couples has been approved and were waiting since 1984 for an older child," said Gonzalo, "and that was six years ago. We had a client who already had a four-year-old son who was rejected by the county because she commuted from L.A. to Santa Barbara to work each day. They told her they were eliminating her application because she would have to get the adopted child up at 5:00 a.m. with her birth child to take them both to day care near her job."

"But lots of kids from non-adoptive families have long commutes similar to that," said Walt.

"That's what we said. She would have had to take a $400 cut in paycheck if she moved to a closer job." Gonzalo shook his head in disgust. "Sixteen years on the job at senior level. She'd have to start at the bottom again on the other job. Fortunately she came to us and we placed a child with her because through our screenings we found out the woman was a great mother."

"You know I live in Ontario," said Gonzalo. "I get my boys up at 5:00 a.m. to take them to Catholic school in the city."

"You wouldn't have qualified to adopt them if they weren't your biological children," said Celia, giggling as she looked at Gonzalo.

"Absolutely right. The standards are different for foster kids."

"They don't have any rights," chimed in Celia. "Especially siblings. There are a lot of great social workers out there. But some seem to look for ways to reject a prospective family rather than ways that they can help make a placement work. We had two foster kids, Eddie and April. Brother and sister. We took one of our clients to a DCFS adoption party and she saw Eddie. She loved him at first sight. She saw a little girl that Eddie was playing with and she asked us whom she was. It was Eddie's sister, April. She was in another foster home. They had never lived together. The lady told us, 'Well, I can't split these kids up so I'll take both of them.' The children's social worker from DCFS didn't want to place Eddie's sister with Eddie because they had never lived together.

"That was her reason," said Gonzalo, chuckling sarcastically. "Can you imagine that?"

Celia continued: "The social worker said Eddie had a few behavior problems, and since they had not lived together it wasn't necessary to place them together. I asked her since both of the children live in foster homes with other kids, what's the problem? They've both lived with other kids before. Her answer was, 'They might not get along.'"

"Now what siblings do get along all of the time?" I asked, my voice shrieking in shock. "They have to learn how to get along."

Gonzalo continued: "I asked her, 'Why are you speculating that they're going to have problems?' The social worker thought about it. We compromised and I said, 'Look, let's place them in the same home but at different times.' So we ended up moving Eddie into the lady's home first, around September. Then we moved April to the home in December. They were reunited for Christmas. And guess what?"

"They got along. Right?" Walt said, smiling.

"You're right."

"Famously," chuckled Celia.

As we listened, Walt and I learned that the system back then didn't encourage putting siblings back together once they were taken from their home. It was becoming increasingly clear to me that there were two types of people working for DCFS: the Sleepers and the Light Bearers. The Sleepers were one of the reasons why children fell through the cracks. Some are condescending, others are overwrought with power, or they may have no power, and for that reason they're bitter. They won't do any more than necessary to keep from being fired, and they often make mistakes. The Light Bearers are the opposite. There are many social workers, like Gonzalo and Celia, who will go to any distance to help children. They are the reason many kids find happy homes.

I began seeing DCFS as the venomous dragon guarding the castle where the Sleepers and the Light Bearers work. Adoptions can drag on for months and years. There was a growing anger that I had with the dragon. One of my greatest lessons was going to be how to overcome this venom that was poisoning me.

To Westerners, the dragon is a fire-breathing demon. But in order for me to have peace, I would have to shift my attitude and see the dragon through Eastern eyes to help Devon. Asians identify the dragon as a spiritual being, a divine symbol of the spirit of change. It would be a stretch for me to see DCFS like that. Back then I was determined this dragon had to be slain.

"Why do you think it's so hard for people to adopt through the County?" I asked Gonzalo.

"Social workers are overworked. Most carry about 90 cases and more. They almost have to do drive-by visits."

"What's that?" asked Walt.

"It's what social workers, if their ranks keep decreasing due to budge cuts, will have to do. Since the social workers have to see all of their children at least once a month, and there is no way they can visit with each one, the best way for them to see their entire rosters is to do drive-bys. They call the foster parents and tell them they will be by at a certain time to see the foster child they're assigned to. The foster parent puts the child in the window, and the worker waves to the kid as she drives by. Now she can record that she saw the child."

"They really do that?" I asked innocently with wide eyes.

"No," said Gonzalo . "It's a joke -- but they may have to."

We all laughed, which broke the mounting tension from the horrid stories. But it wasn't funny that a drive-by might be the only way for a social worker to see all of her children every month. I would learn in the coming years that most social workers were doing their best but simply are caught in the dragon's system.

"There is just so much red tape they have to go through, that's also what slows down the process," says Gonzalo.

"Something is slowing them down," said Walt, frowning.

We talked for about an hour and a half, and it was clear that we were two of the more fortunate adoptive parents by having Barbara as our social worker. She truly championed us despite her getting stuck in the system, too.

When we were ready to leave, Celia gave us her card and told us to call any time for advice. Gonzalo then walked us out, leading us back past the smiling receptionist. Before we went out the front door, he stopped us.

"You must believe you'll get Devon. Refuse to accept no," he said fiercely. "You have to shift your attitude from trying to adopt Devon to rescuing him from the system. Remember, you are on a rescue mission."

CHAPTER SEVEN

March has always been the most electrifying month of the year for me, probably because it's springtime and my birth month. When I met Devon I felt that my life was blooming like the new spring flowers. I had a new lease on life.

I remember feeling then that all of nature was harmonizing with life. Birds chirping, dazzling flowers blooming, and those softly caressing breezes felt like love. The Om, the powerful energy that flows through and animates every single thing and person in the universe, seemed to be pulsating at its highest level and I could sense God in my every step and breath. At any moment I felt that I could fly. I felt that nothing and no one could take away my natural high except the Department of Family and Children's Services.

On March 16, 1990, Barbara called our home. "You've been approved."

"I thought we were approved before."

"Yes, but now the child workers' supervisors and my supervisors have approved you."

I didn't want to try to figure out what this meant compared to our first approval. Instead I tried focusing on the fact that we were steps closer. But even though we were closer, we were still dragging on in the dragon system. The next day I found out that Barbara had a personal emergency and would not be in the office for at least a week. One week stretched into several weeks, and there was no one else to work on our case. Devon's file, his life and my nerve endings were sitting idly on her desk.

~

On a quiet Wednesday evening, April 4, 1990, Walt was sprawled on the couch reading the *Los Angeles Times*. Ryan and I were on the floor playing the Ninja Turtle board game for what felt like the 80th time. Our black cat, Chakra, was stretched out nearby, lazily batting one of the extra dice with his paw almost in time to the soft jazz playing on the stereo. From the dining room door, Prana, our big beautiful German shepherd puppy, whimpered softly, watching us from a safe distance, longing to join the family circle. He was intimidated by Chakra, who had established ground rules when the shepherd moved in. A quick claw swipe to the puppy's nose had sent him howling for cover. He learned instantly that the Jackson home was the cat's territory. It was only when Chakra got bored with us and left the room that Prana would venture in for hugs. But Chakra's reign lasted only a few months. Prana grew to small pony size and discovered he was both the top dog and top cat. They would both live up to their different names that meant the same thing. Energy. I named them that because they constantly flew through the house chasing and running from one another.

Suddenly Walt swung his feet off the sofa and sat up, clutching the paper close to his face as he began reading aloud: "'Angry County Prods State About Foster Homes.'"

I jumped off the floor and plopped next to him on the sofa, looking over his shoulder as he continued reading. "'Stung by allegations that they have failed to protect foster children from abuse, L.A. County supervisors Tuesday told their critics in State government that if they think they can monitor foster homes any better they can take over the job.'"

"They should," I snapped.

Walt continued reading, "'Supervisors voted three to two to terminate the county's contract with the State to license and monitor foster homes, effective June 30, unless the State agrees to provide the county with more money.

"Because of the alleged poor performance by the county, the Department of Children Services State officials also are considering terminating the $3.3 million-a-year contract that gives the County authority to license and monitor 3,800 foster homes housing more than 10,000 children.

"Robert Chaffee, director of the County Children's Services told the supervisors, 'You can't have high expectations on one hand and on the other hand not fully fund the activities to achieve that.'"

"High expectations?" I said. "What does he mean high expectations? That the kids would not have to be abused in the system? Is that a high expectation?"

"Or how about just staying alive in the foster homes," added Walt.

That night I went to bed the way I was becoming accustomed to since beginning the adoption process. I was curled in a tense ball, fists clenched with anger and my mind racing. This was after I had prayed, asking for Devon to be protected. In those days I was like so many people who wonder why God doesn't answer prayers. I still wasn't willing to let go and believe that my higher power would take care of it all. Evidently I thought God needed my help, so I stayed awake worrying about Devon. I thought about calling the reporter who wrote the article to see if he wanted our viewpoint for a follow-up story, but then I thought again. DCFS would be angry, and we could lose out on adopting Devon. But, more importantly, he would lose out on having a protective, loving home.

It was now May. Pandemonium and heart attack time at the networks. The fall lineup had just been announced. One hundred and thirty-two national television critics had just left Los Angeles after days of press conferences at the Century Plaza Hotel with each network. We paraded talent and producers from our new and returning shows before them, shamelessly promoting our new line up, an expensive dog and pony show. Small groups of these reporters from newspapers around the country would meet in a conference room, and the actors with their producers would come in and answer questions about their shows, then circulate to another room to answer more press questions.

This was also the time of the year when ABC's photo gallery would be jammed with back-to-back photo sessions. The photos would accompany the articles reporters wrote reviewing the new shows. These pictures would appear in every major national and local publication around the country and many publications in countries around the world.

It didn't matter how many of these photo sessions I had arranged, I was still nuts the night before. Would the limos pick up the actors on time? Did I remember to hire a special hairdresser an actress requested? Would the studios deliver the right wardrobe? Every session was uniquely different, especially when you were dealing with temperamental actors and their handlers. You never knew what to expect.

Back then the photo sessions mirrored my personal life. I never knew what to expect from my family. I was the youngest of my Los Angeles relatives, who ranged from late '60s to 94 years old. I had cared for them and then, one by one, they died. Five deaths in four years. I was the only one strong enough to pick out their caskets and make funeral arrangements. My fast-paced show business life helped me to forget the grief that seemed to follow me from childhood into adulthood. In the coming years Devon would make me remember.

Actresses Halle Berry and Michael Learned were in individual rooms, sitting patiently as make up artists and hair stylists readied them for the photo session. I thanked them both for coming, and we speculated about their upcoming season. ABC had just given the green light to their show, "Living Dolls," a comedy spin-off of "Who's the Boss," starring Tony Danza, another show I also handled. On "Dolls" Halle played one of four young, struggling models and Michael played the owner of their modeling agency. I was thrilled to be working with Michael again. We had worked together for years at CBS on the first big series I was assigned to promote, "The Waltons." Michael performed as Olivia, the mother, which won her three Emmys.

Halle was the ingénue then. She was excited over the publicity fuss and the show. "Dolls" was her first television role. Not only was she one of the most beautiful women I had ever met, she was definitely one of the nicest. I recognized that it was just a matter of time for her career to take off. What I enjoyed about being a publicist is that you meet actors who are average Joes off the street, and you can sense which ones will become major stars. You help them to get there.

Hollywood publicists work like crazed maniacs begging reporters to write about actors, and then the next day it seems you're hiring security to protect them from throngs of fans when they're on publicity tours. The downside is that some actors, like rebellious teens, grow big heads and try to distance themselves from you. They don't want to admit that a publicist has helped them become famous. They prefer to think the world just discovered them.

By 10:00 a.m. the entire cast had arrived. Everyone was in great spirits. Organized pandemonium. Hairdressers, caterers, costumers, personal publicity agents, and photo assistants all mingled as we watched the ladies strike poses before the cameras. In between wardrobe changes people scurried around like mice searching for cheese. Photo assistants ripped down backgrounds, costumers snatched clothing off racks, makeup people touched up the actors while hair-dressers teased and sprayed their hair.

I was talking to Bob D'Amico, ABC's top studio photographer who was going over the list of the various combination shots we still needed to have done, when we were interrupted by a phone call for me.

I took the call thinking there was a problem on one of my other shows since those were the only calls I had asked to be transferred to the photo gallery.

"Ms. Jackson?"

"Yes." I barely recognized Barbara's bubbly voice. Usually she's reserved, controlled and soft spoken.

"You've been approved by the computer." Her voice was trembling with excitement. I didn't know a computer would determine our fate.

"Great," I said frowning with confusion. I plopped myself on top of a desk, grabbed a pen and paper and started writing down everything she said. So far I had documented the entire adoption process. I would write on napkins or anything that was handy. It was part of my journalism training at San Jose State University. You never know when notes will come in handy. I had a sense that I would need them later.

I had hoped that Barbara was going to say that Devon was coming home. I didn't feel overjoyed that a computer had approved us. Should I thank it? I could only think of one thing: How much longer? We wanted to celebrate special days with Devon, but we watched his birthday, my birthday, and Easter pass. Now Mother's Day was coming up, and I knew we would miss celebrating that day together, too.

"What's the next step, Barbara?" I said with a cut-the-crap tone.

"We're taking him to get his medical exam."

"That includes an HIV test, right?" I was sure that it would automatically be included.

"An HIV test?" All the joy and enthusiasm suddenly drained from her voice.

"Yes." I frowned, sensing her hesitation. I put my finger in my ear trying to block out the commotion and the loud music in the lounge where I was taking the call. Food was laid out on two long tables, and a few of the crew members had meandered in. They were munching and talking loudly while watching a segment of a mid-morning news program. Since the session would be breaking for lunch after the last photo set-up, I transferred the call to a private office next door.

"Barbara, his mother is a drug addict," I said, my voice turning harsh.

"I know she is -- " I didn't let her finish. I refused to hear any excuses, so I spoke bluntly and louder.

"No telling who she had sex with or what needle she was using. In fact, she doesn't know the father. We don't know what has happened to Devon in foster care. If he was physically abused he could have been sexually abused, too."

This was at the time when people were first whispering about HIV, and no one knew much about the dreaded condition. One of my friends had just attended a funeral of someone who had died of AIDS. The closed casket had been draped in black netting, and a rope barrier had been placed around it to make sure no one could come within five feet of it.

"You do test for HIV, don't you?" My voice now dramatically lowered.

Barbara excused herself to ask her supervisor while I hung on the phone,
squeezing it like the neck I wanted to wring. About 30 seconds later she came back on the line. Her voice was soft but tense.

"Ms. Jackson, we don't do HIV testing as part of these types of medical exams."

Up until this time I had been cordial with Barbara because she was a Light Bearer and doing everything that she could to speed up our adoption. I had also been careful to make sure I made a good impression. But this was the last shred of patience sputtering and sizzling inside of me. I didn't know it was about to explode or that anyone in my way was going to get blown away.

"Get me your supervisor," I barked, surprising her and myself.

"She just left."

"I need to talk to her," I shrieked, "get her… please." I was shaking with dammed up rage. Was my Light Bearer now lying to me?

Barbara and I had been dancing nicely with one another, and she had been leading. But now I was going to decide what song would be playing. As I waited, I expected Barbara to come back and insist her supervisor was not available. In Hollywood we played those games often, so I was shocked when I heard someone else get on the line.

"Hello, Ms. Jackson?" The strange voice was a sugarcoated calm.

Instantly I knew it was Barbara's supervisor. As she spoke I became calm, too. I knew she was handling me like staff would do with a patient in a mental hospital. They're trained to remain cool and calm to keep the patients calm. Some spiritual teachers will match their breath with the shallow, rapid breathing of a troubled seeker who comes to them for guidance. The teacher will then slow his own breath down. Miraculously the troubled person's breath will slow and calm. Whatever Barbara's supervisor was doing, it worked, because I wasn't demonic anymore. But I knew I was being manipulated. I could feel my face hardening.

As she spoke I sized her up, nicknaming her Ms. Dingdong. I hoped a bell would wake up this Sleeper. When she spoke I listened intently, wondering how she would justify not giving Devon an HIV test. I began calmly but firmly explaining all the reasons why Devon should have HIV testing.

"Ms. Jackson, I've had an AIDS training course. If symptoms haven't come up by now, and he's three years old, then he doesn't have AIDS."

"Oh, so you know the incubation period of AIDS?" I snapped. I was losing it again. "That's more than scientists know." I knew I was sabotaging my chances to adopt Devon, but I was focused on winning this fight. I was now an unleashed wild animal, remembering words: "Remember, you are rescuing Devon from the system."

"You'll have to petition the courts to get him tested," she said. "It's a matter of confidentiality."

"How long will that take?" I was stabbing my pen on the notes I was taking.

"About two to three months,"

"You're kidding! Why isn't this part of your regular medical exam?"

"It's a privacy issue." I remembered a friend who worked in the County Children's Court once telling me that some social workers say things are privacy issues with foster kids when they don't want to -- or can't -- give an answer.

"So let me get this straight." My words dripped with sarcasm. "You can let me know the results of his medical tests that tell if he's anemic, a diabetic, has allergies, and no telling what else," my voice was strained with rage. "But you can't tell me if he's HIV positive because that falls under a privacy ruling?"

She was exasperated, and she pulled out her big guns.

"So are you saying that you won't adopt the child if he's HIV positive, Ms. Jackson?" Her verbal bullets knocked me flat on my back. I couldn't speak to Ms. Dingdong's ignorance for a few seconds.

Suddenly my body became a foreign object, recoiling, and again shaking. My stomach burned with anger acid. I had no fear. In the years ahead, fighting the system, I would learn that there was something I could do to always be in calm control no matter how angry the dragon system made me. But I wasn't in that consciousness yet. To me fighting still was just as important as winning.

Ms. Dingdong, I wanted to call her, "I have buried five family members in four years, and if Devon has AIDS or is HIV positive, I have a right to know so we can make an intelligent adoption decision." Our hearts had already decided, but I didn't tell her that.

"You gave me a choice telling me he was drug exposed. But I don't know if I'm strong enough to bury my child if he had AIDS. If we knew this, we might decide to walk away from the adoption, but we can't decide unless we know his state, then I'll decide. I do know we should at least have that choice. What if we adopt him and he is HIV positive? Our health insurance carrier may drop us because of that. Carriers drop people with life-threatening illnesses all the time. How would we pay for his treatments? They're expensive." I didn't take a breath. "I don't know what we would do if he turns out to have AIDS, because we're already so connected to him. We'll just have to deal with it when we come to that road." I stopped talking, but my engine was still in high gear. Vibrations shook my body like an idling race car.

"I still feel it's highly unlikely," she said calmly. I imagined, from the condescending tone of her voice, she had long, blood red nails and rings on each finger. She probably had a personalized license plate that read, "Hur Majesty."

Ms. Dingdong, I resisted the urge to call her, "He could have been sexually abused in foster care. Besides, if we don't know if he is HIV positive, he could infect our entire family. We should know the risks." At that time no one knew how AIDS was spread. There were rumors that drinking from the same glass or just being in the same room with someone with the virus was risky.

Finally the supervisor had nothing else left to pull out of her ignorant bag of tricks. "Let me have you talk to the county nurse," she said, now clearly frustrated. I knew she was hoping that the nurse would calm my fears. It pleased me that I could rattle and stand up to the ice queen. The networks had taught me how to stand up against the toughest actors, producers and directors on the planet.

"How will I get in touch with her?"

"She'll call you." Now I was sure I was getting the brush off.

"When?"

"Hopefully this afternoon. As soon as we can get a hold of her."

"I'll be waiting," I said dryly. When I hung up I dropped my head in my hands trying to lasso the fury that was galloping inside of me like a run away horse. I began deep breathing to slow down the bucking bronco inside of me. I couldn't let the actors see me like this. I needed to be cheerful and happy. I fought the tears that were brimming in my eyes. I hated that they always came when I was furious. It had been that way since I was a little girl.

Laughter and loud talking filtered under the door. I could tell everyone was now eating lunch. I heard someone call out my name, but I ignored them. I needed to get a hold of myself before I went back out there. I took slow, deep breaths and began slipping back on my publicist's happy-go-lucky face. Publicists are often great actors. How many times have we found ourselves up to our elbows in egos and had to grin through it all to get a job done for the networks? But sometimes I felt more like a prostitute than an actor.

Just when I was about to leave the office the phone on the desk rang. "I'll get it," I yelled out. I heard someone, say, "Oh, there's Janet. I didn't know she was in there."

"Hello, may I speak to Ms. Janet Alston Jackson?" said a sweet, delightful voice on the other end of the line. Could this be the county nurse?

Instinctively I became a blowtorch, ready to fire out my reasons why Devon should have HIV testing. But the nurse completely disarmed me by immediately taking my side. I relaxed, lowering my emotional artillery. What do you know? A Light Bearer.

Unfortunately, the issue was out of the nurse's hands. It was still in the dragon system. After she reiterated what Ms. Dingdong had said -- that we would have to petition the courts -- I called Barbara back. I told her to start the ball rolling -- or dragging as in the dragon system's case.

Deflated, I hung up the phone and called Walt to relay the stupid DCFS conversations through my tears.

"It could take us two to three more months to get through the courts just to have him tested. It's insane, Walt. Devon could end up like those kids we're reading about in the paper who are killed in foster care. It will be too late then. I don't want us to be too late. We already may be. "

Whenever I am down I can always depend on Walt to take my side and give me new hope and strength.

"Let's call Jessie," he said in his calm, deep voice filled with conviction.

It was his war tone. "It's time to talk to the press."

CHAPTER EIGHT

I finally stopped fearing that our adoption would be hurt if we called the press about the Department of Children and Family Services. My focus was only on getting Devon out of a possibly abusive foster home. I imagined that press exposure would put our problem in the spotlight and that the Department would be anxious to speed up our adoption to silence us. At least I hoped they would. But why wouldn't they? The state was investigating the county. Negative news stories were constantly surfacing about foster care children dying in the system.

What worried me was that I probably told Barbara our plans to call the media too early. I should have called the press first and surprised DCFS. Now I worried, did DCFS have time to cover their tracks? Being the efficient employee that she was, I was sure Barbara had.

I fought off thoughts that something could happen to my family and me. Every sound was amplified in my head as I tried sleeping. My mind replayed all of the government plot movies that I had seen where whistleblowers and their entire families disappeared after they challenged the system. Friends' fears echoed in my mind: "You'd better be careful with those people. They don't play."

Could a knock on our door in the middle of the night change our lives or take our lives? I managed to neutralize my anxiety by remembering that corporate whistleblowers go to the press all the time. My other mind said that they were in a witness protection program and we weren't. Still I argued with myself. If you're in the media's eye, you are safe. The problem is that the press has a voracious appetite for stories and the public has a short attention span. Twenty-four hours can make you yesterday's news.

I drew my strength from Walt, who has a fearless attitude toward life. No one and nothing ever seems to frighten him. If there is a problem or injustice against us that we cannot do anything about, Walt has this innate ability to turn things around and convince me not to worry. Many times when I had been anxious over a problem, he succinctly gave me advice to move on, "Screw them!"

I knew that Walt's strength stemmed from his surviving a perilous car accident and a coma. He had kicked death in the face and he was not going to spend life's precious moments in fear. He had already been to hell and back after his fateful car accident which took away all of his sports scholarships and a shot at the pros. I, on the other hand, had to struggle to overcome my fears. I tried to do it through prayer.

In Walt's more compassionate moments he reminded me of our spiritual training in the ministry. "Where attention goes, power flows."

Finally, I decided not to give DCFS any more attention than necessary. Instead, I thought of Mark Brown, the reporter coming to interview us who is today a popular TV news anchor in Los Angeles.

Then, he was the new, rookie reporter at the local ABC station. He reminded me of a road not taken in my life. There is something about news people that has always fascinated me, probably because I once wanted to be one. But I couldn't get a news job despite my broadcast journalism degree or my CBS radio news internship. It also didn't seem to matter that I had been a community reporter for a San Francisco public access television station. The market was so competitive, and black reporters then were as infrequent as comet sightings. It would have been easier for me to become a rock star.

Despite my high paid, glamorous publicity job, I always felt that I had missed out. I remember being at a place in my life when I was happy in my publicity career until one day I was assigned to shepherd a couple of the biggest CBS news stars at one of our press events. I took a limo to the Los Angeles International Airport and picked up Don Hewitt, longtime executive producer of the "60 Minutes" program, and Charles Kuralt whose "On the Road" segments for the CBS Evening News was a big hit then. They talked about the news business as we traveled to meet the press. I fell into a depression.

I felt like a failure never having achieved my college dreams as a broadcast journalist. It didn't matter that I made more money than some of the newspaper reporters who would interview Don and Charlie that day. I tried rationalizing that the reporters got their celebrity news from the press releases I wrote. In reality, it wasn't news, and I wasn't a journalist.

It would take years of working on hundreds of shows and traveling with celebrities around the country before the "if only" thoughts finally disappeared and I became truly grateful for my publicity career. It also helped that over the years I saw the integrity of many news outlets go down the drain as reporters moved closer to yellow journalism and tabloid news.

The day finally arrived when Walt and I would talk to the press about Devon. I was nervous and yet I felt powerful at the same time. We were the little everyday people who were going up against the dragon, DCFS.

I was looking out the window when a white satellite van with "ABC, Channel 7 News" on the side, pulled in front of our house. My heart was pounding. Those old news regrets, mixed with the excitement of exposing the injustices of the County adoption system, were swirling in my chest like a mini-tornado.

Mark Brown, a handsome, large, chocolate complexioned reporter dressed in a gray suit and tie, sat in our living room interviewing us while his cameraman, dressed in jeans, was videotaping. For 20 minutes on camera, Walt and I regurgitated all of the injustices we felt about our adoption. I knew our interview would be boiled down to a 10 second sound bite.

Later we all walked onto the front lawn while the cameraman attempted to get B-roll of Ryan riding his motorized yellow car in circles. I chuckled to myself, seeing the cameraman seemingly getting dizzy trying to film Ryan. Frustrated, he stopped filming and smiled at me through gritted teeth.

"Boy, he doesn't stop, does he?" I smiled back and whispered, "Try living with the little hyper thing."

Before leaving, Mark told us he was setting up interviews in the next few days with DCFS. "The story should air within a week," he said as we walked him to the ABC van.

Two weeks passed and our story had yet to air. Finally, I called Jessie, our news producer friend who had arranged for the interview. "Your piece has been cut for a bigger story," he said. "I'm sorry. I'm as frustrated as you are."

I felt like a soldier lost in enemy territory. Back then, I didn't have a clue how to control my anger, and it flared like a rampant forest fire, burning with bitterness.

Did DCFS pay off Mark, and what story could be more important than an abused homeless kid trapped in the system? I ran the race card through my head, which I've tried not using unless I suspected a blatant injustice. I always hate it when some blacks overuse it to stay victimized or as a cop out. Besides, to my knowledge, I had not been discriminated against at the networks. I once heard Sammy Davis Jr. say that whites in entertainment were more accepting than other whites of his color, and I felt the same. I feared that if I left the unique world of show business, where the color that matters most is green, I could be in serious trouble.

Still, color was an issue for me with the Brown interview. Was the story killed because we were black? I even blamed Mark. If nothing else, why didn't he push this story to air to help his people? Moreover, he knew that DCFS had created a special unit to speed up African-American adoptions since more of our kids were in the system. That alone would tell anyone there's a serious problem. My imagination ran wild. Was Mark trying to play the corporate game, being the ambitious new kid on the block? Had he forgotten who he was? I also wielded ageism against him. He was young, unmarried, and childless. Those single, cool, swinging brothers don't have any family values I fumed to myself. How could this young brother feel compassion for these babies in the system if he wasn't a father? He walked in another world.

My mind continued to spew poisonous, paranoid thoughts as I fantasized about why the story had not run. I didn't want to accept Mark's innocence or the nature of the news business. There are just so many minutes in a news show, and bigger stories always get priority. In reality he didn't have a choice, or maybe he simply didn't have enough proof or substance for the story to air. Even though deep down I knew it was out of his hands, I wanted to blame someone.

Finally, I collapsed in a sorry heap on my bed, balled up in the fetal position in the middle of the afternoon, and drifted into a teary sleep. No one else seemed to care about the foster kids trapped in the system. They certainly could not care less about Devon.

A few days later when I was still wallowing in depression, we got another call from Barbara. "The Jackson name is being whispered up and down the hallways here."

"What do you mean?"

"The reporter? Mark Brown? You know that he had been asking people around here a lot of questions about your adoption, don't you?"

Suddenly Mark was my hero. God bless him. He was my black Walter Cronkite. I thought of the anger I vented at him and felt guilty. Looking back, it reminds me of a teaching from Buddhist Zen master Thich Nhat Hahn, whom I studied and deeply admired.

"Every day," he taught, "We have at least 21 false perceptions." Obviously, I had at least 21 wrong perceptions about Mark. He did his investigation as promised and it was effective. It got DCFS's attention. But it was my inflated ego that wanted our story blasted all over the news.

Walt and I were thrilled, but only for a couple of days until reality set. The system was still grinding at its agonizingly slow pace. I kept imagining an evil foster mother who only wanted County money to keep him, abusing Devon.

I came home early one day from a location shoot, and again I melted into my now too common fetal position on our couch. Out of sheer desperation I called Gonzalo to commiserate. I didn't know why. He could not help us, but still I was driven to call him. I found myself bending over as if to throw up, rubbing my forehead as I spoke in a soft, hopeless voice. "… and they're not going to air our story after all. Now we still have to wait months for a court date to get Devon HIV tested."

"You don't have to wait that long," Gonzalo said with strong confidence.

"We don't?" My eyes widened. I jumped up and pressed the beige phone receiver to my ear so tightly that my ear began throbbing.

"No, of course not," said Gonzalo. "A social worker can walk that request into a judge's chamber and get an order signed instantly."

I felt blood rushing into my face like a rising thermometer on a hot day. I didn't feel happy about the news, instead I felt sheer rage. "Why didn't Barbara's supervisor tell me this when I talked to her?" I shrieked. "She knew this!"

Gonzalo didn't have a chance to answer. I ranted while he quietly agreed. I realized that this was inside information they didn't want prospective families to have. If people knew this little tip, all of the families would want immediate judge's rulings to rush an adopted child into their homes. But it was this kind of hidden inside information that fueled the "them" versus "us" mentality. Bureaucrats pick and choose what they want to speed through the courts.

"I'll tell you whom you can call," said Gonzalo. "Let me give you Sarah Berman's number."

"Who's she?"

"Second in command at DCFS. A super lady. I've had a lot of help from her with clients."

Despite Gonzalo being the expert on these matters, I doubted his advice. I felt that if I called Sarah, it would be like going to the enemy asking for strategies on how to win the war against her side.

"You mean there's someone in that department who actually wants to help get kids placed fast?" I said sarcastically. I knew my social worker Barbara, and Valerie Wong were sincere, but I didn't want to try to rely on anyone else associated with DCFS t at this point. They say that anger is like burning your house down trying to get rid of the rats. At times I felt there were an awful lot of rats in DCFS, and I didn't care if the place blew up into an inferno.

"Yeah," said Gonzalo. "She gets things done. She's different."

Skeptically I hung up and called the wonder lady whom I really didn't believe existed. Maybe Gonzalo had his head on crooked, too.

"I've been waiting for your call Ms. Jackson." Sarah Berman's voice was cool and mellow. I thought of Mark's investigation and smiled before a frown wiped it away. If she was waiting, why didn't she call me? My inflated ego took over. She had to know that we were not the average accepting, passive, adoptive parents waiting for DCFS to bless us with a child. We answered only to a higher power.

As we talked my hopes began to rise, hearing how open she was --

until she hit me with the same line Barbara's supervisor told me. "You will have to petition the courts to get Devon HIV tested." Suddenly it wasn't about only the HIV test, it was about power.

"I don't have to wait for months Ms. Berman," I rasped. "I know you can walk the request through a judge's chamber and get an order signed immediately." I felt the adrenaline pumping in my veins wildly.

Dead silence on the line. Sarah was busted and she knew it. I had played the trump card. I had the information and information is power.

"I'll call you back," she said softly. When I hung up I was mad. I knew that she wouldn't call me back at least for a few days and only to give me another excuse. But not in my wildest fantasies did I expect the call that came several hours later.

"Good news, Ms. Jackson," said Barbara. "A judge has signed an order. The HIV testing has been approved by the court."

"You've got to be kidding!" I squealed with delight. Sarah was okay after all.

"But you know what?" said Barbara, "There was a mix-up." My joy dropped with a thud that must have been almost audible.

"What?" I growled.

"I found out that the foster mother accidentally took Devon for the test. She did it about a week ago through a mix-up. We told her that she would have to do it soon, but she did it right away. So, it's already done. We just have to get the results to you."

Was this really happening? Were we really gaining momentum on the adoption finally? After months of errors and delays, suddenly everything was beginning to move quickly.

CHAPTER NINE

A week later Walt and I sat in Los Angeles' Griffith Park. We were waiting at the pony rides oval for Devon to arrive. It was to be our first "get acquainted" meeting since the adoption party. His HIV test turned out negative, and Sarah had propelled the adoption procedures forward with lightning speed. I had to get an emergency leave from work. Where our lives had been a wheel spinning futilely in mud for months, suddenly we were freed and screeching out of the ditch at 100 miles an hour.

When little Devon finally arrived at the park, hand-in-hand with Valerie Wong, his social worker, I fought hard to keep from crying with joy. He was even cuter and sweeter than my memories. His dark, sad, banjo eyes were mesmerizing.

Walt talked him into his first pony ride, anxious to expose him to all the wonders of childhood of which he had been deprived. The small, slow ponies from which we chose one for Devon were roped to a huge, rustic wagon wheel. The larger ponies trotted loose, following a circular trail. Valerie watched intently as Walt placed Devon on a white pony, saying how amazed at how light he was compared to Ryan, our little linebacker.

While other kids on the ponies were laughing with excitement, Devon kept his solemn eyes riveted on us. I knew that we three anxious adults hanging over the wooden fence and cheering him on must have looked like slaphappy clowns to him.

The next weekend Walt floored our gold Volvo through South Los Angeles and Compton. We passed small, multi-pastel painted shotgun houses with aluminum sidings and bars on every widow. It was known gang territory.

Finally we arrived at the foster home and stood on the steps, waiting for someone to answer the doorbell. I should have been dressed in army fatigues. I wanted to rush in and snatch Devon like the police did in Florida with the little Cuban refugee, Elian Gonzalez.

When an elderly woman came to the door I was completely disarmed. She introduced herself as Lula, Devon's foster mother. Lula wore a faded green apron over a blue, flowered dress that tinted her large body. Her stockings were rolled down to the calves, meeting her dress hem. She waddled slowly, holding onto a chair and a table as she labored back into the small, dark living room with us following her. Lula apologized for her arthritic knees that often stiffened up on her. This was the child abuser? The bronzed woman looked like a harmless grandmother.

We sat on her lumpy, worn-out couch that was evidence of the 22 foster kids she said she had raised over the years. While she explained that the other three foster kids currently living with her were still at school, I looked around at the immaculate, little dark house crammed with old mismatched furniture. She couldn't be Devon's abuser. My mind struggled to comprehend her hurting anyone. Maybe it was the other, older foster children. I began to suspect an adult she had raised as a foster child, who still visited, might have abused Devon. Later I would learn that abusers come in all ages and cross all ethnic, social, and financial lines.

"Devon," Lula called, "the Jacksons are here."

While we waited I watched a large roach race up the living room wall that was peeling faded blue paint. It had to be visiting from next door. Lula's house was drab and tiny, but it was definitely clean.

When a small figure appeared in the doorway, Walt and I lit up. Devon was dressed in mismatched, worn-out clothes that did not fit him. He wore too-short, gray corduroy pants that were much too hot for the 90 degree weather and a large, faded T-shirt with long sleeves. A small rip in the shoulder exposed an inch of his skin. He stood quietly with his arms pinned tightly to his sides.

I walked over to Devon and stooped to his eye level. "Guess what? We're going to see the 'Sesame Street on Ice' show." He didn't say a word but he readily took my hand as I reached out for his. A few minutes later we were headed toward the Los Angeles Forum and the ice show. All of the memories of fun outings that I had as a kid came rushing back to me. I was so grateful that Ryan was in school and that I did not have to divide my attention between the two boys.

As we walked through a tunnel in the stadium and down concrete stairs, looking for our seats, I could see confusion in Devon's eyes. The brilliant colored lights, the aroma of popcorn, the laughing crowds, and the happy music was overwhelming him. Suddenly Devon stopped, frozen with fear as he looked ahead. People were piling up behind us as his eyes locked on the clowns performing in the pre-show. I had forgotten that clowns frighten some little kids. When a fake cannon went off, Devon jumped and grabbed Walt's leg. Walt swooped up the little tyke and continued walking down the stairs to our seats. Devon clung tightly to his neck, burying his head in Walt's chest.

Twenty minutes into the show Devon's little head constantly turned back and forth as if it was mounted on a swivel. I couldn't stop watching his reactions, and he became my main attraction in the show. Devon's deadpan face and darting dark eyes were soaking in all the dazzle. I thought back to when I asked Lula if Devon had ever gone on an outing like to the ice show.

"Sometimes we get out of the house," she said in a slow drawl, "some days we don't." It was clear that Devon's outings had been limited to attempting to catch the ice cream truck coming down the street.

I was mesmerized by the beautiful ice performances as the skaters in glittery costumes glided magically across the ice under a rainbow of colored lights. The smell of popcorn, the kids shrilling with excitement, and the tantalizing happy music made me feel like I was flying. When intermission came I looked back over at Devon to see his reactions. He was fast asleep in Walt's arms.

Devon was age three when we took him to the ice show that morning, but when we returned him to his foster home he made an eerie transformation into a haunting young creature.

"We'll be back to get you," said Walt as we pulled up to Lula's house. Devon's eyes suddenly blazed with anger. When we opened the car door he quickly scooted out the door and flew up the porch steps like he was on fire. He pounded his little fist on the door.

"Lula, it's me," he said in a hoarse, small, voice. "Open up." We were surprised how loud his voice projected. He was so quiet before. We hadn't been sure he could talk.

When the door creaked open Devon rushed past Lula. We walked in behind him, puzzled over his instant transformation. "Where did Devon go?" I asked Lula.

"We want to tell him goodbye."

"He went in his room," she said with her slow drawl. "You can go back in there if you want."

Walt and I walked into a dark tiny bedroom containing neatly-made twin beds with mismatched green and blue spreads. It saddened me. Not one toy was in sight.

"Devon!" Walt called. A rustling sound came from under the bed. We both kneeled and peeped underneath it. Two large brown eyes peered out at us like a squirrel hiding in a tree hole. Obviously this was Devon's regular hiding place. But what did he hide from?

"We're going to leave now, Devon," I said softly. "We just wanted to say goodbye. Can we get a hug?" He didn't move. His eyes flashed contempt.

"Bye, champ," said Walt. "We'll be back to get you real soon." When he scooted further under the bed we decided it was best to leave him alone in the room.

After quizzing Lula for a few minutes about Devon's reactions, we said goodbye. When we walked out to our car and were about to drive off, we turned at the sound of the creaking, swinging screen door that slammed open, hitting the side of the house. It was a stoned-faced Devon. He stood on the porch, hands by his sides, his feet planted wide apart like a cowboy coming through saloon doors and ready for a shoot-out. My heart caught the bullet. He refused to give us eye contact or any energy, but he made sure we saw him. As he stomped down the porch steps, a couple of teenage boys called out from across the street.

"Hey, Devon!"

"Hey, little man."

He ignored them and us. I wondered why these tough looking teens knew him so well. How much time did they spend together? Walt, an ex-probation officer, knew immediately they were gang members. I suspected that they, too, could have abused Devon.

"He thinks we're not coming back for him," said Walt as we watched Devon heading to the side of the house toward a small unkempt back-yard. "Probably feels we're lying. I think he thought he was coming to live with us today." I nodded in agreement, barely able to speak with the lump in my throat.

The next week we sat at a round table in a small DCFS conference room with a therapist, Barbara, and Sarah Berman, who normally didn't sit in on the last steps of a family's adoption process. I was surprised at meeting Sarah in person. This ash blonde lady with a warm smile was so petite. I kept thinking she was so tiny to be so powerful, running such a large agency.

When the social worker began her report with Devon's complete medical records, I pulled out a tape recorder, placing it in the middle of the table. I knew they were uneasy at this distrustful sign, but no one stopped me from taping the conversation.

One of the first things they told us was that Devon's birth date was wrong in the documents. He wasn't four yet. The smudged, faded birth numbers on the documents that were hard to read may have been a small error to them but were major to us. I remembered how sad I was when I thought we were missing celebrating Devon's fourth birthday with him because the system was moving too slow.

We learned that Devon had been in two other foster homes besides Lula's home.

His mother was a drug addict who had no intention of getting help for her problem. His father was unknown. Devon was born with PCP, cocaine, and alcohol in his system, but he passed all of the psychological tests. In fact, his psychiatrist wrote that he was a "perfect candidate for adoption." Despite his history, we were even more anxious to get Devon home. His social worker read Devon's words in the report: "Mama (foster mother) hits me with a black cord." After she finished, we quickly signed the adoption papers without hesitation.

When the meeting ended I was grateful that Sarah had ridden shotgun on the last of our proceedings to make sure there were no more mistakes. She had an obvious compassion for children and her job. I was surprised and appreciated her candor as she walked us out of the door and down a gloomy hallway.

"Your case was one of the most poorly handled proceedings that we've had out of this office."

Finally someone admitted to the errors. As we talked of Devon's suspected abuse, which was why we called the media about DCFS, Sarah said that she was shocked by statistics she heard in a recent training. "The department suspects that 90 percent of the kids in foster care are being abused in foster homes, emotionally and physically."

Walking to the elevator, Sarah spoke with passion about her mission to place foster children in permanent loving homes like ours, and when we parted I had new respect with her at the helm.

Two years later, Sarah would be hit by a bus and killed at the Los Angeles airport. Her death would be a great loss to the thousands of foster children and to us. I was devastated over the news.

The next week I stood on our front lawn, anxiously waiting for Devon's arrival. This was the day he was coming to live with us. Ryan was playing a game of tag with the little girl who lived next door while I kept looking anxiously down the street for Walt to bring home our new addition to the family. My heart jumped with excitement at every passing car. I was the little kid waiting for Santa Claus to bring my gift.

Finally, I saw our gold Volvo coming toward us. "He's here, Ryan" I said, barely able to contain myself. "Devon's here."

"Gotta go," Ryan yelled to the little neighbor girl. He then ran to my side screaming, "My brother's here! My brother's here!" He was jumping up and down.

When the car pulled into the driveway I was shocked. Walt was alone. "Where's Devon?"

"Well, there was a problem," he said solemnly as he slowly got out of the car.

"A problem?" My voice cracked. "What kind of problem?" My mouth could barely formed out the words. "But they told us we could get him today."

He sighed, dropped his head, and then took in a long, deep breath. Suddenly he snapped his head up. "Surprise!" he yelled, breaking into a broad grin.

A tiny head popped up on the passenger's side. Devon was smiling at me. I wanted to kill Walt, but I was too happy to see our new son. I leaned into the car window and kissed the little tot on his forehead.

"Devon, were you hiding from me?" I smiled, tickling him. He giggled and grasped my hand.

"You're home, sweetie. You're home!" I said.

Ryan dashed to the car, nearly knocking me out of the way as he swung open Devon's door so hard that I thought it was coming off the hinges. "Come on, Devon, let's go," yelled Ryan as he ran to get a red ball lying near the red roses.

An excited and happy Devon, unlike the Devon we had seen previously, slid out of the seat, anxious to play with Ryan. His eagerness outran his little legs, which could not move as fast as he wished or as Ryan would have liked. I would later learn that Devon was like many abused kids in the system who had poor, underdeveloped motor skills.

For an hour we watched the boys play. I felt so blessed. All of the hell we went through was dissolving into pure happiness. My family was now finally complete, and our house was buzzing with joy -- or so I thought.

Later that evening Walt went up the hill for his daily run while I bathed the boys. A normal childhood ritual was about to turn into a nightmare. After Ryan's bath it was Devon's turn. I had planned it that way in order to spend more time with Devon while Ryan settled into bed with his favorite book.

As I lowered Devon into the warm bathtub he began screaming as he clawed and fought me like a cat trying to get away from the water.

"Devon, what's wrong? It's not hot." He didn't answer. He just looked at me with his little lips quivering and big crocodile tears, which told me what he could not. He had a deep fear of the water. But why was he scared of bath water? It only came up to his belly button.

Then it dawned on me. Could someone have punished him with scalding water? It was a common child abuse tactic. That had to be it, or maybe he had never taken a bath before. I could believe that easily, judging from the caked dirt inside of his ears and the ring around his neck. Lula's house may have been clean, but she was not a stickler for child hygiene. I remember that the first time I touched his hair I jerked my hand away. It was dry and brittle from a lack of proper care and washing. His hands felt like a reptile's back. They were scaly and rough from poor nutrition. I thought back to the adoption report. Devon had told his social worker that Lula fed him and the other foster children only crackers and rice.

Finally, after a few minutes of soothing and holding Devon to my chest tightly, I was able to cajole him into sitting in the water. I sang to him softly as I slowly and gently washed his shoulders, then his arms, and then his neck.

"Let's turn around sweetie, so I can get your back." Devon was getting use to the water and was now even singing "Jingle Bells" with me, the only song we both knew together.

When he let me turn him around, suddenly my world stopped. I saw it for the first time and internally I screamed. A big, raw, nasty scar ran the width of his little back. It reminded me of a slave's wound from a whip. He must have bled a lot.

"Devon, what happened here on your back?" I said trying to sound calm. Where he had opened and relaxed around me, he now stiffened and became mute. I could almost hear the gate to the fortress around him slam shut. His face went blank, and his little chest swelled up like a puffer fish for protection. He did not have to say a word.

I tried remaining calm and finished washing him. After drying off his little body and helping him get into his new Sesame Street yellow pajamas, I hugged and kissed him. I read a book to both boys as they drifted off to sleep. My mind raced, thinking of Devon's fresh wound.

After leaving their bedroom I poured a glass of red wine and sat in the living room, waiting for Walt to return from his run. When I heard him stick his key in the lock, I ran to the door.

"We now have evidence," I said. "Devon was definitely abused."

CHAPTER TEN

Walter stood before me, perspiring from his long run, and I was flushed with anxiety over Devon's abuse.

"We've got to cover ourselves. They could say that we hurt him," said Walt. "Call his social worker."

That night I left a message on Valerie Wong's answering machine. Two days went by without a response. Walt and I agreed that I should next write Sarah Berman to protect ourselves. There's something about the power of the written word. It propels people into action. Perhaps the fear promotes the action. Since I knew I was a good writer, having several decades of experience writing for the television networks, I felt a sense of power sitting down to the computer. But why did it have to come to this? Why didn't Valerie return my call?

I felt myself turning on the woman whom I had admired for saving Devon and finding him a home. But I was also like many people. Fickle. As long as you are doing something for people, they like you. But make an error, and they quickly forget the positive things that you have done. I justified my turning on Valerie thinking this was serious abuse. She needed to shut down that home fast. The other kids left with Lula were in danger. I quickly forgot any loyalty to Valerie. Now I was in full-fledged anger.

In the letter to Sarah, I pointed out the law. If a child's appointed agent, including a teacher, police officer, social worker, or anyone who deals with children for a living, does not report child abuse, they are subject to the law's punishment -- six months in jail, and/or a fine. I also mentioned in the letter about Devon's other behaviors that made us suspect abuse. He was hardly eating, although it was clear he wanted to when he came to the table. He had reported to a social worker that Lula wouldn't let them eat sometimes.

There was also the day he kept yelling "cocaine!" in the store with Walt. Shoppers looked around at my embarrassed husband, who immediately left his filled cart at the check stand and left the store with Devon. In addition, there was the time Devon was hysterical when I tried to bathe him.

We had complete faith in Sarah. She had dissolved some of my suspicion that there were people in the system who didn't care about children. We knew people cared, at least some of them, but by the way they handled business it was hard to believe that they did.

Looking back, these workers were simply caught up in the Dragon system. Draggin' on and on. No one could move faster than the Dragon allowed.

A few days later our family was excited, scurrying through the house getting ready to attend Ryan's pre-school graduation. We had no idea that our joy was about to turn into terror.

We couldn't have been more proud of our boys as they crawled into our Volvo. The boys looked like little businessmen in the tiny suits Walt had bought. He got the greatest pleasure buying clothes for his sons. If he bought Ryan a yellow shirt, he would get the identical shirt in blue for Devon. It seemed that every other day Walt came home with new outfits for the boys. Devon had begun looking amazingly like our birth child. He and Ryan had the same haircut. His skin color was somewhere in the middle of Walt's chocolate brown and my coffee latte color.

After Ryan's graduation we went to dinner. It was about 8:00 p.m. when we returned home. It would take Walt and I at least two hours to get the boys bathed and into bed after a joyful, exciting evening.

Devon's personality had finally blossomed and he and Ryan were like two tiger cubs, forever romping and rolling about in the house. On this night their excitement was at fever pitch. They couldn't seem to calm down.

It wasn't until 10:00 p.m. when we finally got the giggling boys into bed. Despite Walt and I begging for mercy, wanting peace and quiet, it was good to see Devon coming out of his shell. He was now as loud and as rambunctious as Ryan was. We had our hands filled with two screaming kiddies with happy feet running through the house.

Just as I was leaving the boys' room a loud banging rattled the front door. I went to answer it, meeting Walt in the hall, coming out of the kitchen. He frowned and motioned that he would answer the door. Who was calling this late, and why were they trying to knock the door down?

"Who is it?" barked Walt in his toughest voice.

"Open up… " the voice called back, "Police!" I knew Walt's reaction was like mine. The news junkies that we were, we seldom missed a story. Instantly I recalled a recent news headline: "Police Impersonators, Knocking on Doors Late at Night, Rob Homeowners."

Walt didn't say a word as he peeked through the window near the front door as the persistent banging continued. He suddenly turned to me, his face drained, "Jan, call the police!"

"Wha - - " He didn't give me time to question him.

"Just call them," he snapped. "Ask if they've sent a unit to our house."

My heart pounded as I ran to the kitchen phone. I trusted Walt's instincts as a former probation officer. I always thought he was somewhat psychic, but he shrugged off the term and preferred streetwise instead.

I could barely punch in the phone number, my hand was shaking so badly. I looked up and saw the boys standing on the landing of the steps. "What's wrong Mommy?" asked Ryan. "Who you calling?"

Devon stepped down behind him. Kids can sense danger.

"It's okay, honey. You guys go back upstairs."

But it wasn't okay, and the frightened look on Devon's face told me it wasn't. Earlier Devon had mentioned that a couple of teenage boys at his foster home were shot at while running from the police. As they ran through Lula's house and out the back door, a cop's bullet hit one of them. Devon was foggy on the details, but it was clear what made an impression on the three-year-old. "Paramedics came." How could a little boy say such a big word when he hardly could talk?

I waited for the Foothill Division police dispatcher to answer, and when she finally did, I was immediately put on hold. We could have been murdered while I waited. Suddenly Walt flew past me and opened up the kitchen door, letting Prana, our four-year-old German shepherd dog, inside. Prana shook his head as Walt struggled to put on his leash. The dog obviously sensed something was wrong and he began to cower as Walt dragged him back past me into the living room. Normally Prana races anyone to the front door at the sound of his metal leash, but this night he was like a reluctant soldier forced to fight for something that he didn't believe in. He didn't want to go.

Meanwhile the boys had inched further down the steps, looking at Walt. I wanted them to come to me so I could hold them both, but I didn't want them in the path of potential danger. Why had I procrastinated at buying that cordless phone? Walt dragged the rebelling Prana to the front door.

"What's wrong, Walt?" I hissed.

"Two men are out there. One's sneaking around the back of the house." I didn't have to ask Walt's plans. He was going to try to scare them with the dog, who was really the scared one.

This was exactly why Walt didn't want us to buy Prana. He wanted a watchdog that showed his teeth and could protect his family. We had sought out a man who raised dogs for the police force. His litters came straight from Germany with papers to assure no interbreeding had taken place. While the other puppies in the holding pen were jumping at us, Prana was sitting quietly at the back of the cage, watching the action. He was absolutely the most beautiful German shepherd I had ever seen with his jet-black saddle, tan head, and snow-white ruff on his chest. Reluctantly Walt paid $500 hundred dollars for our new "watch dog" after Ryan and I begged to take Prana home. Walt was convinced that the only thing Prana would watch was his food.

Perspiration was pouring down my back as I continued to wait on hold. While Ryan was asking his usual zillion questions and chattering away, Devon was still displaying fear. He was drifting away, fading back into the same dark cave from which he had recently emerged.

I watched in horror as Walt suddenly snatched open the front door with Prana in tow. He stepped face to face with a man dressed in dark colors. Walt was still dressed in his P.J. bottoms and a white T-shirt, and he was barefoot.

What was Walt doing? Why in hell did he open the door? Was he crazy?

Through the open door I could see past them. A car was in the middle of the street with yellow parking lights on. The other man, who apparently was snooping along the side of the house, suddenly appeared.

Just when Walt closed the door behind him the dispatcher came on the line. I panicked at being unable to see Walt.

"Two… two men are at our door, saying they're police," I blurted out. "Did you send police to our house?"

"Calm down, miss. What's your address?"

I rattled it off so fast she had me repeat it twice.

"I'll look," said the dispatcher. "Don't hang up."

I could hear the men's gruff voices through the closed door. The dispatcher came back on the line.

"No, ma'am, we didn't send a unit out to your house."

"You… you didn't?" I said, horrified.

"No, but hold on. Don't hang up."

I started trembling. I couldn't see Walt. I could only hear his raised voice barking at the men. Finally, I couldn't stand it anymore. I put the phone down and rushed to the window. I could see Prana cowering and two white men looking at Walt as if he was nuts.

"What do you want?" Walt kept saying. I couldn't hear the men's answer, but they began moving back to their dark blue sedan in the middle of the street. I ran back to pick up the phone. Now I couldn't see or hear anything except the boys.

"Ryan," I shouted, "take Devon upstairs, now!" The boys were surprised at my harsh tone. Devon was paralyzed. Ryan tried pulling him up the stairs.

A voice crackled over the phone line, "Ms. Jackson, there was a unit sent to your house. It's from the Compton station. That's why I didn't see it on the screen right away."

"Oh, God, thank you. Thank you."

"Ms. Jackson, don't hang up. Ask one of the officers to come to the phone."

I ran out the door and saw neighbors peeking through their

curtains. A few came outside.

"It's okay," I said, rushing up behind Walt, "they're police. The dispatcher said they were sent here."

Walt's face flushed. He then turned to the men, looking relieved. "I'm sorry, officers," he said. "I didn't know… all of these impersonators around."

Surprisingly the men didn't take offense, but I could easily see why they had retreated, which is totally out of character for police. They hadn't known quite why they were sent to our house.

One officer unfolded a crumpled piece of paper. "Are you Devon's foster parents?"

"No," said Walt softening, "we're his adoptive parents."

The officers looked at each other, puzzled. The taller one spoke up. "We need to see if the child is okay."

Was it one of the grown adults Lulu raised taking revenge for her? Did she raise gang members? Someone was obviously playing games.

I followed the officers and Walt to the house with the still-cowering Prana trailing behind us. Now I could see their unmarked car had a police light on the side. When the men turned around, for the first time we saw "Police" written in bold white on the back of their dark blue windbreakers.

Inside we offered them coffee and soft drinks, which they politely declined. While Walt told them about the abuse we were trying to report, I ran to get a copy of my letter to Sarah.

"We need to see the child," said the shorter cop. I called Devon and Ryan led him down the stairs hand-in-hand. Devon was barely navigating the tall steps with his little body. As the taller officer stooped his jacket flapped open, and Devon's eyes were transfixed by his gun and handcuffs.

"Can I see your back, son?" The man was gentle with Devon, who was frozen.

"Come on, sweetie. The nice policeman wants to see your scar." Devon turned slowly around as I lifted up his red ninja turtle pajama top.

The officer tried questioning Devon, who continued to be mute.

I explained that Devon withdrew into a shell whenever I mentioned his scar. The officer understood. Devon hadn't fallen as he told me. Someone did this to Devon.

"It definitely looks like the scar was inflicted," said the officer.

Meanwhile the other officer was on the phone with the police dispatcher, trying to unravel the reason they were sent to our house. Initially they thought they were coming to the foster home to check out Devon. They didn't know he had moved in with us.

Finally, the officers had to leave. They apologized for the mix-up and shook hands with Walt, who walked them to their car. It was clear they had a communication problem with the child abuse unit that apparently asked they check out Devon. Back then agencies didn't share information concerning children, some across the country still don't.

When Walt and Ryan went to bed I sat up for a while holding Devon, who had retreated to a place I could not reach. He refused to talk. Finally, I carried him to bed and sang to him while rubbing his back. Would his new nature return in the morning after being traumatized?

I sat up with my mind racing. Was the foster mother angry? Of course she was. Was she trying to retaliate and bring us up on charges, too? Who knew?

After another hour of turning everything over in my head a zillion times, fatigue set in. I had to go lie down. Just as I began turning off the lights I stopped to see if we had any phone messages. There was one.

"Mr. and Mrs. Jackson, this is Valerie Wong. I got your letter about Devon. I am calling the police."

Thanks, Valerie, for the warning.

CHAPTER ELEVEN

Rage poured over me like hot, bubbling witches' brew. I couldn't believe Ryan's graduation night turned into a nightmare because of the lack of communication between DCFS and the police. Back then there wasn't an integrated computer system for multiple agencies to share criminal information concerning juveniles. Kids like Devon simply get lost in the juvenile justice information gap.

I was terrified when the police came to our door late that night. They had acted only after I phoned Valerie, and then suddenly we became the criminals. Had everyone gone mad? Making matters worse, a week later, not far from our house, the Los Angeles police stopped Rodney King. The beating turned our backyard into the world's focus. Suddenly it became uncomfortable seeing the same police from our neighborhood, the Foothill Division, in the local 7-Eleven store. For years we said morning greetings to them as we got our coffee there, but now I felt uncomfortable when our eyes met. I could feel their tension. I knew they thought that every black person was scrutinizing them, and back then I was. I wondered which cops I saw at the store were at the beating, either watching or participating.

Traditionally blacks have feared the police racial profiling blacks. If a family member of yours had not been unnecessarily stopped by them, then you knew someone else who had.

While people were shocked and incensed over King's beating, I kept thinking what could have happened to Walt. He was nasty to the police, fearing that they were really imposters loose in our neighborhood. Those cops could have blown up anytime, handcuffed him and taken him to jail or beaten his butt in some alley. Fortunately the officers who came to our house were respectful and extremely under-standing, but what if they had not been?

I was even more livid at the thought that after we had finally pulled Devon out of his shell the police incident had set him back. Our home was supposed to be his shelter, but instead he was exposed to the kind of threatening activity we thought we were protecting him from. How could he trust us now? In the years to come, trust would be the issue behind his behavioral problems.

During the next couple of weeks I talked to a small army of abuse workers. It was during this time that the state was temporarily taking over some of the county's child- related divisions until they felt that DCFS was operating efficiently again. This played out to be a nasty war in the press.

"Do you know it took me nearly 12 phone calls to locate Devon?" said the tall gray-haired state investigator who was sitting in our living room, talking about his frustrations with our case. Usually the county investigates these things, but this particular investigator had come down from Sacramento to interview Devon because of the big county mess. He explained that he prided himself on being competent in his work, and that's why he was especially appalled when he couldn't locate a small child in the county system. This was one reason for the state investigation. The child welfare system was losing kids. Unfortunately it wasn't just a Los Angeles problem. Throughout the years I would read about other county agencies across the country losing children in the system, especially in Florida.

Several weeks later we got word that Lula's home had been closed because of our charges. After further investigations, officials found that other foster kids had been abused in her home. I was thrilled to learn that they closed the home and several of the children had been immedi-ately adopted. Because of faulty county records we never found out if those other children were Devon's siblings. Valerie suspected that at least one of the children was related to Devon. However, she couldn't tell for sure because of the county's fuzzy record keeping.

After the investigations we started to see strange behaviors in Devon. For weeks he got up quietly in the morning, dressed himself, and then went to get a broom and started sweeping. This would please any parent, but at three-years-old he was much too young to be this responsible, I thought. Why was he doing this? It was obvious that Lula had trained him, but I sensed that he was trying to please us.

When the family was watching television, Devon would sit with his back to the screen and stare at us as if we were his entertainment. Then there were the times when I gently touched Devon to wake him up and his little body shook violently as if he were being electrocuted. We took him to the doctor and it was determined that his shakes were the residual of drugs in his system from his addicted mother. We also suspected this was why he wet the bed every single night, way into his teens. His nervous system had not fully developed because his drug-addicted mother never got pre-natal care.

I took time off from work to be with Devon before finally putting him in pre-school. During that time we cuddled endlessly. He constantly wanted me to carry him. It was as if he was trying to catch up on his lost baby years. I knew that in foster homes with multiple kids and a lack of emotional attachment, he didn't get this kind of love and attention, so I submitted myself completely to his needs.

I also knew that like most drug babies, Devon had probably cried all of the time. A foster parent may not have had the time or the emotional bonding to tolerate his needs. Besides, since he had been in three different homes, I guessed that he wasn't given the time to attach to his caretakers. Now that he was living with us, probably for the first time in his life he had total attention. In the coming years I would learn that was not enough.

There were times when I felt that I was suffocating from Devon wanting to be held and his constant neediness. I had a hard time learning to sit still long enough to breast feed Ryan because of the fast-paced lifestyle I led at the television networks. When Devon came I knew I had to get outside of myself to take care of his needs. I did it, but it wasn't easy. It was like going from 100 miles an hour in the entertainment world, to zero, just sitting holding a toddler.

After feeling that Devon was physically all right, we realized that he had some mental issues we needed to address. We spent months on the waiting list for Hathaway Children and Family Services, a therapeutic behavioral clinic, before we were finally assigned to a young intern. I was highly insulted. Alicia was a child. The tall, dark- haired, raving beauty was still in college. What did she know?

Hathaway has a great reputation, and works extensively with foster care children, so I decided that I needed to put my objections aside for Devon. It could take months for him to be seen if we waited for an older, more experienced therapist at the agency.

My angry disbelief wasn't directed entirely at the glitches in the system. Drug mothers were my targets, too. How could a mother choose drugs over her child? According to the Department of Children and Family Services report, Devon's mother had refused to give up drugs to keep him. She also had other kids who were in the system. I cursed her and mothers like her.

I knew it was my job to explain to Devon that his mother was sick, so I felt that I needed to forgive her, but I was too angry. I had to do something about the venom I was carrying, so I contacted a home for drug-addicted mothers. It was during the time I had decided to write " Cry for Light." I desperately needed to understand how mothers could let the system raise her children. Didn't they know the system was abusing their kids while they were abusing drugs?

One bright Saturday afternoon I was on my way to a home for addicted women in Pasadena. I had arranged earlier that week to visit Crystal Stairs, with the director of the home, and the women were expecting me. I told the director that I wanted to hear the mothers' stories for the book I was writing but I really needed to hear their stories to get over my anger. Why did they abandon their children?

I found the small, yellow-painted home in a residential bedroom community in the San Gabriel Valley about a half-hour from my home. As I walked around the back to a tiny pool, a three-legged dog greeted me along with a very affectionate black cat that followed me. When I arrived at the back door, the cat rubbed against my leg.

Ginger, the red-haired director, greeted me, shooing the cat away. She was a large lady with an open smile. She invited me into the immaculate house, introducing me to the women.

Ginger called us into the living room they used for house meetings and group therapy. The women filed in and warmly greeted me, unaware that I held contempt for them in my heart. What kind of selfish people were they? It didn't matter that they were in the home to get help; I blasted them in my mind for being in that predicament in the first place. I had no idea how judgmental and self-righteous I was back then. I expected everyone to have my values.

As the women took their seats on mismatched chairs, I was amazed at the rainbow of different ethnicities and races that appeared together. It touched me that they all seemed to help and support one another.

After my introduction I told them about myself and quickly launched into my questions.

"I want to know how you got separated from your children," I announced. I wasn't expecting the fountain of rage and sorrow that filled the room. Kathy, a black lady with corn rows, began.

"I was on drugs and they took my kids away, and they put them in different foster homes." I remembered hearing that siblings were separated after they were put in the system.

"The judge told me I had to see them at least once every week to prove that I still wanted to be their mother, but I didn't have a car. Hell, they put one in Riverside, another in Lancaster, and another in Los Angeles," said the woman. "It takes me three buses and a half-day just to go to Riverside." The other mothers in the circle nodded their heads, sharing her plight.

"And then I'm trying to work. I can only go see one kid on the weekend," her eyes dropped to the floor. "They're in school during the other days."

The other women chimed in with "uh-huhs." It was their story, too.

"So if I can't get to see them, they say that I don't care about my kids. That ain't true."

The lament fired up the women. A few dabbed tears from their eyes.

"And the social worker is constantly telling you that you aren't a good mother," said Kathy.

"Your social worker told you that?" I was shocked.

"Yeah."

Others nodded and told of their social workers' insensitive remarks toward them.

"Don't forget about the drug testing, ya'll," said Edie, a young white mother who appeared to be no older than 20.

"What about it?" I asked.

"Well, some judges want you to get tested once a week."

"That's $40 a pop," said Juana, a Latina.

"Expensive."

"Hell, yeah."

"Well, if you don't have a job, how do you get the money?" I asked.

A couple of girls looked at one another and rolled their eyes, mumbling under their breaths. I read their faces as they exchanged knowing glances.

"You prostituted?"

"You do what you have to do," said Kathy in a matter-of-fact voice.

"And when you're trying to get your act together, the social worker and the judge will make you jump through so many hoops," added Edie." "Finally, you just say it's easier to let the kids go. Just take them, damn it!"

"At least they'll have good homes," said Juana.

I could see how fragile these women were. They wanted to be good mothers, but their self-esteem was so low fighting the system. A few would repeat their own mothers' mistakes; others didn't know their mothers or had bad relationships with them. Some of these moms had also come from emotionally and physically abusive homes. A few were from upper-income families whose members modeled the same low self-esteem.

"You know, I felt so bad about myself," said Juana, "that I couldn't even see myself holding a job at K-Mart sweeping the floors. I thought I was the lowest thing in the universe, especially when they took my kids away."

"And it seems the system just kicks you when you're down," said Edie.

Two of the women left to start cooking dinner, following their regular chore schedule for the house. The other women kept talking as if relieved to tell someone on the outside their plight without being judged. They wanted me to hear their side of the story.

They were not the uncaring mothers that I had imagined or that the media depicted. They were mothers who had made wrong choices, including loving the wrong men. I learned that many drug mothers fall deeply in love and transport dope for their partners. Since police don't catch the drugs on their men, the guys walk scott free, and it is the women, like a few of these moms, who end up in jail on drug charges. When they do their time and get out, their man is gone.

I learned that their happiest moments were when their children visited them in recovery. Unfortunately a few of the women said they had lost their children to the system forever.

Many tears fell in that circle, including mine. After spending several hours with the women, I left with a totally different attitude toward drug mothers. I saw myself in them. As I had listened to their stories I realized that as an emotional eater I had used food like these women used drugs. How could I look down on them? These mothers were fragile, sensitive, and loving beings who had been hurt too many times. This was the reason some of them got on drugs -- to numb their pain. They were not bad, insensitive people as I had pre-judged. They were the opposite, so sensitive to life's hard blows that they didn't know how to shield themselves except with drugs.

Before leaving I led the women in a prayer for strength. As I hugged each mother, I felt unconditional love pass between us. Tears rolled down my cheeks as I walked back to the car. I asked God to forgive me for wrongly judging them, and to help me to help them. In the days ahead, they would help me.

CHAPTER TWELVE

A year after meeting the mothers recovering from drug addictions, I was promoted to West Coast publicity-photo editor in charge of the ABC Television Network's image. I remember when the rehab director at the drug-recovery cottage asked me about where I worked, the ladies were fascinated that I not only was a career woman, but a mother, too. It was their dream to do both, something that seemed so natural to me.

In my new job I was responsible for hiring photographers covering our shows and choosing the best still pictures, which would be released to the press. I loved that job. It gave me a break from some actors who were constantly complaining that they didn't have enough publicity. I felt fortunate working with top celebrities, but sometimes the drama that comes with working closely with the demanding ones could be overwhelming.

I felt a sense of power, seeing photos that I selected end up in magazines that I saw while waiting in grocery store lines. I also was grateful that I didn't have to travel as much as I did during my earlier publicity years. I could be at home with my family. The extent of traveling I now wanted to do was my 90-minute round-trip commute to work and home, which kept me exhausted. But one of my perks was being able to grab a quick nap at lunchtime on the beige sofa in my new, large office.

With all of the adoption drama behind me, my life was becoming manageable again, until one day I received a flyer in the mail from the Department of Children and Family Services. They were looking for volunteers to drive foster children to an adoption party.

I thought back over the words of Devon's social worker: "The foster mother didn't want to bring him." This common, I learned through other social workers. They told me that some foster parents didn't want their foster children to be adopted because they would miss the monthly paycheck. They also said that many hard-working, wonderful foster parents simply didn't have the time to drive them to adoption parties because they were taking care of so many children. Some of their foster kids had disabilities. With this in mind, I signed up to volunteer and was approved to take three children to the upcoming adoption party.

I left messages at several of the foster homes where the children were living, but I was frustrated because they didn't return my calls. A DCFS worker told me that I needed to keep leaving messages, which I did. Finally I made contact and arrangements with all three people in charge of the kids up for adoption.

That Saturday I left Walt with the boys and I picked up my mother, who wanted to go with me to the adoption party. When we arrived at the first group home no one was there although I knew 10 foster children were living in the home. I went around to the side of the white, two-story house and knocked on the back door.

No answer.

The director of the group home knew I was coming. Where was everyone? I realized that this man was obviously playing games with me, and I was livid. Earlier he had been the hardest of the guardians to track down.

At the second home, a tall, solemn-looking woman said the boy I was suppose to pick up was sick. I got back in my car doubting that she was telling the truth, and I was still fuming over the empty first group home.

We headed across town to a section of South Los Angeles, that was noted gang territory, to pick up the last child, a four-year-old girl. I knocked on the door of the two-story, framed, green house with anti-burglar bars on every window, wondering what obstacle would I be faced with now. But to my surprise the foster mother had the child dressed and waiting for me.

Jada, who was tiny for her age, was absolutely adorable. She had long braids and was dressed in black patent leather shoes, a red velvet dress with a big petticoat that bopped up and down when she walked. I could tell that she was proud of her party outfit. Jada and I walked down the front steps as her foster mother, whose name was Ella, looked on sadly after us. I could tell by the girl's confidence and chatty nature that Ella was a foster mother, like many I would meet, who dearly loved her foster child.

I would learn later that Ella had raised over twenty foster children, but she was most saddened by Jada being up for adoption. Ella wanted to adopt Jada, who had lived with Ella since babyhood, but DCFS wouldn't allow the adoption since Ella was going to marry a man about to get out of prison. Ella had met him in the California State prison when she was doing missionary work for her church. Jada's social worker wouldn't let Jada continue living in the home since the ex-con was about to move in.

"Janet Jackson," said Jada, looking up at me as we crossed the street to the car. "Are there going to be clowns at the party?" Jada called me by my first and last name because she was a big fan of Janet Jackson, the Grammy Award-winning singer.

When Ella told her that Janet Jackson was coming to get her, she got excited even though she knew I wasn't the entertainer. I also knew that since Jada readily went with me, a total stranger, that Ella had painted a wonderful picture of the great party Jada was anticipating. My hope was that it wouldn't be as drab as the one where we met Devon. I could tell by Jada's excitement that she probably didn't fully comprehend that she was going there to find new parents. She seemed so well adjusted with Ella.

When we arrived at the festivities I was amazed at how much this type of DCFS party had changed within just a year. It was a little carnival held outside on a church property. There was a large moon bounce, clowns painting faces, games, music, and loads of food. The prospective parents, foster kids, and even the DCFS workers all seemed to be having a great time.

When we joined the party prospective parents, white and black, immediately came up to me to ask about Jada. I couldn't tell them much, but I gave them her name so they could inquire through their social workers.

Jada was oblivious to people questioning me about her. All she saw was the moon bounce filled with giggling, screaming kids bouncing like balls.

"Janet Jackson, can I go over there?" she said pointing to the moon bounce.

No sooner did I get "Yes" out my mouth than Jada let go of my hand, flew over to the moon bounce, ripped off her black patent leather shoes and her white, frilly party socks, sending them flying in all directions. She didn't care that her ruffled panties were showing as she clambered into the moon bounce like a cowgirl. Screaming with delight, she bounced herself into a frenzy with the other kids.

After we had been at the party for about an hour, Jada and I joined my mother, who was sitting on a bench eating popcorn. Mom was retired and enjoying any moments we had together. Jada was still wired from all of the excitement and the games, and when I sat down, she quickly climbed on my lap facing me. I held onto her hands as she leaned back, giggling, pretending that she was falling. As we swayed back and forth together laughing, it was like a rhythm of life that felt so natural. It was as if we had known one another for years.

"Are you enjoying yourself, Jada?"

"Yep, Janet Jackson," she said, leaning back again and giggling. I pretended to drop her further backwards, and her eyes widened with delight. "Do it again, Janet Jackson. Do it again."

I don't know where the magic dust came from, but, just as with Devon, I fell in love.

"Mom," I whispered, leaning to her ear, "I think I want to adopt her."

"Really?"

Mom's eyes lit up as if I was telling her that I was pregnant again. She smiled, looking adoringly at Jada, who was now hugging me to catch her breath. "That's wonderful. She's a beautiful little girl. So friendly."

"Yeah, but I gotta let Walt see her."

Whenever I get an idea I'm like a runaway train.

"Let's go home." I lowered Jada from my lap, grabbed her hand, and headed for the car with Mom trailing behind us. As far as I was concerned my mission was accomplished. I had found Jada new parents.

Twenty minutes later we were on the freeway, going to see Walt and the boys before I took her home. Walt was raking leaves in the front yard when we arrived.

"Walt, I want you to meet Jada." I opened the door for her, and as she climbed out I whispered to him, "What do you think about adopting her? We never did get our daughter." It was Walt's decision that we should be looking for a girl when we found Devon. He still felt that we needed a girl to balance out the family, and he was right. Lately I was feeling overwhelmed with all of the testosterone in the house.

Walt smiled briefly at the little girl as they shook hands, but he was somewhat aloof. Ryan and Devon came out the house screaming, "Mommy's home," as they stopped dead in their tracks wondering who the new kid was with Mommy and Grandma.

"We've got two kids already," said Walt, dumping leaves into a can. After hearing about the adoption party he went back to doing the yard work, but I saw him looking at Jada as the boys ran around the yard with her. Her giggle was infectious, and she seemed to adapt easily wherever she was.

"Well, what did he say?" whispered Mom as we got back in the car.

"Nothing really," I whispered back. "But I know he is going to want to adopt her."

"How do you know?"

"I just know my husband," I said with a smile. I dropped off Jada and Mom at their homes. By the time I returned home to Walt he was in the curious state I had predicted.

"Well, are you going to call DCFS?"

I acted coy, "About what?"

"About adopting the little girl."

"Oh, really? I thought you said we had two boys and that was enough."

"I didn't say all that."

He frowned, growing impatient with my game. "Are you going to call, or do you want me to call?"

We both knew that Sarah Berman at DCFS could make it happen for us, and she did. We were put instantly in contact with Jada's social worker, Maria Sandoval, a wonderful lady who worked diligently to get Jada into our home immediately. There was no red tape, drama, or other problems like those that we had with Devon. Jada was in our house with lightening speed.

We learned that Jada entered the child welfare system as an infant, when she was living on the streets of downtown Los Angeles with her three-year-old and six-year-old sisters. After their drug-addicted mother left them to find drugs, Jada's eldest sister carried her from store to store begging for food when one shocked merchant called the authorities.

I'll never forget the heartbreaking day Jada was leaving her foster mother. Ella loved this child so much that it was difficult for everyone involved except Jada, who was eager to go with Walt and me. Even though Ella explained to her that she was going to be adopted, I don't think at that age she really understood that she was leaving Ella forever. I think Jada was just thinking of the good times she had at the party and about playing with our boys.

Walt and I hustled back and forth like worker ants loading Jada's boxes into our two cars. It seemed like an endless amount of stuff for a four-year-old. It was quite different from Devon, who came to us with a small, tattered, yellow suitcase filled with rags for clothes and no toys.

I was trying to avoid the heavy emotional scene, but it was difficult. Three church ladies had come over and were comforting Ella, who was crying. She was trying her best to be accommodating to us and my heart went out to her. One of the church ladies passed me and growled, "That's a shame they're taking that child away." She was angry at DCFS, but I knew she was mad at me, too.

Despite Ella's experience of being a foster mother for 20 years, this was the hardest separation for her with a foster child. My only consolation was knowing if we didn't adopt Jada, she would go to another foster home if DCFS couldn't find adoptive parents for her. Jada had to leave Ella's home before Ella's new husband moved in.

Later, when I unpacked Jada's belongings, I found a letter addressed to Jada from Ella's fiancé. "Daddy loves you." He included an elaborate abstract drawing. I couldn't determine what it was, but something about it seemed creepy. I never asked what the man did to be put in prison, but I surmised it must have been severe if DCFS wanted Jada out of the home immediately. Was he a pedophile?

I was always amazed that while Jada's social worker wanted Jada to leave, Ella's other foster child, a boy nicknamed Smurf, was left with her. He had a different social worker. Didn't she see the urgency, too? Smurf was a two-year-old and mentally challenged. Why wasn't he moved? In the coming years I would learn that special-needs children would often fall through the cracks.

When Christmas rolled around, Jada had been in our home a few months. I was so happy to be wrapping gifts with my new daughter. I hadn't had female companionship and intimacy this close since I left college, and with a house full of men this was refreshing. As we wrapped gifts, Jada, who was turning into a real-life Chatty Cathy doll, talking non-stop, told me about her old home, her school, and her friends.

I don't remember how it came up, but as she chatted she told me about an incident that made my heart feel as if it was dropping into my stomach. A man in Ella's house had touched her inappropriately.

I couldn't sleep that night after Walt and I discussed what to do. We were going to the child abuse authorities, but first we agreed I should talk to Ella to see if she knew about Jada's accusations. Had she already reported the incident? The next day I called.

"Ella, did Jada tell you that some man molested her?"

"Yeah…yes, she did. But that was a while ago," she said cautiously. "I wasn't home when it happened."

"You knew?"

"Yes," she said quietly.

"Did you report it?"

"No, I couldn't figure out everything Jada was telling me. I didn't think I had enough information." Ella went on to explain that she left Jada and Smurf for about 30 minutes when she ran to the store. The molester was a handyman working on the kitchen sink.

I couldn't get off the phone fast enough to place the next call to the child abuse hotline.

"What makes you think she has been abused?" asked a child abuse worker who answered my call.

I was shocked, not by what she said but how she said it. She had an attitude as if I had just awakened her. I kept thinking that this woman was supposed to be on the side of the child.

After having some harsh words with the woman over the way she questioned me, I asked to speak to her supervisor. He wasn't there. Several days later, when he finally returned my call, he, too, was defensive and growled something about being understaffed. It was his excuse for how the woman treated me. I got off the phone with him and researched how to get his supervisor's name. I was going straight to the top again.

The higher you go up the ladder the more people pay attention. The problem is trying to find the right ladder. When I spoke to the main person in charge of that division, I found him to be open and understanding, and he promised to take care of the issue right away. I pleaded with him not to send the first woman, whom I knew was biased, to investigate, especially since she knew I went over her head and complained. He kept his promise.

Within a week Lydia, a young, slim, soft-spoken DCFS child abuse investigator, came to our house. I found her easy to talk to and empathetic. She got right on the case and suspended Ella's foster care license. This was common procedure during these types of investigations.

"The man who abused Jada lives around the corner," Lydia said. "Ella called him her handyman, but I think there was a relationship going on."

"Really?"

I was super intrigued, especially since Ella, a Christian woman as she called herself, was suppose to be getting married.

In the meantime we got our court date to finalize Devon's adoption. At that time, there was no child friendly court like today's Los Angeles County Children's Superior Court in Monterey Park. Instead we went to the criminal court and stood just feet away from a prisoner in shackles, wearing an orange jumpsuit, and with two deputy sheriffs at his sides.

Little Devon kept staring at the inmate and the deputies. I sensed his fear, so we placed him between us, holding both his hands. When we were finally called into the cold and austere mahogany-paneled courtroom, his adoption was quickly finalized.

Days later an excited Ella phoned me. It was the first time I had talked to her in the weeks since DCFS started investigating her, but I had made sure that Jada called her about once a week to tell Ella how she was doing so Ella didn't have to call our house. Ella acted as if nothing had happened.

"Hi, I just wanted to say hello to Jada,"

"Sure, I'll get her."

"Oh, by the way, I got my license back." I don't know what shocked me more, the casual way she acted toward me or the news that she was getting her license back without the case being closed. After Ella spoke to Jada I immediately called Lydia.

"Well, Ms. Jackson, we can only take the license away for three months during the investigation, and the time is up."

"But what happened? What did you find?"

"Well, there was no paper trail. Ella didn't take Jada to the doctor after it happened, so it's hard to prove."

"But it wasn't a full three months," I reminded Lydia. "You had to stop the investigation while you went to a training session for two weeks. Doesn't that add time to our case?"

"I know. I'm sorry. The training had been set up months ahead of time, and it was mandatory."

"Well, did you talk to the handyman? I know you said you had a hard time catching up with him."

"Yes, it took me weeks. He kept hiding from me. But I got to talk to him."

"And... ?"

"He said he didn't do it."

"And you believed him?" I shrieked. I was now shaking my head in disbelief. I could tell she was dumbfounded by my reaction and the tone that I used with her.

"I have to prove --," she began. I cut her off.

"Okay, okay!" I said, exasperated, holding my head. "Let me just ask you one thing, Lydia. Do you believe Jada was molested by that man?"

"He certainly acted guilty, especially the way he kept hiding from me, and I believe Jada."

"Lydia, for my own piece of mind, do YOU believe he did it?" She was silent for a few seconds.

"Yes, I do," she said softly. "We just don't have enough evidence to put him away."

"Okay. Thanks." I hung up and dropped down on the living room sofa, staring off into space. I wondered how many other children the man had molested. How many more would he molest?

The case was closed, and so was my heart.

CHAPTER THIRTEEN

They say that after six months an internal clock goes off in some adoptive children's heads, and their true selves emerge. It's about this time that many children stop fearing that they'll be sent back to their foster homes, and they test their new parents. They want to know, "Do you really love me? Do you really care? Or are you going to give me up like my birth parents?" In other words, the adoption honeymoon is over and real life begins.

When the alarm went off within Devon, it was as deafening as a siren. A different person emerged from the shy, demure little boy who just wanted to be held and cuddled. A strong, obstinate personality began to surface, and I didn't know how to handle him.

When Devon reached six he started attending pre-school at the same predominately-white private school Ryan was attending. Jada was still in daycare.

I remember that when Devon first arrived at pre-school, his teacher and several of her aides took special care of him. He had that effect on people. Devon's charm brought out the empathy in people who wanted to give to a needy, abused child. Not to mention that he was so adorably cute.

After a couple of blissful months, whenever I picked Devon up from school, I began to detect from the strained look on the faces of his teacher and the teacher's aides that something was wrong with my child. Devon's obsessive clinging was draining them. They talked of how he demanded their constant attention, and when they tried to attend to another child, Devon would interrupt, demanding their affection.

The once "Oooh, he is so sweet," turned into "You have to do something about his behavior."

Devon's personality change was not only unnerving to them but to our family. I remember the first time I saw a difference in Devon. It was when one day I told him to pick up his toys. He just stood there, staring at me. I bent down to his eye level and repeated the instructions several times, but he didn't move. His face seemed frozen and his emotionless eyes locked onto mine. It wasn't like some kids who have a stubborn streak and pout or rebel in anger. He was amazingly calm and eerily still, like a statue.

As he stood before me, I watched his little chest swell like a puffer fish. It was as if a shield was dropping down around him. I learned much later that defiance and obstinacy are ways an abused child maintains control since he can't overpower his oppressor. But I wasn't oppressing Devon; I simply expected what any parent wanted -- obedience. I worried, was this just "The Terrible Threes" that often lasted until a child is six? Deep down I sensed that it was something much more serious.

The teachers at the school reported that Devon's obstinacy seemed to grow worse with each day. He also was developing a unique ability to antagonize other children, who would quickly retaliate. Little did I know then that this was the beginning of Devon's self-abuse stage. Subconsciously he wanted kids to beat him up. He knew how to exist in chaos, but not when life was calm. Abuse was familiar to him.

After months of complaints by teachers, one day our neighbor came over to see me. Her olive-green eyes were blazing with indignation. Walt and the boys were eating dinner when she asked me to step outside. I worried, what did Devon do to her daughter now? Those kids were like two live wires together, sizzling with trouble.

"I'm taking Susan out of that school," she barked.

"Why?"

"When I went to pick her up today I saw kids hitting Devon."

"Really?" My stomach shriveled. I wondered aloud, "Why didn't Devon or his teacher tell me?"

She took a deep, exasperated breath and ran her finger through her short, brown hair.

"They were not just hitting him, Janet, they were pounding on him, and I saw several of the teachers just watching them beat him up," she sputtered. "Do you know I had to ask Ms.Grenbaum to stop the kids from hurting Devon? I was so angry."

The next day Walt took off from work and took both boys out of the school. We then enrolled them in a public school, with minorities, not far from our house. I thought the teachers there would be more tolerant and understanding. But I was soon to learn that it wasn't a race problem I had to deal with in the schools, it was blind discrimination toward special-needs children.

One day I went to pick up Devon from his new school, and I was alarmed to see a three-inch-wide dirt streak running from the back of his head down to his bottom.

When the kindergarten teacher saw me, her face went ashen. She took a deep breath and stormed up to me.

"Mrs. Jackson, I have been teaching for 25 years, and I have never had to do what I did today."

By this time, I was accustomed to expecting negative Devon reports.

"What did he do?" I could tell she was defensive and ready for a fight.

"He refused to leave the storybook area as I asked all of the children to do. I wanted him to come back to his table and start on another project, but he refused." Her nostrils were flaring. "He's been like that all day. I had to drag him across the room."

I could not believe what I was hearing. "You had to what?"

"I had to drag him across the room," she said bluntly, as if daring me to say she was wrong. "He wouldn't leave." Her voice was raised in disbelief.

As I was thinking lawsuit, I saw other parents picking up their kids and watching us with puzzlement. I felt flushed with embarrassment and anger. I didn't have these problems with Jada or Ryan.

"Mrs. Jackson, he's constantly antagonizing other children and he refuses to follow directions. You need to talk to him."

I had just finished fighting so many people at the Department of Children and Family Services that the thought of waging war with this teacher was overwhelming. It's one of my big regrets today. I should have stood up for Devon despite the teacher having an outstanding reputation, but back then I simply didn't have the energy for another battle so soon. I was feeling exhausted as a working mother of three, but I was also sensing something more devastating that was occurring. What was disturbing Devon? I would need all of my strength to find out.

That day when I left Devon's classroom, I also left my innocence behind. Two different teachers in two different schools were giving me a wake-up call about Devon. When I got home and told Walt what had happened, he gave me two options. I needed to handle the situation and go to the principal about the teacher, or he would. I didn't want Walt fighting my battles. I needed to stand up for myself or people wouldn't respect me.

"You have to deal with people directly and tell them what you feel," he said. I thought I had done that well with DCFS, but I realized that was different. When I stood up because of Devon's delayed adoption and both Jada's and Devon's abuse, I was fighting against blatant injustices. But what I would have to learn was how to stand up against the everyday, small attacks people make on one another subtly, which can easily eat away at your soul. A part of me just didn't want to make waves in the children's new school.

I realized that I was going to have to develop a tough skin and stand up to anyone who mishandled Devon, even though he was the one provoking it. I would make him accountable for his behaviors but I wouldn't let anyone further abuse him. It was the beginning of what was to become a long battle.

In the years ahead Devon plagued Ryan and Jada, which meant the constant bickering and fighting was wearing on Walt and me. Devon would take their toys, steal their money, lie, and endlessly provoke them. Time outs, extra chores around the house, and suspended privileges started to be a constant in Devon's life. I hated giving him the consequences for his behaviors, but how else would he learn?

The strange and sad thing we discovered was that Devon didn't seem to mind having his privileges taken away. Missed birthday parties or other events were almost a neighbor-hood known.

"Devon's always on time out," said one little boy coming to play with Ryan. He was right. Suspended privileges would devastate Ryan and Jada. The mere threat of taking their toys away would make them behave, but Devon didn't seem to care. I would learn later that his problems were so deep that normal behavioral modification measures used for most kids didn't faze him. Besides, he came from a foster home that didn't expose him to these types of privileges, so it wasn't like he was missing anything. He did not treasure toys because he never had them before. Some kids would have appreciated them for that fact, but Devon managed to break his new toys immediately.

Devon's exasperating and complex behavior sent us running to Alicia, his therapist. Walt and I couldn't determine what was normal child behavior or the red flags from his abusive past.

My solace was being able just to tell Alicia about Devon's weekly behaviors. It was then that I realized that parents need support groups or someone else to confide in to take the strain off their families when a child is out of control. It was comforting knowing a third party was concerned about Devon's behavior and that gave us hope. Looking back, I knew we were getting desperate because black people back then were almost the last people to go to therapy. I think it was because African-Americans had a general mistrust of the establishment. My mind was flooded with doubts. "How can a white therapist like Alicia treat my son? She doesn't understand my culture. She's too young even to know what life is about. How can she tell me what to do? "

I now realize that it was Alicia's youth and inexperience that were the very qualities that were helping us. She would try harder to understand my family, more than the jaded, "experienced" therapists I would meet later, who were caught up in their own egos. I remember thinking when I first met Alicia that she seemed timid, quiet, and too laid back for me. I wanted things to happen like at the CBS and ABC networks, fast if not instantly. I wanted to see a change in Devon immediately. Fix that kid. Over time, what I saw was a change that was occurring in me.

I started looking at my time with Alicia as my Zen break, even though Devon was with me at the sessions. The low lighting in her office and her calm demeanor were relaxing. The way she gently spoke to him and asked me questions reassured me that things weren't as bad as I imagined. My ego would remind me that she could afford to be calm about Devon since she wasn't emotionally invested like I. Still I found Alicia to be like a comforting warm blanket that helped me to feel more optimistic about Devon's future, even though Walt and I still didn't have a clue as to why Devon was provoking kids.

It was difficult for anyone, including his teachers, to figure out what was making Devon act out. Was it the drugs his birth mother had put in his system? His abuse? Or was it because his mother abandoned him as a baby? Perhaps it was because of what Alicia suspected, that he had Attention Deficit Hyperactivity Disorder (ADHD).

It was a label that gave us something tangible to hang his behaviors on. Most of our frustration came from not being able to pinpoint the problem. If you can find the problem, you can fix it. We would soon come to learn that ADHD was not the problem. It was deeper than that.

What was most disturbing was when Devon had "good" days. In that case we praised or rewarded him. But the next day he would create hell in the classroom. It was a strong predictable pattern. I could have had a luxury vacation if I took bets on how many times he would act up after he had a good day. Devon never failed.

For months we worked with Alicia on getting teacher's reports, trying to pinpoint the exact time of day Devon would act out. I recorded everything he ate to see if it was an organic problem. Nothing gave us a clue.

I remember one period when Devon had been at his worst for a few days, like an alcoholic on a self-destructive binge. I was so grateful that we were scheduled to see Alicia. I rushed Devon to her office, thinking of the peaceful energy that she exuded. I knew I would have relief from the insanity and I would leave with a better outlook.

Devon and I sat in Alicia's tiny office, looking up at the various cartoons on her wall that she, like most therapists, used to help children identify their feelings. I was identifying with the anger, hurt and anxiety-ridden faces when she began to speak softly.

"I have just completed my internship."

"Really? Great Alicia," I said with a smile.

"Well, not so great," she said looking sullen. "I'll be leaving Hathaway."

My first concern was not for her future, it was for ours. What are we going to do now? Alicia explained that they would assign us to another therapist. But as I would quickly discover, good ones would be hard to find.

Devon didn't take the news well. This was just another person in his life who was abandoning him. Alicia's news would also bring up my own abandonment issues dating back to my own childhood. The people I seemed to grow attached to always seem to leave me, usually by way of death.

In the following days Devon acted out his anger in class. I couldn't blame him. At the time I wished I could just go berserk too. It probably was liberating and released a lot of energy just to go crazy. It would be one of the many ways that I would see myself in him.

What I didn't know was that this was just the beginning of more painful days ahead.

CHAPTER FOURTEEN

Aside from Alicia and my mom, we told no one of our problems with Devon. Walt and I didn't want to hear "I told you so's" from friends and family members who didn't support our adoptions. They simply couldn't understand why a fertile couple would adopt rather than have another child of their own.

My mom was the only one who encouraged us. "Don't worry. Devon will be all right." They had a special bond. They understood one another. Maybe it was because during this time she connected with Devon's feelings of being disconnected to life. She had just lost my stepfather her second husband, suddenly from a car accident.

I don't know which was harder to deal with: seeing the strong career woman I grew up with succumbing to depression or Devon out of control, making me depressed.

Fortunately Walt and I operated as a team. He would pick up the kids from school and feed them the dinner I had cooked in the morning, since I didn't get home from ABC until after 7 o'clock. The kids attended after-school care until 5:30, when Walt came to pick them up, so he didn't see their teachers. Therefore, when I dropped them off in the mornings I met with Devon's teacher before school started to get his behavior report.

Every morning began the same. I would take the kids to school, and then walk across the schoolyard to see Devon's teacher. The little note system we had with Devon bringing home reports, often did not work because they simply didn't get home.

"Ms. Jackson... Ms. Jackson!"

A small herd of children ran from across the schoolyard to greet me as Devon and I walked to his class. "Do you know what Devon did?"

"Devon hit me!" "Devon stole my pen." "Devon took my lunch." "Devon pushed me."

I wanted to scream.

It was like walking through a jungle and hearing screeching and howling creatures. The kids were so furious with Devon they could have easily attacked him like wild animals. I probably was his saving grace.

Despite accusations coming at us like native spears in the jungle, Devon calmly denied each one of them, deflecting them like a shield. He didn't get upset with the kids, even though they wanted to tear him apart. He simply refuted what they were saying, which only worked the kids up into a lynching mob. As they grew louder he seemed to grow calmer. I thought one little girl was going into an apoplectic fit she was so enraged.

I knew too well the children's frustrations. At home I would ask Devon about something he did wrong and he would calmly say, "I didn't do it." I knew that he did the deed. It was mind-boggling how I could watch him do something and he would calmly say, "I didn't do that," even though Devon knew I had been watching.

There were times when I had to ask the family, or whoever was witnessing Devon's behavior with me, "Didn't you see Devon do... ?" They did, but because Devon lied so flawlessly, with a blank expressionless face, I doubted my own vision. These were the times Devon engaged in what I learned mental health experts labeled "crazy lying"-- lying about things when there was no reason or benefit to him. It wouldn't be long before I would wonder if Devon actually had a split personality.

Walt and I went out of our way not to punish him if he told us the truth after he had lied, just to prove to him that telling the truth was the right thing to do.

"Devon, I know you lied about this, but if you just tell me the truth," I pleaded with him, "you won't get into trouble."

But Devon didn't seem to care. He seemed to want to get caught in a lie. In the years to come I would learn that this is also a form of self-abuse -- to get caught and punished. Devon's lying was almost spooky in that he did it so seamlessly. It was his one behavior that could send me jumping into flames just to get away from him. I had zero tolerance for lies.

As the days passed and Devon's behaviors festered, I continued to doubt my self-confidence. I had prided myself on rearing Ryan and Jada, who were now honor students, and I had handled difficult stars who acted like children, but I couldn't handle Devon. The hardest part was because we didn't know why he acted out, so how could we take steps to help him? The more we tried to love him, the more he would push us away.

Since we had three children we knew that individual time spent with each child was extremely important, so we had "tea-time" with each of the kids on certain nights, which they loved. The child whose turn it was would fix tea and bring it to Walt and me in the bedroom for privacy from the other kids. We then would do whatever that child wanted, play a board game, read, or just talk. They were such special heart-warming times. In addition, I can remember feeling such a strong connection to Devon on his special nights. We would laugh, hug, and feel so good in one another's company, but the next day, like clockwork, we would get a teacher's report that Devon was at his worst.

Why was he pushing us away? Why wasn't our love for this child enough? Just when we connected so well, he distanced himself from our love. I felt so helpless.

We desperately needed help. It had taken us months to get Alicia at Hathaway, and when she left we found ourselves back on the waiting list, so we went to find other therapists in a fruitless search that would take us from one end of Los Angeles County to another. Devon saw therapists in Barbara Hills, and when that didn't work out, we took him to one we heard about in Lancaster, nearly 70 miles away, and another in between. No one seemed to have an insight into Devon's troubles.

The hardest part about taking Devon to a new therapist was the periods in the beginning when a therapist spent the first sessions to try to get to know Devon by playing board games with him. They wanted to gain his trust in hopes that he would open up and give them insight into how he was thinking. It was a gut wrenching time, especially when they tried to feel Walt and I out as parents to see if we had problems that made Devon act out. People automatically assume when a child is troubled, it's the parents' fault. I always felt I was being scrutinized -- and I was. Often I found the female therapists sizing me, mentally, emotionally, and to my chagrin, physically. They would scan me up and down, so I made sure I was dressed nicely, and I resented having to do that, but I knew it was important as well as superficial. But I knew appearance was part of their analysis of me.

Because no one seemed to be able to help us, I started educating myself by going to meetings and reading what few books there were on troubled adopted children and on kids coming from the system. I desperately needed to understand Devon's background. Sadly, I found little or no information on the foster child in those days. Instead I found one blunt comment from a UCLA therapist: "We're waiting for the '80s drug babies to grow up to see the effects on children born with drugs in their systems."

After we went through a small army of therapists -- and our savings -- what we finally realized was that the usual child therapy didn't work on kids from Devon's background. They were extremely bright and they knew how to play the therapy game because they were moved so many times. Living in the system, these kids had to be a quick study and read people if they wanted to stay in their new foster homes. If they wanted to be moved from a home they played that game, too.

I was always amazed that the therapists did not know Devon was playing them until I opened their embarrassed eyes. He sat before them angelically and calmly as if all that I had reported to them was in my imagination. When they would call his teachers at my request to validate what I told them, they were shocked that he had played them for fools.

Despite his problems, Walt and I loved Devon deeply and we knew that he loved us. He simply had problems, and we were determined to help him. It was at school and with other children where Devon had the most problems. At home with Walt and me he was an absolute delight. I always felt that he would have done best being an only child, but that wouldn't necessarily solve his problems with other kids whom he would antagonize. Where therapists agreed that he adored us, he seemed to loathe his peers and would be strictly anti-social to them and his teachers.

126

"Darling Devon," I wrote in my journal, "we love you so much. We just don't know how to help you. Please tell us what we should do. How can we help you?" It was a constant entry in my journal. I hoped that I would hear his Higher Power directing me in some way. Walt and I knew he was in pain, but over what? That was the missing piece of the puzzle.

The morning reports I received from Devon's teachers were taking a toll on me along with the calls from school I would get at work. Devon was quickly becoming known in the school as the kid with big problems.

Walt spent many days and nights talking to Devon and trying to raise his self-esteem, which was an obvious problem. Devon seldom gave anyone direct eye contact, so Walt would place him in front of a mirror and tell him to look at himself in the eyes and say, "I love Devon." At first Devon couldn't get through those three words without dropping his eyes, but soon he got the hang of it and loved the exercise. He even began singing the phrase around the house. He told perfect strangers that he loved himself and it seemed that his self-esteem was elevating, but unfortunately, so was his penchant for getting in trouble at school.

Mornings would be hell after I received the negative reports from Devon's teacher. I would sometimes leave the school in tears. Walt's and my social life was now becoming non-existent because we couldn't find anyone to baby-sit all three kids, since no one seemed to be able to handle Devon. They would take Ryan and Jada, but only one friend, Velvatine, would welcome all three with open arms. And we couldn't keep imposing on her, especially since she lived 45 minutes away by freeway.

I will never forget the winter of 1993. Some nights I wouldn't get home until almost 7:30 from work because of the heavy rainstorms, which left me inching along the notoriously-jammed 405 freeway. I remember some life-changing experiences that season. In the mornings I would stand in the shower, hearing the kids screaming and arguing. Most times I would be ready to get out and into my robe to stop a fight. My mind would think of the busy pilot season at work, and I felt heart palpitations. In the evenings coming home from work, I would line up behind at least 10 other cars stopped at the red light that led to the on ramp of the freeway. I wanted to fly home to my family, but I could see the cars already on the freeway were completely stopped, and I kept thinking, "Life is much too hard."

Something had to give. I couldn't take it anymore. Our lives had become uncontrollable. One morning I came unglued in the shower.

"I can't do all of this, God. This is too much. Please help me. I can't manage my job at ABC, and I can't manage Devon and raise Ryan and Jada. I can't do this all at once. Please, God, show me the way. Please."

I stood there with the tears pouring down as fast as the shower water. Then suddenly it came over me. Peace.

I never believed in pleading to God. I knew my Higher Power had already given me everything that I needed, and I don't believe that my pleading helped. But I do believe what happened was that I surrendered my burdens to something greater than me, making room so an answer could come. Surrendering would be a lesson that I would learn repeatedly in the coming years.

A week later, a memo came down to all of the ABC employees about a buyout. The network needed to cut back on employees because of some failed shows, which added up to a bad schedule that year. Before laying off employees, ABC offered us a chance to take our benefits and run.

After discussing this with Walt, I was one of the first to sign up. I was grateful that we have always backed one another's career decisions, even if they were going to lead to big financial sacrifices. We didn't have a lot in the bank to fall back on, but I knew I couldn't continue coming to work crying on the freeway. I needed to be home to help Devon. At that time Walt had written his book *Sporting the Right Attitude: Surviving Family Violence*, so I figured I could promote the book and be more accessible to our kids.

My co workers were shocked. I had made manager almost a year before and inherited a large office, and here I was walking out. Titles mean everything in entertainment, including more money. I told them that I was leaving to promote Walt's book even though the driving reason was raising Devon. I felt that they wouldn't understand why I was leaving for my family since most of them were single. I also shrank from confessing to them that Devon was driving me crazy. I had already driven my colleagues crazy by whining to them about our slow adoption process. I feared they would say, "You got him, now you're paying for it," or "You have to be careful for what you pray for."

My move was something that I had to do if our family was going to survive, but in the coming years our family's survival was still going to be questionable.

CHAPTER FIFTEEN

After my leaving ABC the financial sacrifice would prove to be tremendous for our family, but we couldn't see any other way to deal with Devon. No one but Walt and I could handle him around the clock, and no one wanted to.

Keeping copious notes, I journaled about his behaviors and therapy treatments. Writing has always given me peace and a sense of order in my life, but the more I wrote about Devon the less sense I could make of his actions. At night, when the children were asleep, I wrote furiously of my anger in my journal, at times ripping the pages. I found myself writing repeatedly, "Why God? Why is this happening to our family? Why is this happening to me?"

I threw myself into the search for information on the '80's drug babies. Through this search it dawned on Walt and me that there were far too few programs to help high-risk children. There was no support for them. Before we knew it, we found ourselves on a mission to help these children and emotionally support their families. We knew that children like Devon fell into the system because parents were stressed and turned to devices like drugs to relieve the pressure. But looking back, I probably wanted other parents supporting me.

In 1993 we opened the doors to Believe In Yourself, Inc., a tutoring and self-esteem building program for children and their families. The non-profit organization was born out of the talks we had with parents, including the drug mothers, who simply didn't know how to help their children. Suddenly our struggle with Devon began to make sense. It was leading us to a higher mission beyond ourselves and beyond our own pain.

Believe In Yourself was the hardest job I had ever had in my life. Walt was the CEO and financed it by working, and I was the Executive Director, running the daily operations. Each week approximately thirty children came to us for after-school care at an L.A. Recreation and Parks Department Center. Local high school students came to our program to tutor and put in their civic hours for credits. Adults came to volunteer.

I called on celebrities I had worked with, who all gave money, including Mary Tyler Moore, Edward Asner, and Lee Bell, the co-executive producer of "The Bold and the Beautiful" and "The Young and the Restless," ongoing television series.

When people didn't give money they gave their advice about what a non-profit like ours can do to survive. I learned the hard way that there are so many options to pursue, but it all boils down to this: the established non-profits were successful; we were brand new and starting from scratch, and we had to compete with them for grants.

Walt and I were so naïve on the political scene. We thought we would get support just by helping people, but we quickly learned it's a game, a personality contest, and Walt refused to "kiss ass" and "play the game" for politicians' support. Coming from my entertainment background, I thought at times he was wrong, but he kept the organization with strong integrity and refused to bend for what he called "chump change." We supplied money out of our own pocket.

I remember Walt and I sitting in the office of our district councilman, who headed a board that was in charge of a community project that would give moneys to organizations like ours. "We didn't want handouts -- just a hand."

"You should be receiving funds for your organization," the councilman said earnestly. I smiled inside because that was just the reason why Walt and I had made the appointment to meet with him. We had heard that money, set aside from land developers, was designated for children's programs in our area, and we had the only after-school program going.

"You know I'll work with you. I lead the board. My staff also has connections with *The Daily News* and *The Los Angeles Times* newspapers," he said. "I'll make sure you get exposure in them to get donations."

Walt and I left his office and floated back home, assured that when his committee voted in the next couple of days we would have the funding for our program, and the support of the council member.

I could barely concentrate as the hours ticked away. Every time our phone rang I snatched it up, expecting to hear that we received the funding from the board. Instead, we got a call from a friend who was a long-time community activist.

"You know that when Believe In Yourself came up on the agenda, you lost the vote."

I was frozen but managed to mouth some words, "But why?"

"The councilman said that he didn't want to support a program run out of someone's kitchen."

"Kitchen?" I was livid. "We're not holding the program in our house; we're holding it in the recreation center. I just have our office in the house."

"I know Jan, but that's what he said."

"So we don't get any money?"

"No," she said softly.

It would take me years to get over the anger with that council member, and as I write these words I realize I still haven't healed from the pain. Why did he lie to us? Why didn't he just say that he would see what he could do? Why pump us up?

"He's a politician, that's why," said Walt. "He didn't know that you had someone on his board who would tell you the truth."

This was a moment of decision. We wouldn't go after any more government money. We had already seen that running a non-profit makes you dependent and you have to grovel for crumbs. Walt, being proud was not about to put us in that position. "We're about purpose," he said. "We don't have to beg anyone for anything."

And with that we began to charge families a small fee for the program. Some couldn't afford to pay, but we let their children attend anyway because the kids were so enthusiastic about coming.

But it was the support of volunteers that gave us the emotional lift to keep our doors open. I would leave our house to go to the program and nearly trip over a huge bag of snacks that Carolyn Monroe, a high school counselor, donated constantly to the program. Then there was Claudine Harris, a mental health expert who donated her time teaching crafts to the children. I couldn't have run the program without Deborah Olin and Danielle Hanchett, two blondes who could give supermodels Heidi Klum or Claudia Schiffer a run for their money. They were by my side every day, running the program with me.

Then there was the financial and huge emotional support from our devoted board members, mostly from the entertainment industry. Geramy Quarto, Suzanne Gordon, Marlene Mattaschiam, Joan Dunning, Velvatine Sykes and Jim Mceuen, they believed in Walt and me and supported every move we made, including the decision to forego applying for government money.

It wasn't long before word spread about our program. The local school even asked us to move BIY to their campus. We did, but our joy would be overshadowed with embarrassment.

The school was where our own kids, including Devon, attended. Here I was, teaching other children how to do the right thing and trying to build up their self-esteem, and Devon was swinging from the rafters. He was continuously in trouble, even disrupting the kids in the program so much that I constantly ordered him out of the classroom until he could control himself. Everyone knew Devon was our kid, and I found myself under such strain not only to get Devon to cooperate because it was the right thing to do, but also because now his behavior was tarnishing Walter's reputation and mine as community leaders. I imagined parents and teachers saying, "How is she running this program if her own kid is out of control?"

When thinking about Devon's oppositional defiant behavior, I kept asking myself what did I have to learn from this? I needed to find the answer or I would continue to stumble into the same hole. I had to find out what in my consciousness attracted a child like Devon to me with so much defiance? What was interesting was that teachers and parents brought kids who also were out of control to BIY. We managed to help them and received tremendous praise, but, sadly, I couldn't help my own son.

I couldn't help Devon, because we didn't know what inside of him needed help. He had so many issues -- from sexual abuse to being born with drugs in his system -- that we couldn't pin down what was disturbing him. Over the hears all of his therapists agreed that we needed to work on only one of his problems at a time, but no one could single out a predominant source of his behaviors. I couldn't "fix" Devon, so I began to concentrate on fixing myself, trying to find out what I needed to learn from all of these trials and tribulations with Devon.

One evening while I was praying and journaling to seek answers within myself, I had a revelation. I had graduated from college and landed great jobs at the networks. I had traveled, worked with and partied with some of the world's biggest celebrities, but Devon showed me that no matter how far I had come in life, if I didn't handle important issues from my past, they would come back to haunt me.

What feelings inside of me surfaced and were most intensified by Devon's behaviors? The answers thundered back to me. Deep embarrassment and shame. I quickly did an exercise I was taught in the ministry and wrote about the first times I remember having those haunting feelings. I remembered when my stepfather, a hard-working baker, used to drink excessively on the weekends. He morphed from a loving, kind, generous man to a monster, and numerous times I remember fleeing with my mother out of the house in the wee hours of the morning before one of them killed the other. I stopped inviting my friends over, and when my parents had their friends over and their arguing erupted, I felt what most kids feel, living in that environment: somehow it must be my fault.

Suddenly I had a shift in consciousness. It wasn't only about Devon. He was sent here as mirror to help me clear up some major issues that were never resolved for me. It had to do with the power of forgiveness. I knew I had to forgive my stepfather and Devon and his parents. But I didn't know how. I didn't know how to reach peace over this. I did know that if I was going to survive this, it was up to me to find a way.

CHAPTER SIXTEEN

It seemed that whenever things were going well in our family -- as terrible as it sounds of me -- Devon would sabotage our joy with deplorable behavior. Could an eight-year-old be this calculating? At first I thought it was my imagination, but as I observed the timing closely, he never failed.

I remember after one exceptionally wonderful afternoon with the kids in our Believe in Yourself program, Devon's teacher called to tell me that he had started a new school behavior -- stealing. He stole not only from classmates but from her, as well.

At home we had already started hiding everything of value. We suspected when things came up missing that Devon was responsible. The proof came out days later. I remember how shocked I was when I first discovered it.

I began regularly to comb his room when he was at school. One day I found Ryan's missing CDs and my credit cards under his mattress. I plopped on his bed as the wind went right out of my lungs. When I gathered myself, I pulled open his dresser drawers and was shocked to see they were filled with snacks from the kitchen. This was particularly bizarre because he didn't eat much at all. Sweets didn't really interest him, but they were stockpiled, like socks, in his drawer.

I was relentlessly driven to research this behavior, and after pouring through psychology books on children, I learned that hoarding is common to some foster children. Many lose their belongings by being moved from home to home. In some overcrowded foster homes they don't get enough food. I then remembered that Devon said his foster mother fed him only rice and crackers. I'm sure he got more than that, but I was also sure that if he had brought up the subject, she was rationing out the food.

With each passing year things with Devon got worse. New teachers, new therapists, and new friends would come into our lives with plans to "help" him.

Everyone thought that his or her way could change our son. He had that effect on people. Despite his mischief, he was extremely charming and engaging. I thought these were his redeeming features until one day when I was talking to his psychiatrist.

"Charming," she said looking at me deadpan, "can be extremely dangerous. Serial killers are charming." It was a wake-up call. As you can imagine, I didn't sleep that night.

Over the years I watched those who wanted to help Devon fade in and out of our lives like phantoms, quickly withdrawing their energy out of frustration. They just knew their way was the right way, but their tactics failed. Before they abandoned us we often heard them say, "You and Walt are saints for putting up with that kid," or "Devon doesn't know how lucky he is to have you guys as parents," and "I could never live with him."

"People come and go in Devon's life," said Walt. " They change, but he stays the same."

He was right. I saw some of the nicest teachers, whom Ryan had before Devon, turn into vicious witches when they got Devon in their class. Where I had praised those teachers in the past, a few times I ended up reporting them to the principal because Devon pushed them to blurt something inappropriate.

Every new semester began the same. Devon was always on his extreme best behavior at the beginning and our hopes were high with a new teacher and a new semester. We told him that he could start over with the past now in the past. We kept thinking that he was maturing and maybe this year he would finally settle down. These honeymoons lasted only about a month before the "old Devon" emerged. When the new teacher and Devon clashed because he couldn't keep it together, the school called me, Devon then turned on them to retaliate. His bitterness was in his eyes when he spoke about his teacher. I used to wonder, "What life lessons is that teacher learning? Devon would definitely be the teacher."

Looking back, we had plenty of teacher conferences. There were times when Walt took off from work and went to bat for Devon only to find out he had lied about his teachers and pitted us against them. After several times of being extremely embarrassed, finding we were wrong because of what Devon told us, we learned to build strong alliances with teachers, making it clear to Devon that we were not going to be "played" by him.

Still Devon pushed a few teachers to a point of raging anger, especially when he told Walt and me that a teacher was lying about him -- and this right in her presence. People simply lost their cool with him. I knew exactly how they felt. Over the years of trying to help Devon, I watched myself turn into an uptight bitch with a bundle of nerves and short temper. My beeper went off constantly about Devon's school problems and when it didn't, I was a wreck wondering when it would. Sometimes, out of anxiety, I would just go up to the school to check on him because I knew that any moment I would be called.

There were times that I, too, like the teachers, would say things to Devon out of anger and frustration that I wished I could have called back. I would never say them to Ryan or Jada. But I was just that angry.

There were also a few times that I regretfully spanked him when behavioral modification, endless reward systems, therapy, begging, and pleading didn't work.

I remember the first time was when we had company. Three other children had come over with their parents. Immediately Devon started antagonizing them, so we put him in our room on "time out," since the kids were playing in his bedroom that he shared with Ryan. When I came back in the room to check on Devon, I smelled something burning. Looking down I was horrified to see a hole burned in the carpet. Devon looked at me sheepishly with matches still in his hand.

When the company left, his bottom was mine. He was eight-years-old, and he knew better about matches. I was more afraid than mad. He could have burned himself to death as well as everyone in the house. Where I had been patient with years of Devon's therapy, I wasn't going to take this up with his therapist and suffer through months of worrying would he understand. I knew the next time Devon lit a match could be the last time for him or any of us, so I immediately gave him consequences.

But spanking Devon, or any child, is not the answer. I am opening myself up on these pages for criticism because I understand parents' frustrations. I also want readers to know spanking is a form of abuse and I was wrong.

While spankings may result in the child changing his behavior, often it's temporary. The child may act out later in hatred, revenge and hostility what they learned from their parent's spankings. Spankings can damage the self-esteem of the parent and the child. I wanted Devon to do things out of love, not fear. I also realized that Devon was merely mirroring the abuse he received in foster care. Devon pushed every button that I had. He knew the right ones.

During this time I learned that DCFS could step in and take Jada and Ryan from us, if they felt I was abusing Devon with spankings. From then on I put him in his room, taking privileges away. These sacrifices didn't seem to faze him. He continued his mischievous behaviors.

I was amazed how stubborn Devon was when his privileges were taken away.

When Ryan and Jada misbehaved, which they rarely did, timeouts were a catastrophe to them. I often thought that God gave me two other kids who never gave me any trouble because He felt sorry for my misery over Devon.

No type of behavior modification worked for him, as every therapist and psychiatrist he visited over the years realized. We had tried extensive reward programs, and they were exhausting, just trying to make sure we were consistently following through. In the end, they failed, too.

We had tried putting Devon in sports, which he loved, to channel his energy and learn teamwork and respect. I spent endless hours sitting with him in his classes to make sure he controlled himself. We took him to piano classes religiously since he wanted to play and had an insatiable appetite for music. We bought him whatever instrument and music he wanted, but nothing helped. I took him to Sunday school and youth church during the week, hoping God would intervene. But through all of this he continued with his favorite sport which was tormenting other kids at home and at school.

I prayed constantly for his healing and for my patience. I could easily see how parents can lose total control and I was determined not to let him know that he got the best of me, which he did. At night, while everyone slept, I often cried myself to sleep.

I think what was just as unnerving as some of Devon's behaviors were the constant, frightening reminders we received from people.

"If Devon doesn't get his act together," they said, "he will end up behind bars."

Would that come true? Was what they said right? Maybe his birth parents were criminals. We had no information on their backgrounds. During that time I read articles by experts who wrote that people can inherit sociopathic traits from their parents. Was there such a thing as criminal genes?

The bottom line was that we had to stop Devon from becoming a train wreck. We knew that the world didn't care about his sad background or that he had been diagnosed with oppositional defiance, Attention Deficit Hyperactivity Disorder, and sexual trauma, which we later learned was not correct. If he committed a crime he would go to jail. Period. It certainly seemed by the way he defied authority that he was headed in that direction.

I distanced myself from friends who said he could end up behind bars because, after all, I was his mother. Walt and I loved him deeply. Why else would we go through this madness? We just needed to find him the right help. I knew that there were people who quietly gave their adopted children back to the system because they were extremely difficult, but Walt and I were not about to take that road even though it was tempting. We knew deep down it was not Devon's fault he had these problems. We had made a commitment to raise and love this child, and that's exactly what we were going to continue doing.

My salvation was taking long hillside walks with our German shepherd while the kids were in school and before I went to our Believe In Yourself program in the afternoons. There I would ask God, "Why haven't you answered my prayers to help Devon? What do you want me to do, God? Why is it that despite our best efforts and people calling us angels for taking Devon in that he doesn't get better? What am I doing wrong?"

I don't believe God punishes people. I believe in a loving God and that things happen in the universe as part of the yin and yang of life. I knew that I just needed to maintain balance as life sent me through these treacherous twists and turns. Sooner or later things would get better. But it became harder as the years progressed and Devon's behavior became more serious. I found myself reevaluating my spiritual beliefs. Was I being tested?

It seemed every few months Devon started something alarming. Now he began harassing and even stalking little girls he liked. What made it mortifying was that he was doing this during the O.J. Simpson trial, and some of the girls Devon refused to leave alone were white. From his teachers I learned that the stalked girls ran home crying to their parents about our son. Walt and I were at wits end. Devon was feeding into the fears of the whole media-fixated country that was mesmerized by the Simpson trial. Walt and I understood parents being upset over Devon. If Jada came home crying because a boy constantly harassed her we would be irate, too. Taking away privileges simply didn't work. He continued his anti-social behaviors until finally, like a meteor flying across the sky, it died away.

One night, while Walt and I were in bed, Ryan and Jada came in together to see us. Devon was in his room on punishment. He had developed another pattern. Whenever he got off time-out he would immediately do something to get back on. At times we let his behavior slide because I didn't want him living jail time at home. But when we did, he would simply do something else extreme that we couldn't possibly ignore. It was another way of sabotaging himself.

"Mom, Dad," said Ryan, peeking into our bedroom. Jada was close behind. "Can we talk to you?"

This was serious. Usually they just pounced on the bed to talk about whatever was on their minds. We had a nightly ritual. They would crawl under the covers with us and share their day.

"Okay," said Walt, "about what?"

I patted the bed and they crawled on, their faces solemn.

"It's Devon," said Jada, her lips quivering. She was on the verge of hysterics.

"What about Devon?" asked Walt, turning to Ryan, who was more controlled.

"Some kids said they're going to get their big brothers to beat up Devon because he keeps messing with them, and their brothers are going to hurt me, too, because I'm Devon's brother."

"And me, too," said a visibly shaken Jada, who suddenly burst into tears. "They said they're going to get me, too," she shrieked.

Ryan looked at her and started crying, too. My children were terrified.

I sat up in bed with a five-alarm bell ringing in my head. While Walt comforted the children, my mind raced. Not far from us, as in many San Fernando Valley suburbs, there was increasing Latino and African-American gang activity. The city problems were spreading to the suburbs. Tensions were growing and gangs were opposing one another. Devon may be bothering the wrong girl. We had to do something to stop him, but what?

The next day I was confiding in Ms. Duran at school about Devon and my family's fears. She was the special education teacher who was adored by all of the children, including Devon. She had soft, compassionate brown eyes and a soothing voice. Ms. Duran, like others, didn't have solutions, but she was a good listener. She had allowed Devon to come into her class after lunch since she only had 10 special needs children to teach and an aide to help her. Devon was not eligible for special education because he had high test scores and he was extremely bright, but the small class size seemed to work. He became calm in her class.

"When Devon comes off the playground from lunch or recess his motor is still running," said Ms. Duran. "In his afternoon class he can't seem to switch gears to calm down like the other kids. And with those 30 other students it's like mixing fire and gas. Kaboom!"

Devon was getting along fine with the special needs children. I knew that his regular teacher was relieved to have a break from him, if only for an hour during the day. She could then do what she was paid to do: Teach without interruptions.

At first I was concerned that Devon was missing math. But how could he learn anything disrupting that classroom? How could the other kids learn? How could the teacher teach?

"I have a special needs daughter," said Ms. Duran. "I know what you're going through." Tears rolled down my face. Thank God. Someone else understood our problems.

The relief of being able to drop my mask was so freeing. In my mind I had this strong image to uphold in the community. Ryan and Jada were both honor students, so I felt that people looked up to my parenting skills as an example, but Devon's antics blew that theory away. Even though I had loads of respect, and people kept bringing their children to BIY, I felt judged by others because of Devon. It was a tough balancing act. No one seemed to understand but Walt. Hearing Ms. Duran talk about the challenges she faced with her daughter was the additional support that I desperately needed and at the right time.

"Do yourself a favor," she said, staring at me intently while placing her hands on both of my shoulders. "Put Devon on medication." I looked up with my mascara-streaked eyes, and something clicked in my head.

"Do it for yourself," she said, "do it for your family."

Therapists and other teachers had suggested medication to me years earlier but I refused. I even got angry with them for bringing up the subject. I had been adamant about putting drugs in my own system. I certainly didn't want my kids drugged. When they got colds I juiced fresh fruit and vegetables rather than giving them decongestants or cough medicines. That worked fine.

Before meeting Walt, I was a vegetarian. After we married, we became periodic vegetarians together. The thought of chemicals in our bodies was repulsive. After Ryan was born I drove his daycare director nuts because I sent fresh squeezed juices and vegetable dishes for his lunch and insisted he be fed them. It made her job more difficult, not being able to feed him the processed foods with the other children.

I had even gone the organic route with Devon, hoping that would help him. I also took him to a chiropractor who specialized in herbal treatments. She had an incredible reputation for working with kids with behavioral problems. News articles were written about her successes. Hundreds of dollars later we realized that herbs were not working either.

Now as I looked into Ms. Duran's comforting eyes, it was clear. We had run out of options. Maybe medication could help him and stop our family from being controlled by his actions. When Walt and I were angry at Devon's behaviors, that anger carried over to our relationship with Ryan and Jada. We were in foul moods, or we didn't have patience with them -- and that wasn't fair. Speaking with Ms. Duran, I realized we had an obligation to the entire family, not just Devon. Ryan and Jada deserved the full attention of their parents, too. One person should not manipulate our entire family. I believe that a family is a team -- and in those days our team was losing the game.

Within several days his psychiatrist, consulting with his therapist and me, placed Devon on Ritalin. He was 9 years old. They both felt I should have put him on it long before. Still, you would have thought I was giving him poison because I was riddled with guilt.

I brought Devon to school late after we saw his doctor and I gave him his first dose of medication. As we approached the front gate Devon did something that I had never seen him do before. He started running in circles. He stopped only to turn cartwheels, which I didn't know that he could do. To my horror I realized the Ritalin had speeded him up, not calmed him down. Since I knew this sudden spurt of turbo energy was a recipe for another classroom disaster, I promptly turned him around and took him home. That night it was sheer hell as he became more hyperactive and antagonized both of his siblings.

"Remember, these medications do not change behaviors," said his psychiatrist as she wrote him another prescription, this time for Dexedrine. "They just help the child to be more in control." Damn! I was praying for a miracle drug.

Several hours after giving Devon the new medication, I couldn't believe how much calmer he was. I also was surprised by his reaction.

"Thanks, Mom."

"For what?"

"The pills."

"Why do you say that?"

"Cause I feel I can control myself."

Looking into his eyes, I was reminded how much I loved this child despite his actions. I reminded him that it was his behaviors, not him, that people didn't like, and that maybe the behaviors would change with the medication. He shook his head yes, and we hugged for a long time.

I knew Devon didn't want a reputation of being the school's terror. I also knew that he had become the school's scapegoat and his behaviors also reflected the fact that he knew people didn't like him. But like all kids, he just wanted to be loved. He couldn't help it if his actions, which he didn't seem to be able to control, pushed people away. I realized then that the medicine could be a miracle drug if it helped him display to the world that he is a wonderful soul. It was the reason we adopted him.

Unfortunately, in time the medication, like therapy and our love, simply would not be enough.

CHAPTER SEVENTEEN

Believe in Yourself, Inc., captured the attention of two major newspapers, *The Los Angeles Times*, and *The Daily News*. Needless to say, we were thrilled when reporters visited and wrote stories about our program. We had high hopes that the media attention would bring funding. It didn't.

Meanwhile Devon seemed calmer since he started taking his medication. He was not as disruptive in the classroom and he didn't seem to antagonize children as much. I found myself lulled into a false sense of relief until other symptoms began emerging that were even more disturbing.

"Did you call me, Mom?" Devon was breathless as he ran inside from the backyard to see me.

"Nope, I didn't." I smiled as he shook his head in confusion, turning around to return to the backyard.

The first few times he asked me if I called him when I hadn't, I didn't think too much about it. Then it was evident. Devon began hearing voices. Every horror movie I had seen in my life began haunting me.

"What are these voices saying?" asked Susan with a frown as we sat in the therapist's office. I suspected she was probably thinking what I feared. Would the voices tell him to do something terrible?

"Nothing. It's just I hear my mom calling me," answered Devon.

We had taken a break from therapy after finding no benefit, but now that the voices had started, Walt and I had brought Devon back. It wasn't too soon. Although there were now weeks when Devon was on his best behavior and we thought he was improving, he would suddenly begin some bizarre new behavior that would astound me. I could not relax when he was constantly in trouble, and now I couldn't relax when he was on his good behavior. We didn't know when the other shoe would drop and what he would do next.

After two intense weeks of psychological testing, Henry, Devon's psychiatrist with a heavy black beard, told me, "It's amazing. When Devon is told to focus visually on a picture, he seems to grasp the tiniest details." He showed me a drawing of cars parked on a busy street that he also had shown to Devon.

"He picked out the parking meter."

"The parking meter?" I said, taking the drawing from the doctor's hands and pulling it close to my face. "Where is it?"

"Here," said Henry pointing, "You can barely see it at the edge of the paper. This is what Devon fixated on," he said with a perplexed look on his face. "I kept trying to get him to see the whole picture, but he kept seeing the parking meter."

Suddenly I felt light, as if a huge rock had rolled off my chest. Someone understood what I experienced.

"That's just what he does all of the time!" I said, my voice shrill. "That's exactly how he is when we talk about his behavior at school. He does not see the overall picture, just some small thing that happened. When anyone at school or at home confronts him on something he did, Devon picks out a small detail and clings to it, overlooking the big issue."

It felt like the sun had burst through the clouds. Someone else finally had a glimpse into Devon's mind. I had often wondered if he was lying or truly saw life differently from the rest of us. I thought many times that he was schizophrenic. I retold an incident to the doctor proving the psychological tests were right.

"Devon, did you eat all of the Tums?"

A couple of weeks earlier I was showing him a nearly empty bottle of anti-acid tablets. It had been three-fourths full on the bathroom counter earlier that morning, according to my mother, who was visiting. She felt bad that she had accidentally left them out with children around. I had already questioned Ryan and Jada but then I stopped, seeing the telltale evidence of pastel-colored residue around Devon's mouth. After calling the doctor's office to see if we should rush him to the hospital, we were relieved to learn he would be okay, and I resumed questioning him.

"No," said Devon. "I didn't eat all of those Tums."

We all stared in disbelief, watching Devon as he denied eating the tablets. I had even placed him in front of a mirror to see what we saw on his mouth. Still he kept vehemently lying even when he knew he had been found out. Again his privileges were taken away, and he was given weed-pulling duty. Later I took the Tums bottle and went to talk to him in the backyard, where I caught him singing into the rake handle like a microphone and dancing away.

"Okay, Devon, you can get your privileges back if you just admit the truth." My body was heavy from weariness. "For the last time, did you eat all of those Tums?"

He took the bottle from me and shook it.

"No, Mommy, I didn't eat all of those Tums." He opened the cap. "See, there's still some left."

I couldn't help smiling. I realized this was an example of how he fixated on the smallest detail, ignoring the big picture. In the future we were careful how to phrase things to him.

During the weeks Devon underwent psychological testing, even though there were no solutions to his problems, it was a relief having someone in the professional mental health world finally understand our plight.

"Dealing with Devon," said the psychiatrist, "is just like dealing with ghosts." He went on to explain his testing and I kept thinking he was so right. There seemed to be no rhyme nor reason for Devon's behavior problems or when they would surface. If we couldn't find a reason or a pattern, how could we help Devon?

Often I felt like many other parents I met, sitting endless hours in therapists' waiting rooms, filled with frustrations. When Devon would come out he would be all smiles while I was wrestling with pent-up emotions and feeling more stressed from waiting in a small room filled with hyperactive kids crawling over me.

Who was listening to me? What about my feelings? Yet it was such a relief to hear that the psychiatrist was putting a finger on what I felt.

I fumed at child-raising experts on afternoon television talk shows. Children were the most popular topic on the rash of new talk shows then, and they still are. I remember watching shows on unruly children, hoping I would find a clue to Devon's behavior. Instead, experts, the host, and the audience would turn on the parents. Everyone had their opinion on how to raise children. Yes, in some cases they were right, but clearly in other cases a parent had tried to help their child and failed. The audience, like a pack of wolves, would attack the parent. They couldn't know the whole story in a three-minute segment.

If a child is acting out, should we automatically assume it's the parent's fault? I was sure if I had gone on those talk shows, they would have persecuted me, too. But I knew not one of them throwing stones could survive living with Devon for a week and I barked back at the television set, telling them so, too.

Still I couldn't totally blame the audience. I had to admit to myself that before Devon's problems I was quick to rush to judgment about parents. I thought many of them were hopelessly inept.

I remember once before visiting Crystal Stairs and meeting drug mothers, I was in a parent internet chat room. I criticized parents who deserted their children. Everyone in the chat room was on my side except one visitor. He was the lone voice, but I heard him loud and clear.

"What makes you think they don't care about their children?" he typed.

"Because they chose drugs over their child's welfare," I replied.

"Remember," he wrote back, "never assume that people are not working on their stuff. To us it may not be enough but they may be working hard to change."

After that internet chat, I softened my self-righteous attitude. Maybe he was right. If some parents knew better, they would do better. Observing Devon in our house, one could assume we, too, were not good parents when, in actuality, we did everything, including searching the earth and the moon, to help him. Those who knew Walt and me -- friends, therapists, and teachers -- applauded us. But to the outside world we must have seemed like failing parents.

My search to find answers to Devon's behavior problems led me to an organization called CASA -- Court Appointed Special Advocates for children. I saw their ad in the *Los Angeles Times* asking for volunteers to help children who were wards of the court. During those days any child coming from Jada's and Devon's background got my immediate attention and if I could help, I felt like it was my duty to save them from the system. So despite my jam-packed schedule, I volunteered.

Many of the children that CASA volunteers help are foster children. Just being around the volunteers was healing because these people understood foster children, who were very much like Devon. It was liberating just being in their presence. They didn't judge a kid with emotional problems and didn't judge me as a parent when I told them Devon's problems. I quickly and surprisingly found out that Devon's behavior was typical of a child living in various foster homes.

After a few weeks of training I had a case assigned to me. I was to be the voice of a child in court and the eyes and the ears of the court to help the child who, as Devon was, may be trapped in the system. As a CASA advocate I made recommendations to the court for placement or anything else my CASA child needed.

Judges appreciate CASA volunteers because they know social workers are overloaded with cases. Back then they carried approximately 90 cases apiece. An extra pair of CASA eyes could help the child get the needed special services. At that time, there were 50,000 children in Los Angeles County who were wards of the court. Often they had suffered abuse and neglect. But with so few CASA advocates we could take on only about 1 percent of the cases.

My first court case was nothing short of victorious. Grandparents of seven-year-old I will call Libby, knew she needed special help that they couldn't provide. But out of guilt they didn't want to be responsible for sending Libby away from their home. The grandparents were already taking care of other grandchildren. These were two small boys and a teenage girl who belonged to the couple's drug-addicted daughter. She was currently in a treatment facility. The children's fathers were unknown, except for one who was in jail.

Libby was severely mentally challenged. She ate her own feces, constantly banged her head on walls, pulled out her hair by the handful during continuous temper tantrums, and struggled to walk with a leg brace. Libby could not speak, so she grunted loudly. The elderly couple didn't know what to do to help her. The entire family was constantly on alert because they didn't know if the girl would harm herself. No one slept peacefully in the house.

Libby's social worker insisted that the girl needed to be with the grandparents but they were exhausted with four children in their custody. The grandmother, who worked at night and took care of Libby and the others during the day, confided in me that she had to take tranquilizers and was on a verge of a breakdown while trying to deal with the children. Her marriage of nearly 30 years was on the verge of breakup from the tremendous stress. Both grandparents juggled their jobs and caring times for the children.

I remember nervously waiting to plead Libby's case before the judge, an attractive Latina with a quick no-nonsense air. I sat perspiring, watching the case before mine. Two deputies brought a leg-shackled father into the courtroom from a small holding room. He was obviously serving time, dressed in an orange jumpsuit with his hands handcuffed behind his back. I felt sorry that his small kids, anxiously looking at their father, had to see him that way. I recognized the anguish the kids were suffering as I watched the nine-year-old, standing next to the five-year old, wring his hands while rocking back and forth.

As I watched the hearing of permanent placement for the children to stay in their current foster home, which took approximately five minutes, my mind drifted back to something I heard in CASA training. It often takes days to settle the property in a divorce case, but in the matter of child living arrangements it often takes all of 90 seconds for the judge to decide. This is why it's important for a CASA to give her evaluation of a child's case along with a hard-working social worker's report to the judge. The judge can see a bigger picture with the report of the CASA, who has the time to spend with the child and to do investigations in depth.

When my case came before the judge, I nervously spoke for the grandparents' concerns. I had found a wonderful facility to help treat Libby. To my amazement, the judge ordered the girl to be placed in the facility at my recommendation.

A few months later the trained staff at the facility had managed to stop Libby from eating her feces. The head banging was reduced to a minimum and Libby's hair had grown out beautifully because she had stopped pulling it out. The staff was teaching her how to communicate through sign language but she also could now say simple words like "yes" and "hello".

Needless to say, the grandparents were deeply grateful to me, and when I went to see Libby, I nearly didn't recognize this glowing, happy child who came up and hugged me. Why couldn't I find help for Devon, too?

I learned a lot from CASA. It was just comforting being around those who cared. But between BIY and raising my own children I was drained, and I didn't have much time or strength for more cases. When I was asked to join the Friends of Child Advocates fundraising board because of my publicity background, I jumped at the chance since it would be less demanding of my time and less emotionally draining. I found myself immediately immersed in promoting "The 50,000 Lights" project. The outside of the children's Superior Court was to be lit up with white lights representing the 50,000 children who were wards of the Los Angeles court. Most had been neglected and abused. I was thrilled being a part of the promotion and contacting the media -- and at the success of the program that is still a tradition today.

Working with CASA not only helped me to see that there were many kids out there like Libby who needed more help than their parents could offer, but also that their emotional problems were just as crucial as their mental disabilities. It was the reason why Walt and I pushed so hard to keep our Believe In Yourself, Inc. doors open. We were dealing with children's emotional issues with our self-esteem and meditation classes.

We saw those emotional issues in Devon and we tried to educate people on the problem. But now we were more determined since my volunteering for CASA. It was like a tale of two cities. People who worked at the DCFS and the children's courts knew there were emotional issues, but outside of that group, it was a foreign concept.

Enter the Columbine High School massacre. April 20, 1999. Suddenly the world took heed of the secret life of children's emotions. When teens Eric Harris and Dylan Klebold killed and wounded their schoolmates, people were now saying what we already knew and had been preaching. Children have stress and emotional problems that can lead to disaster.

I remembered a *Los Angeles Times* reporter's questioning of me on children having stress.

"Stress? I can't believe these children have stress," he told me, taking out his pad and pen, snickering to himself. "They're too young." I didn't argue. I simply seated him in our class for our "sharing" time. One little nine-year-old girl was anxious to share first. Her grandmother had just died.

"I have to go live with my dad now," she said, swaying from side-to-side holding back tears. "I don't want to. I don't know what's going to happen." Her voice lowered. "He drinks a lot."

I looked over at the reporter, who was obviously struck by this little girl. I knew what he was thinking. He verbalized it to me later. "You're right. Children really do have stress."

Yes. They do have emotional drama going on that's often under the adult radar. The Columbine boys' profiles were like Devon's. I was rocked when I read about them after the massacre. I began feeling more paranoid about Devon's behaviors and horrified to think that we, as parents, could be responsible for Devon's actions that we couldn't control.

One of the Columbine boys had been adopted and was on medications and in therapy just like Devon. During the news coverage my mind raced with fears about our son's future. Was he capable of the same crimes?

But the national awareness of children's emotions developed a few years after BIY was closed. Back then, I was feeling my own emotional storms and deep resentment because BIY was struggling to keep the doors open.

"Don't they know that BIY and organizations like ours could save tax payers millions?" I ranted to Walt. We were in our daily meeting, bouncing fundraising ideas off one another as well as our frustrations.

"What they don't realize is that if they don't help kids now, they'll be paying for their mistakes later," Walt said bitterly. We both knew that meant prison, murders, robberies, or simply welfare. We had no clue then that three years later the Columbine massacre would happen. We just knew that our little program was helping prevent kids from living a life of crime by teaching them to believe in themselves. Our mission was to help them to become productive, law-abiding citizens with dreams they could reach.

I often felt that the government made the people running non-profits feel dependent and humiliated like some of the clients who depended on these programs. I hated the pre-proposal information meetings that grant funders held to inform organizations about how to apply for their hoped-for grant. It reminded me of coins being thrown into a crowd and people scrambling to pick them off the ground. I attended these meetings alone and saw well-connected paid representatives of big organizations who had political endorsements. BIY didn't have a chance. The stipulations and the red tape of grants are another kind of dragon, like DCFS. On the other hand, when grant money comes too easily, it's a warning.

Over the years we met representatives from several large organizations who offered us a portion of their grant money, but the terms were suspect. They were going to integrate our program with theirs, or worse, steal our ideas, which meant stealing BIY.

It was the time of the sharks, and we found ourselves swimming for our lives. The large, successful organizations were told that funders didn't want to keep giving to old tired programs. These organizations needed to be innovative. To attract funding they needed a program like BIY with fresh new ideas. We became a target for a couple of uncreative heads of organizations who were looking for some new component to their program to get the grant dollars. We also enlisted a couple of aggressive volunteers who wanted to take over BIY. It's a common problem with many organizations. More than once we showed these volunteers to the door.

"We're not going to compromise the program," Walt fumed. "We have to stand on purpose and integrity." I admired him for keeping BIY on the high road. I have to admit that when finances were dry and I was extremely fearful, I was tempted to collaborate with a couple of organizations without looking at the consequences. Walt always woke me up.

"Believe In Yourself will attract the right private funders. We don't have to grovel and lose sight of our mission. We don't need their money."

We don't? I often wondered. But I was proud and thankful that Walt was so strong. We stopped running after government money, which we never got anyway. The private money we attracted didn't have the stipulations, and the celebrities whom I had worked with at the networks donated freely. No questions were asked. Our board people gave us donations, but still we needed outside funding. Every penny we raised went into the program. Even two small stipend checks I received over three years I promptly put back into the program.

As the days rolled on BIY continued to take its toll on me. Before we had opened our doors we talked to many heads of non-profits. They assured us that we could get the financial backing because ours was a good program. Looking back now I realize that they didn't have a clue. These were CEOs and presidents who were hired by their respective organizations. We had overlooked the small fact that, unlike us, none of these people had actually started a program from scratch. They didn't know how agonizing and how difficult it was to go through government processing to qualify for non-profit status. These leaders had walked into existing positions in established programs that were running on automatic. They didn't have the foggiest idea what it took to struggle in the beginning to form an organization and get credibility.

I was at a point once again where I was about to crack. The stress and strain of politicking, begging for donations, seeking publicity, putting together and delivering presentations, doing speaking engagements to get support, organizing our volunteers, writing our handbook, being a mother and wife while running the organization, was ripping me apart. I had no perspective anymore. I was feeling like a failure for not being able to pull in the money since the program basically rested on me. Walt participated when he could, but he had to keep working to financially support our family and the program.

Although we were blessed with wonderful volunteers, including adults and high school and college students, what we needed were paid employees to consistently and dependably do the work.

Back then I was doing what I had always done in my life -- playing super woman. I was afraid to let go despite my sleepless nights and my ballooning weight from emotional eating and stress. The organization had become my fourth baby. I had invested too much of my soul to let go. But when we don't willingly yield, sometimes we are forced to.

CHAPTER EIGHTEEN

During the last days of 1995 our family hit huge financial problems. We were near bankruptcy. While bill collectors haunted and hunted us down, our house was falling apart from needed repairs that we couldn't afford. We managed to work around things that were broken but that only created more stress -- trying to live with a leaking refrigerator, leaking pipes, and broken drawers to name just a few. It's amazing how you can improvise when you don't have things you take for granted.

Looking back, we probably should have closed the doors on BIY then. But how could we shut down a program where so many children were benefiting? Besides, we kept telling the children to believe in themselves, and I kept thinking that I had to do the same, despite the bleak financial picture.

Still, secretly, I looked around for a part-time publicity job. I couldn't go back full-time to any job because no one wanted to take care of Devon after school. Even the few people I had approached whom I thought were strong enough to deal with Devon rejected the idea. Apparently, they weren't strong enough.

I didn't tell Walt that I was looking for a job. I figured he could digest the thought if I landed one. He believed in the dream that BIY would be financially secure and he wanted me to believe, too. To him, my getting a job would mean giving up the dream.

I quickly found out part-time publicity jobs were hard to come by. There were many publicists out of work then and they were snatching up any available jobs. Plus, I had been away from Hollywood for three years and much of landing entertainment jobs is networking. The only people I had networked with lately were under age 12.

I was appalled at being turned down for even clerical part-time jobs when they saw my history in glamorous Hollywood and running a non-profit with Walt. They knew I wouldn't stay around but for an eye blink and they were right. Who wants to train someone who would be leaving?

With increasing financial pressures, we hung on, hoping each day for a miracle. But all we seemed to experience was Murphy's Law: "If anything can go wrong, it will" -- and it did. Just when we started our financial spiral downward a hit-and-run driver backed into the side of our blue Ford mini-van. It was a week after our insurance briefly lapsed because of a late payment. In those days it was a matter of our choosing between first paying the mortgage or paying the car insurance. I just couldn't see living in a van with two adults, three children and a dog.

We may have been broke, but we still had our pride, and our van was an embarrassing eyesore. One day Walt was putting groceries into the van outside a supermarket when a man approached him and said that he could fix the van inexpensively right at our house. The next day a couple of men who spoke only Spanish came and after shaking hands with Walt, they began working on the van. When Walt was inside he heard a drill and looked out the window. He nearly had an apoplectic fit.

The men, who had been sanding the dent, now were drilling holes in the side of the van. They didn't have to speak English to know that Walt was mad. He asked them to leave, pointing to their car. Now we didn't just have a dented door, we had a half-sanded van with nine holes in the side. It wasn't until later that we learned this is part of a common, quick-fix body repair job. Holes are drilled into a dent, and then a tool is put into the holes to pull out the dent. They then fill the holes with cement and follow this with a paint job.

For nearly a year we drove that van around sporting those holes and an unfinished body job. I was extremely embarrassed, especially the first time one of the kids in the BIY program saw the van when I was parking.

"Who shot at you Ms. Jackson?"

I hadn't realized the van looked like it was shot up with bullets. No wonder people constantly stared when I pulled up next to them. After that I made an extra effort always to park with the holes not being visible from whatever establishment I was about to enter. When I went to a business meeting I parked way down the street. It didn't hide my shame. I kept remembering a remark I heard from motivational author Terry Cole Whitaker. "If you want to know what condition your life is in, take a look at your car. It reflects your state of mind."

My mind, like our van, was filled with holes. Fear can eat holes right into your brain. I couldn't find a part-time job and bills were mounting. Devon was still more than a handful and the last thing I wanted us to do was give up on BIY. I had never worked so hard in my life starting that organization, and it was running smoothly except for lack of funding. I kept thinking that we could influence these children to believe in themselves and stay off drugs so they wouldn't have babies like Devon and Jada that would go into the system not knowing their biological parents.

Along with fear comes resentment. I felt guilty for not being able to take our children on fun outings, weekend excursions or vacations. During three-day holiday weekends or school vacations we all sat at home with Devon driving us nuts. I bought games and tried entertaining the kids, but I hated those claustrophobic times. I felt like a failure for not being able to give them more.

Back then I burned with envy when our kids told me about their friends' trips.

"Jessie is going to Mammoth to ski for Christmas."

"Do you know that Sandra is going to Chicago to visit her grandma for the summer?"

"Where's Chicago, mom?"

"Nick is going to Hawaii for his family vacation."

How could they afford to do this? I tried justifying my jealousy. Well, they didn't have three kids like we did, and they certainly didn't run and financially support a non-profit. They're probably in over their heads with credit card debts. In truth I was describing our situation.

We could barely afford to take the kids out of the neighborhood, let alone out of town. When I did take them on outings to the movies or to an amusement park, I had to salvage coins from under every cushion in the house, delighted when I found silver and not just pennies. When we took them to the bank, I let the kids stand in line and ask the teller to change them into bills. I wanted it to look as if they had saved the pennies themselves.

The kids were proud to have this big responsibility and I was too embarrassed, being a grown woman, turning in coin rolls, especially pennies. Other times I let the children put change into the supermarket coin-counting machine that was located directly in front of the checkout counters. When the noisy, clattering pennies poured into the machine, I didn't want the people standing in checkout lines to realize that I was broke. Instead I hoped the shoppers who saw my children at the coin machine thought it was cute that they had saved their pennies.

I learned to be frugal and creative during these times. When I took the children to the movies, I brought several plastic bags and split a large popcorn serving among them when the lights went down. I also pulled out small bottles of juices that I smuggled into the theater. In the back of my mind I remembered an ABC coworker's comment when someone on a comedy show we were screening did the same thing.

"I hate it when I see people do that in the show. They're cheap," she said indignantly. Cheap? How about broke?

On Valentine's Day, the same day that we had moved into our house eight years earlier, I slipped off my wedding rings and headed to the pawnshop, embarrassed and humiliated, with tears streaming down my face. It was a hell of a way to spend a romantic day. I got a measly $30 for the symbol representing 15 years of marriage. What would be more humiliating was if I didn't claim it within the 30-day limit, they would sell it for hundreds. I got my ring back, but on that Valentine's Day I saw tears instead of hearts. A month later we had to hock Walt's wedding ring. We weren't able to reclaim it before it was sold.

Still we managed to keep our money problems from our family and friends, but that cost me some friendships. I was too embarrassed to tell the truth. It appeared that I was rejecting these friends because I constantly turned down their invitations to birthday parties, lunches and other get-togethers. They were mostly people in the entertainment industry whom I knew wouldn't understand that I couldn't afford to buy them birthday gifts. I couldn't show up without one. They were used to nice lavish presents or, at least, decent ones, which I couldn't afford, either. I simply told them I couldn't come to their affairs, and even though it was my intention, I never could afford to send them a late gift. Who wants a friend who constantly turns you down? I dared not invite them over to our house either, especially since it seemed to be falling apart. Eventually some of those friends faded from my life. Socializing in Hollywood is imperative to making deals and keeping relationships. "Out of sight," as they say, "out of mind."

Fortunately I confided in one friend who became more than a friend. I met Geramy Quarto, a drop-dead gorgeous, well-respected manager, whom I knew when we both worked on "The Young and the Restless" daytime TV series. He looks like the stars he represented, including actor Rob Lowe's brother, Chad, who married Oscar-winner Hilary Swank. Geramy left show business before I did and later sat on our BIY board. He also became Devon's godfather. We called one another sister and brother even though he's Caucasian. It never mattered because we knew we were related in the heart.

One evening I drove around a phone booth at least three times before parking and secretly calling Geramy, not wanting Walt to know.

"Geramy," I said meekly.

"Hey Jan! What's up, hon?"

"I… I hate to ask you this… but… " My throat was closing. I couldn't finish without crying.

"What's wrong, Jan?"

"We're… we're in deep financial trouble," I sobbed. "Walt doesn't know I'm calling you. He'd die."

"How much do you need?"

"You know the reason is… " I tried explaining how we got into the mess, but he cut me off.

"That's not necessary," he said. "You give so much to others. Just tell me what you need. It doesn't matter how it happened.""

"About $800," I cringed. "That'll… that will help cover most of this month's mortgage payment. You'll get it right back."

"Don't worry about paying it back. You'll have it tomorrow. I just want you to have it. You sure that's all you need?"

"Yes," I said, sniffling.

After hanging up, I got back in our van and collapsed, throwing my head against the headrest. Tears streamed from relief and gratitude. I would tell Walt after I paid the mortgage. He had such pride. I knew it would hurt him.

It saddened me, too. I had never borrowed even close to that much money from anyone, not even my parents. I didn't believe in it. But now I found myself with a change of attitude like I had been having about a lot of things. Constantly changing. I was losing my impulse to judge people and developing a tolerance and understanding for others. I was learning that you never know when you could be in their shoes.

My conscience, which was already filled with guilt from not being able to give my children more, now had more guilt for not being able to help my aging mother, who lived by herself. She, too, was going through financial problems as a retiree on a fixed income. She found herself behind on paying bills after getting sick and had astronomically-expensive prescriptions that she desperately needed to have filled. The only thing that she managed to pay on time was her mortgage. I had learned from her that even though you are broke, keep a roof over your head.

Sadly, we could only afford to give her a measly $25 at a time to help. It pained me not to be able to bail her out because not only was she my mother but she had donated to Believe In Yourself in the beginning when we had no other donors. Why couldn't I help her? Why couldn't I help my own family more? I asked that of God so many times.

During those days I found myself drowning my feelings with food. Emotional eating was a symptom of not forgiving myself. My emotions back then solidified in the form of fibroid tumors. I once read that those type of tumors are aggravated from stress and resentment. No kidding. I had plenty of both.

One day while the kids were at school and just before I was due at BIY, I laid on the couch balled up in a fetal position terrified of our family's future. How could my life have come to this? Wasn't I a good person, God? Where were we going to get the next dime?

My mind filled with "what ifs." I found myself looking back over the life I had left as a publicist and wondered if I had made a grave mistake leaving the television industry. I really didn't have a choice. Who could have watched Devon? No one.

Still my mind drifted to my rides in limousines, traveling with stars across the country, staying in luxury hotel suites with talent, dining at the nation's finest restaurants, press parties with celebrities, and traveling first class with them, including aboard helicopters and yachts.

Finally I couldn't take it anymore and forced myself to get off the sofa and into the hills. I had also learned from my mother that the way to get out of depression was to get moving, so I did. I found a deep sense of comfort and solace walking those hills behind our house that bordered the Angeles National Forest. Just me and our dog Prana. I remember that we climbed past tumbleweeds and through acres of brown hills scorched by the hot California sun. Even so, it was beautiful. I felt so blessed to be a witness to the California spring landscape that was a palette of colors. Birds and butterflies fluttered past us under beautiful blue, smog-free skies.

We climbed to the top of steep hills to survey the city below as I inhaled the fresh woodsy aroma. A mystical Santa Ana wind murmured and the distant, rushing freeway traffic hummed below. Occasionally the lonely sound of a commuter train whistle hung in the air.

There's something about being in nature that helps cleanse souls. I once heard that our bodies are made of the same material as the trees and rocks, so we feel rejuvenated when we are outdoors. I certainly felt that way.

I looked around at the hills that Walt and I often walked together. But most often we took the children. These were our outings. Those hills kept us believing, dreaming and seeing how nature provides and how we, too, are part of that divine plan. Somehow, like the plants and the birds, we would be provided for.

These were our mini-vacations. Now that I look back at those times of bonding, expensive vacations would not have brought us so close.

While Prana and I hiked into the hills, I spotted ravens flying over our heads. The Native Americans called them magical symbols and if you believe in the birds, magic will appear. Then I was hoping for the magical funding for BIY. Suddenly a hawk glided in circles, landing in a tree just ahead of me.

After the bird landed, I realized that we can be short on cash and resources, but we can still fly high like the hawk. As my walk ended I saw a radiant, huge yellow sunflower growing alone in a desolate patch of dirt. It didn't care that it was alone. I took it as another lesson. Stop struggling and "just be." We, too, can blossom when life around us seems empty and bleak.

Back then those magical hills reminded me to believe in myself. After returning home that day I was renewed. It was as if I had been to the proverbial mountaintop and my life came into perspective. I flashed on the little faces in our program and how they had developed. A few children were shy and introverted when they first came to Believe In Yourself. Now they had blossomed into effervescent young men and women. I remember smiling Michael, a 10-year-old built like a little linebacker. "When I get upset, I meditate just like you taught us, Ms. Jackson. It helps me to calm down."

Those thoughts and Walt's story about his passing through the schoolyard on his way to the BIY program flashed in my head.

"The kids always scream my name when they see me coming. 'Hello, Mr. Jackson!'" he said, lighting up as he imitated them, waving his hand in the air. "Every time I hear 'Hi Mr. Jackson,' I feel like a rock star," said Walt. "One kid yelled out to me 'Hi Mr. Jackson! Mr. Jackson, I'm coming to Believe In Yourself today.'"

We both felt the same; our hearts were filled with joy working with those children. The kids filled us with happiness that no money could match. And how could we put a price tag on parents telling us how grateful they were to see a positive change in their child? It was priceless knowing that teachers recommended their students to the program.

As my spirits lifted that day, I had no idea that my family was about to descend into pure hell, and the only thing that would help me would be to keep believing in myself.

CHAPTER NINETEEN

Marcelle Gordon, a very special friend who passed away, used to love the famous quote, "Where there's life, there's hope." There was no hope for me in 1996, because there was no life. I have often thought that the date's numbers were symbolic of the heartache I suffered that year. The two nines were upside down sixes. Three sixes in a row. 666. The symbol of the beast and hell.

I remember thinking that if I had met anyone going through the problems that I would experience in 1996, I would have run in the opposite direction, far away from them. Something had to be definitely wrong with anyone who attracted that much disaster. It was like a falling tree. If you stood too close you could get crushed.

Devon was halfway through the fifth grade then and he was becoming at least tolerable. His medication seemed to be working to a certain extent, and he was a lot calmer. Ryan and Jada were getting along with him better.

Donations were trickling into BIY and we maintained a strong base of students and volunteers. Walt and I were even able to refinance our house with a bank that took only a couple of high-risk clients like us each year along with their safer borrowers.

Our monthly mortgage payment was now lower, which eased our financial burden. We had escaped bankruptcy, and it seemed smooth sailing ahead. I had no clue that life was comparable to a quiet tiger sneaking up on its prey. It was about to attack.

In early January we got a call that my godmother, who had been suffering from a lung disease, had suddenly died. At her small funeral I thought back to a year earlier when she gave me her beautiful china. I didn't want to take it since she had entertained with the set since I was a little girl, but she insisted. I couldn't figure out why she was giving away the dishes along with loads of her other personal belongings.

"I'm not going to need these anymore," she told me. I didn't question why, I just followed her through her house as she pointed out other things for me to take as well. "I'm cleaning house," she said, throwing up one hand in the air if as she was dismissing everything. I don't know if she knew something then or her words were simply prophetic, but a few months later Godmom, who was a heavy smoker, was in the hospital. She would live the rest of her life attached to an oxygen tank.

When my mother and I went to visit her, I was startled to see this once spry woman whom her children had named Spudnik, because she moved with lightning speed like the Soviet satellite, now weak and frail. "Evelyn," she wheezed, "you'd better stop smoking."

"Why?" my mother questioned. Mom had always been defensive when someone advised her to stop smoking.

"Just look at me," said God mom weakly, her eyes riveted on my mother's. "I'm your lesson." Mom listened politely, but later, when I, too, asked her to quit, she bristled. "I'm not going to stop smoking," she said indignantly. "Just because she's sick, it doesn't mean that I'm going to wind up like her." It was useless arguing with mom even after Godmom died a few weeks later.

In February, Walt got a call that would bring him to his knees. Linda, his eldest sister, had suddenly died from a brain aneurysm. She was one step away from being the first black female warden in California.

Linda's funeral packed the church in Stockton, California. Dignitaries came, and because of standing room only, uniformed prison lieutenants and correctional officers lined the walls. Attendees at the funeral had to pass two blocks of double-parked cars to get to the church doors. At Linda's graveside a rifle squad fired a 21-gun salute. I had no idea that they did this for prison officials. No one in her family knew that Linda was this well-respected in the penal system, especially not her brother.

I had never seen Walt break down about anything before, but at Linda's funeral, he was crying uncontrollably. I knew it was from more than grief. It was an unhealed relationship. A missed opportunity.

"We used to fight all the time," he once told me reflecting on Linda. "We did what we saw our parents do. Fight." He looked forlornly into space. "They constantly disrespected one another and Linda and I did the same thing."

In their adult years Walt wanted desperately to be closer to Linda. They talked, but they were never able to heal their relationship. He carried that wound for years.

On March 26, 1996, at 9:30 p.m., I called my mother for the third time that evening. No answer. I hadn't spoken to her in two days, which was odd since we talked every single evening around 5:30.

"Let's just go over there and see what's going on," said Walt. Suddenly we were propelled in high gear as we readied the kids for the 45-minute ride to mom's house. On the way there Walt was stopped for speeding, but an understanding officer let us go, hearing our fears about mom.

After knocking for a few minutes on Mom's front door, Walt went around to the back as I pressed my ear to the door, hoping to hear mom stirring inside. One year I found her on the kitchen floor, dehydrated, and rushed her to Midway Hospital. After that she became a regular volunteer there in the emergency room, refusing to miss a day's work. Lately she complained of flu symptoms, and I wondered had she gotten sick again?

Ryan, Devon and Jada were running on Mom's lawn in the dark when Walt, who had entered the house from the backyard, opened the front door where I was still standing. He had a ghostly look on his face.

"She's gone, Jan," he said softly as I stepped past him over the threshold. His eyes were filled with love and compassion.

"What do you mean?" My world froze, but intuitively I knew. I felt it in my gut.

"She's dead?" I shrieked, my eyes transfixed on his with shock. He nodded yes and then held me.

Mom and I were so close. How could she have left me without a warning? Why didn't I know she was going? I know she wasn't feeling well lately and had been fighting a cold, but not this. God, no. Not this.

I don't remember the kids' questions about their grandmother, but, fortunately, a neighbor took them to her home. Meanwhile I had refused to see Mom, who was lying in her bed. I sat rigid at the dining room table with Walt and the coroner, a mere 10 feet from her bedroom, where she lay dead. The house was so still. I kept expecting Mom to walk into the room, healthy and fine.

I couldn't cry. It was as if I was buried alive. I could barely move from shock. Every word, every thought, every feeling stuck in my throat.

"From the look on her face, she slipped away without any pain," said the emphatic coroner. His gentle tone revealed his experience talking to grief-stricken people. "She looks very peaceful."

I still didn't want to see her. I wanted to remember my smiling, loving mother whom I last saw a couple of days ago and who dearly loved her family. I flashed on her always carrying our family portrait in the pocket of her pink smock during her volunteer duties at the Midway Hospital. When people waited in the emergency room visitor section, Mom would serve them cookies and coffee and then comfort them. She would then whip out the picture of Walt, the kids and me and tell them stories about us. When I rolled my eyes at her for doing this, she told me, "These stories help distract them from worrying about their own loved ones in Emergency."

I sat in a fog trying to comprehend what no one can predict. Death. While we sat at Mom's dining room table discussing her arrangements with the coroner, a night bird flew over the sky light directly above us. It was so loud that we couldn't hear ourselves talking. We stopped our conversation, and we all looked up as if we could glimpse the bird in the black sky through the skylight. It was not just chirping loudly, it was screeching as if to get our attention.

I had grown up in that house, and as an adult I had been there too many times to count, but I had never heard night birds scream as that one did on March 26, 1996. I knew instantly it had to be Mom saying goodbye. She was free now of her finances. Free of her body that failed her. Free to fly away.

During the days following the losses, I was scared and extremely needy. But what was most frightening was me. I was a mere shell of myself. I couldn't figure out who this woman was in my skin. Whomever she was, she was afraid to take the next step in life. I was afraid that a land mine would blow up in my face. I felt powerless. I had lost the inner strength that so many people felt was one of my best qualities. It was my badge of honor to be strong, but now I didn't want to be strong anymore. I couldn't. I just wanted to lie down and sleep until the nightmare had passed.

I had always had this ability to sleep whenever I commanded myself, since I traveled the country so much with actors. I could sleep on a plane or in the airport, virtually anywhere at any time, but now I barely slept at night. I was terrified that I was becoming an insomniac. Sleeping when a loved one died was my escape, my solace. Now I had to contend with another loss. My sleep.

I would lie awake wondering where did those people go who died? Where did Mom go? Where did Godmom and Linda go? I had been so close to Mom, and Walt protected her like his biological mother. Why didn't we see this coming? We had sheltered her and kidded that she was our fourth child. When Mom passed I wanted to travel with her on her journey. Not to stay but just to make sure she got to wherever she was suppose to go safely. Did she get lost, as she sometimes did when driving her blue Pontiac? She could barely see over the wheel.

Devon especially was set back by all of our losses. He was acting out what I felt. Abandonment. People always seemed to leave him in his young life. Mom's passing was extremely hard on Devon, since she had been his champion. She was always the one who understood Devon and tolerated him the most.

The evening before Mom's funeral it was hard for Devon to sleep. Ryan was already snoring when I came into their room. "Nana's now your guardian angel, Dev," I said, putting my arm around him as we sat on his bed. His head was bowed. He rotated a tiny toy in his small hands.

"You know you can talk to her anytime you want." I placed my hand on his heart. "She's right here with you always." He sat motionless and muttered, "I know." I felt so helpless, but I surrounded him with love. I had learned through the ministry that sometimes just being with someone who is grieving is enough. We don't have to try to cheer them up, but just hold them in love. That's the true healing power, along with time.

After sitting for awhile, I hugged and kissed Devon good night and allowed him to lay back and sleep in his clothes. It was sad, but it was at times like that I felt most loving to Devon. His barriers were down. Most times I was too angry with him even to want to get close, but on this evening I wanted to hold him like a baby.

At Mom's gravesite I felt sorry for myself. I had only a couple more relatives who were left living on her side of the family now. As I watched them lower the casket into the ground, it dawned on me: there goes the only person in my life who truly loved me unconditionally. Despite the love of Walt and my children, there is something irreplaceable and unmatched by a mother's deep love.

Mom was gone now. She was the last line between mortality and me. I felt like I was standing in life's rifle sight. At any minute I could be blown away.

After the funeral Devon got into more conflicts at school than usual. His frustrations escalated, and nothing and no one seemed to calm him down. One day he got into a fight with a classmate during lunch period in the schoolyard. When the principal tried restraining him, Devon kicked the man and swung at him as the entire school looked on. Reports were that Devon was "going insane," kicking and screaming like a wild bull.

Fortunately Ryan saw the incident and ran to help the principal, throwing his body on top of Devon, knocking him to the ground to restrain him. Later the principal praised Ryan's actions, but Ryan came home filled with embarrassment over Devon's behavior. It would be one of many times that our entire family would be embarrassed by Devon.

That incident was not the first time Ryan would have to restrain his brother. One day I came home from grocery shopping, and Ryan and Jada stormed me at the door. Before I could get my key in the lock the door was flung open, and they practically pounced on me, breathing heavily with excitement.

"Devon's gone crazy!" shrieked Jada. "He said he's gonna kill us."

"Yeah, Mom, you should have seen him," huffed Ryan his face flushed, eyes wide. "He kept saying he was going to kill us!"

"What?" I dropped the groceries on the couch, "Where is he?" I tried to be in control, but the thought of Devon threatening to kill Ryan and Jada scared me. Both kids pointed to the garage door, right off the hallway.

"What happened?" I said, marching to the garage door. As I threw it open, Devon came out, grinding his teeth with anger, fists balled.

It turned out that Devon had gone ballistic over an argument about changing the television channel and threw things around the living room. When Ryan tried to stop him, they got into a physical scuffle. It was the familiar sibling rivalry conflict, but what disturbed Walt and I was Devon's threats. It wasn't the first time he talked about killing. With Devon's problems those threats couldn't be taken lightly.

One time Devon was washing dishes while Ryan was doing homework on the kitchen table. The usual sibling bickering started, but Devon picked up one of the knives he was washing and threatened him. He also threatened Jada with a knife.

We were on tactical alert with Devon after that. Again I found a new therapist who in time, like the others, was just as ineffective with Devon. In the meantime Walt raced with Devon to a juvenile detention center. A former juvenile probation officer himself, Walt was able to get one of the officers to talk to Devon about the consequences of violent behavior. It didn't seem to faze Devon that he could end up behind bars.

Over the years they would visit several such facilities, including police stations, where other officers would talk to Devon. But nothing seemed to make a difference to him.

In April we received another deadly call. My college roommate's mother had passed. I had known her for years.

I simply couldn't believe what was going on. I was living a horror show. Why were all of these people leaving me? Why was this happening? I thought that when I was in my 20s I had paid my dues to death. My small family had virtually disappeared then. Five deaths in four years. Since I was the youngest in the family of otherwise elderly people, it fell on me to pick out caskets. I either made the funeral arrangements, or helped make them. Then, after each funeral, I asked my boss at CBS to send me out of town on any assignment, which he did.

I really wanted to fly to the end of the earth. But running away would be a high price to pay later. Suppressed grief is destructive energy ready to explode. I didn't know that the only way to release pain was to feel it and go through it. Back then I didn't know how, nor did I want to do it.

In the days ahead it felt like our little family was living on shifting sand. One morning when the kids were at school and Walt was at work, I dropped to my knees and laid face down in the middle of the living room floor, crying hysterically. I moaned and screamed to God, "Please... please help me. Just tell me, God, what is inside of me attracting this? Why are all these people going? When is this all going to stop? Please, God... please... help me... help me... " I was so afraid of who else close to me would die. Who was left? Walt? Ryan? Jada? Devon? God forbid.

I couldn't understand why this was happening. I was a good person. I sacrificed so much for others. I ran a wonderful program for the community. "Is there something you want me to change, God? Talk to me," I screamed, pounding the floor hysterically. "What do you want me to do? Just tell me... please."

I was crying for light.

In the following days Devon seemed to grow worse. I knew this would affect any kid without Devon's problems, but it was intensified with him. My pager went off constantly. The school kept calling me to come and get Devon. When they didn't call, I was on edge, wondering when they would summon me. Often I just went up to the school and started organizing for BIY early because I knew that Devon would get into trouble eventually, and at least I would be on the grounds to get him.

A month later, when Devon and our affairs seemed to be settling, we received a letter from the IRS regarding our personal taxes. We were being audited. I knew it was nothing to worry about, but it was just the hassle of having to go through all of the steps on top of my grief.

This was at the same time that I was trying to settle Mom's estate and bills. She had a reverse mortgage on her house, and we hired an attorney because of unreasonable astronomical charges that they added after her death. In the meantime the house was in the process of being sold. Our attorney told us to stop the sale to settle the lawsuit or we wouldn't have leverage with the property sold. The buyers then threatened to sue us. This hung over us for a few months until things were settled out of court. We got only a fraction of what the house was worth. The equity in the home was eaten up by the reverse mortgage. My childhood home, the memories, the dreams, were stolen.

Every day the world was growing more foreign to me. I was now becoming terrified to answer the phone or open mail, fearing more bad news.

The last line of my defense against the world was about to shatter. Walt and I, who have always been close and united on every aspect of our lives from finances to raising our children, were growing distant. We had nothing to discuss except our mounting problems. We didn't have the time or energy for anything else. When Walt came home each day, there were no smiles and no joy. Discussing our problems represented more damned stress to one another. But there were business matters that couldn't wait. They needed our joint decisions immediately. It got so that when we looked at one another we saw all of the problems that plagued us. Home had become a caldron of problems. The pot had boiled over, and we decided to separate.

Now all of my pillars of support had completely crumbled.

A few days before Mom's house was to close escrow, I decided to go there and just feel her energy. I wanted so badly to talk to her, to hug her and feel her arms around me. In short, I needed my mommy to make everything better. I needed to see her huge roses and wildly-growing tomato vines that she prized. I wanted to see the lemon tree we planted when I was in high school. She loved giving lemons away by the bucketful. It was her way of giving people love. When your world is crumbling, you just want to hold on to anything familiar. I would find out there was nothing for me to grip.

I had been skittish about being in Mom's house alone after she died, but now I desperately needed to feel her presence. I needed unconditional love.

When I was walking to Mom's front door, I noticed the forest green gate was opened to the backyard. Did the workers Walt hired to haul away trash forget and leave the gate open? I knew Walt was as protective of her property as he was of ours. He was the last to leave after the workers cleaned up. Nothing would be left open or unlocked.

Cautiously I decided to walk through the gate to the backyard. A wave of fear came over me with each step. Suddenly I saw an adult bike leaning up against the side of the house. I stopped. My jaw clenched and my heart raced. The black bike was leaning up against the large window that had been my bedroom. I was pulled to look inside. I gasped. A large man was lying face down on the floor apparently asleep.

I made a muffled scream and jumped back, almost tripping over the bike. My heart pounding, I scrambled out of the yard, throwing open the gate that crashed against the side of the house as I passed through.

I ran across the street to our van, shaking so badly that I could barely get my key in the lock. Just as I slid into the driver's seat, I saw a huge man rushing through the green gate from the backyard. I recognized his clothes. It was the same man who was lying down in my old room. I had awakened him.

I sank down in the car so that he wouldn't see me, but I could still see him as I trembled behind the wheel. He stood on the front lawn, his brow furrowed as he snapped his head from left to right, looking as if to catch someone on the empty street.

All of a sudden the man started ranting and raving to himself, waving his arms in the air. He was insane. My heart pumped faster as I reached for my mobile phone on the floor, grateful that I had brought the bulky thing. Not only was it big, it was expensive since it was one of the first cells on the market. But we needed it for any BIY emergency with the children.

My lips quivered as I told the police about the intruder while watching him go into the backyard. They were on their way. I then hung up and called Walt.

Twenty minutes later Walt pulled up in front of me and jumped out of our gold Volvo. He had come with lightening speed from his job, which was at least a 35 minute drive away.

"Where are you going?" I screeched, panicking as he dashed past me. "In the house."

"The house? No... no Walt, don't. The man is crazy."

He didn't listen. I looked around frantically, praying that a squad car would pull up. I knew the intruder was much bigger and taller than Walt. He could get killed. It was no use.

"Stay out here," he commanded as we reached the front steps. I knew it was no use arguing, and we did not need to be fighting with one another. We both needed to be on guard against the enemy.

I stood on the steps idly, not knowing what to do but pray for Walt's safety as he disappeared inside. Seconds later I heard Walt and the man arguing. The voices grew louder as they came toward the front door, where I stood on the porch. All of a sudden, the man burst through the front screen door with Walt cursing him, dead on his heels.

"Get outta here, man... #@##$... Get outta here!"

"I don't have to, mother ##!& Screw you!" growled the intruder as he slowly moved passed me down the steps. Suddenly he turned and lunged at Walt. They scuffled as I screamed at the top of my lungs. "Stop it... leave him alone!" I looked around for something to pick up. Nothing.

Walt managed to push him away, and the man almost fell. They stood there, glaring at one another like mad bulls. The intruder thought twice about lunging back and started walking toward the open gate to the backyard.

"I said get outta here." Walt has now picked up the steel rod that turns on Mom's antiquated sprinkler system. "Where are you going? Leave!"

"Yeah, the cops are coming... " I yell. "Get outta here."

"I'm gonna get my bike," the man yelled continuing toward the gate. Walt jumped in front of him, blocking him. Walt then disappeared through the gate with the man hot on his heels. Seconds later

Walt came back with the bike and slammed it to the ground.

The man pretended to lunge at Walt but instead picked up his bike and rode away.

"You pissed me off now, mother #$@, " he yelled at Walt. "I'll be back!"

"Yeah, I'll be here waiting for your ass, too, with the cops!"

We watched him disappear out of sight. Still no police. When we walked in the house, my legs grew weak. The intruder had ripped open several boxes we had left there the other day. They were too much to take in our packed car. Mom's record collection from over 30 years was scattered about. Some records were missing.

But what was most terrifying was that the box filled with my late father's butcher knives, which he used working as a chef in fancy restaurants, was open. My stomach knotted as I cautiously inched into each room. We found the knives placed strategically around the house. The intruder definitely had planned to use them on anyone who surprised him in the house. Walt could have been killed. I could have been killed.

When the police finally came, Walt beat me to the front door. "I'll get it."

As he explained the situation to the cops, I kept thinking how blessed we were to be standing there in one piece.

A month later we were at the court to testify against the intruder, whom the police had caught and later released. He was a vagrant responsible for a number of robberies in the area. He didn't show up that day for court. With no permanent address, there was no way to track him. The police failed to find him again, and eventually the case faded away.

At night I laid awake, my mind racing. What did I need to learn about the break-in? What was God telling me? What was I suppose to learn about all of these problems and losses in 1996?

Reflecting on the intruder, it dawned on me. Let go, Janet. You have to let go. I was battling so many fires, I didn't have time to grieve. I was fighting my way through life, running on empty.

I didn't know it then, but when we are faced with nowhere to go and no solutions, it's a clear message to release and let go. Only then can we begin to step back and get ourselves out of the way so that our spiritual selves can come through and point us in the right direction. When we don't let go, sometimes the universe helps us in ways we can't comprehend.

I thought about Believe In Yourself and the financial strain. We simply couldn't afford to go on. I didn't have the strength or the will. I thought about my impending separation from Walt. I knew I couldn't run BIY by myself even if the program brought in money. I needed his support. My mind shifted to my fragile state. Besides, how could I lift others if I, myself, was lost? I didn't know who this woman was I saw in the mirror.

The next week I told the BIY children and the parents the devastating news that would leave me shattered and hurt for years to come. "When the semester ends in a couple of weeks, BIY will end, too."

There were many people upset, but they didn't know that now I had to go in search of myself.

CHAPTER TWENTY

After we closed Believe In Yourself, Inc. and the escrow closed on Mom's house, I remember standing in our garage staring down at most of what was left of Mom's belongings consolidated into two big boxes. Walt was rearranging the garage to store some of her things along with BIY records. Despite our decision to break up, we were civil to one another while getting our affairs in order and mindful of our children's feelings.

"It's a shame," I said shaking my head. "All of Mom's 72 years are reduced mainly to just these two boxes." It was painful having sold or given away nearly everything in Mom's house except a few pieces of furniture that I kept as reminders of my childhood.

"That's what's going to be left of us, too, one day," said Walt as he continued stacking the boxes. He was right. Once again, he had cut to the heart of the matter. I started wondering, 'What would be put in my boxes that someone would want to keep when I'm gone?' In the days ahead that question would haunt me. What was my legacy? I needed to find out what was I here on the planet to do. But first, I had to crawl out of my own box.

Within a week I was bound for Hawaii on an airplane headed for Kauai. Alone. Tears streamed down my face as the plane roared down the runway and I saw Los Angeles whizzing by my window. As we lifted into the air my mouth suddenly started moving as if I was possessed. I was grateful that no one sat next to me as I whispered words with such power and force:

"When I return from Hawaii my life will change. All of this heartache will stop, and my life will be in order." Where I had begged and pleaded with God to help me, now I was demanding the universe heed my order.

"My life will once again be calm, and all of the confusion and pain will disappear."

It would take me years to learn that the words I spoke that day were a decree. When we decree, it's following an ancient practice, the most powerful form of spoken prayer no matter who says them or what religion one practices. I would learn that decreeing is the most effective way to harness God's energy if you do it with strong feelings and emotion. It's the key to changing yourself and the world. For me, it was the beginning of reclaiming my soul.

When I landed on the spectacular pristine island of Kauai, I felt immediate relief. For the first time since I had been a mother, I had taken a trip by myself, for myself. I knew it was the beginning step of loving Janet. Putting me first for a change.

After selling Mom's house, settling her bills, and buying a new van, I had to get away. I had to find me. When I returned from Hawaii I knew Walt and I would divide our household and tell our kids that we were going our separate ways. If I didn't take the trip now there wouldn't be an opportunity later.

I brought my journal and vinyl paints with me to the island. A few weeks earlier I had visited the beautiful 160-acre Descanso botanical gardens in LaCanada-Flintridge trying to find peace by walking among rows of rose bushes. I visited a small art gallery on the property where I met a slightly-built elderly woman who was a volunteer. Looking back on that day, I know she was one of the angels God placed in my life.

"I would love to paint like that," I said to the lady. She stood by me, anxious to answer any questions about the dazzling landscape painting before us.

"Why don't you do it?" she replied, smiling sweetly.

"Maybe later, when my kids are grown."

"Now is the time," she said pointedly. "Do it now. Don't wait." She was right. On the way home I bought myself art supplies. The next week I was obsessed and possessed, painting a picture of a lion. It was the animal energy in my life that I needed according to Native

American beliefs. The courage of the lion was what would help me get through these dark times.

When I finished the painting my family and friends were all surprised at how well it came out since I had never produced a picture like this before, or taken classes. I was surprised the most. It taught me a valuable spiritual lesson: We haven't begun to tap into our full potential. We have no idea what wonderful creations are inside of us just waiting to come out. But one of the most important lessons was the peace that it gave me while painting the picture. I realized that peace came from being in the moment, taking in the color, watching my fingers command the brush, focusing only on what I painted. The relief of thinking of nothing else was liberating and so calming.

I checked into the luxurious Hanalei Bay Resort on the north shore, overlooking the breathtaking Bali Hai Bay. I chose Kauai for my trip because only 3 percent of the island has been commercialized. There weren't many people populating the island, unlike Oahu. Honolulu reminded me of Los Angeles. Kauai was the Pacific paradise I had pictured -- - soft, white sand beaches, gentle breezes, red dirt, a cobalt blue ocean and plumeria-scented nights. I was as close to God as one could get on earth. That's why I was there to find Him or Her.

The resort reminded me of the privileged life I lived while working for CBS. I had traveled with a production crew to Oahu to shoot the television movie "The Island of Beautiful Women," starring Peter Lawford and Jane Kennedy.

The view from my condo was unbelievable. In the distance a sheer green wall of mountain towered thousands of feet over Hanalei Bay. In the foreground was a forest of thick tropical vegetation that led down to the water's edge.

As I walked on the property I took in lush tropical landscaping, cascading waterfalls, and dramatic rockscapes. The main dining room had walls of glass that rolled back so guests could feel the tantalizing, soft trade winds.

After such pressure running BIY and constantly policing Devon, I couldn't believe that I had nothing to do but sit back and take care of

Janet, which is exactly what I had planned to do for the next week. I found myself back in my early 20s, indulging in my favorite sport of scuba diving and spotting a shark underwater.

Scuba diving on that trip was a big step back into regaining my courage. When I was working on the CBS movie I stayed an extra day to go diving. I nearly lost my life when I got excruciating ear pain 65 feet under water. But now I was back in the water again, symbolic of what I needed to do in the days ahead. I would have to dive back into life with new courage.

In the evenings I wrote furiously in my journal and painted. I began to see myself from a distance. I realized that in the last few months before the deaths happened I hadn't been really concerned about how I looked. I had also become a control freak. Devon and the responsibility of BIY had turned me into one raw nerve.

I found myself meditating and praying for hours, asking for direction on those purifying shores of that spiritual island. I also found myself trying to cleanse my body as well as my mind as I ate nothing but pineapples and other fresh fruits of God. I knew an internal cleansing would help me wipe away the dirty window of life I had been looking through lately. When your body is cleansed and healthy, your mind is clearer. Suddenly life began to come into focus.

I realized that I had been so busy in my work that maybe I hadn't seen signs that my Mom was leaving. I had been flying around like a cat whose tail was on fire. I was afraid the volunteers would not run BIY as I would have liked, so I kept control. I held angry grudges against the politicians and grant funders who denied us monies. I was so constantly worried about Devon's erratic behavior that I stood in constant vigil. I was so dogmatic trying to get all of the business straight with Walt that I never asked him how he felt, or how his day went. I simply snatched what I needed from him. Even though I was with Ryan and Jada physically seven days a week, I wasn't emotionally there for them. Amazingly, I had missed a couple of school years standing right beside my children. I had also watched our house deteriorate from lack of upkeep as we took money for repairs and put it in BIY. I had not only neglected my house, I neglected me, too. I let my weight balloon and my body grow stiff from lack of exercise. I had forgotten how to smile, I took life so seriously lately. But in my defense, I didn't have any joy to smile about. I was so busy trying to help others that I forgot to support my family or myself emotionally. I would learn later that giving comes from the overflow, not from a half empty cup.

During the Hawaiian days I drove my little blue rented Pinto while exploring Kauai's gentle rolling countryside lush mountains. I was giddy with excitement and freedom as I passed magnificent canyons, white sand dunes, and acres of pineapple fields. I hiked through lush valleys with plunging waterfalls, through Haena State Park with it's scenic wild land and into wet, ancient sea caves formed about 4,000 years ago.

At sunset I would return to my condo and sit with the door open, listening to the rain that fell off and on almost every hour. It was nature's beautiful ballet. The musical raindrops pounded the huge banana tree leaves that swayed gracefully in the wind outside of my window. In the distance I could see the 5,075-foot high summit of the mystical Mt. Waialeale, one of the wettest spots on Earth, averaging 444 inches of rain each year.

I started counting my blessings. My eyes, my hands, my feet. The gift of being able to be in God's country. I began realizing that I had been so caught up with living that I had not thanked God. I had kept looking at what we didn't have instead of what we did. I had my health, my wonderful children, even Devon, who couldn't help that he had such a horrible start in life. I had my family. I reflected on the gift of being with Mom during her last 10 years after she moved back to Los Angeles from San Francisco. The gift that my kids got to know their grandmother. I reflected back on my entertainment career, a privilege being with the most famous people in the world, sharing their wealthy lifestyles without having to give up my privacy like they or suffering their public scrutiny.

That night I began giving thanks for everything I could think of in my life. It was an exhilarating experience. My mind was now shifting from lack to abundance thinking. I had complained so much that I didn't know how blessed I had been. Suddenly I became so excited that I couldn't contain my energy in my condo. I put on my blue hooded windbreaker and went walking in the warm tropical rain. On the trail, passing fire red anthodium flowers and stark white hibiscus blooms, I saw the sky turn into a heart-stopping melange of colors with moving clouds crossing the huge, orange setting sun.

And then, suddenly, I saw her.

I hadn't seen this woman in several years. When she smiled I felt her familiar warmth and her joy surround me. She was walking with such confidence and inner strength, radiating love. It was my old friend that I thought I had lost forever. Tears came to my eyes. On this magical evening I saw her again for the first time in years. I found me.

The day that I was leaving the hotel to return to Los Angeles, I went to check out and passed the lobby where people were looking out the huge windows with awe. I could not believe the sight before me. An incredible rainbow that spanned most of the sky was mesmerizing. Never in my life had I seen a rainbow this huge and bright.

As I drove to the airport the rainbow seemed to get even bigger. Finally I stopped the car to watch the astounding spectrum of brilliant colors. It reminded me of my favorite song, "Over the Rainbow," from my favorite movie, "The Wizard of Oz." It was truly another blessing to see this magnificent sight. As I continued driving slowly, reflecting back on my glorious last few days, I felt that I had indeed found myself somewhere over the rainbow.

When I returned home, just as magical as the rainbow appeared, my life, too, seemed to magically change. The decrees that I invoked at the beginning of my trip, demanding of myself that my life was going to change, materialized into reality.

Suddenly I found that my problems were disappearing. When Walt saw me at the front door we both stood there, silently smiling at one another for a few seconds with such love and tenderness. We both knew our separation that we needed had already happened with my Kauai trip. We didn't need to be apart any longer.

That night, as the children slept, we shared our awakenings, which were amazingly similar. We talked for hours about our mistakes but also about the love for one another that we didn't want to lose. We made a commitment to go to marriage counseling as we regrouped and planned our future.

We were what Walt always called us, soul mates. But we discovered that in life's frantic pace we were losing our souls. That night we reclaimed them and our love for one another.

CHAPTER TWENTY-ONE

After my trip to Kauai I began to pursue my spiritual self with a vengeance. I had touched God on that island, and I needed to know how to keep in touch always.

I started thinking on a deeper level about life.

When we're faced with catastrophe in our lives, some of us cry out to God for help as a last recourse. I was no different. This was my last recourse when it should have been my first.

Looking back, sure, there were many times that I called for spiritual help, but I didn't allow my higher power time to work. I kept impatiently trying to do things myself, not waiting for divine intervention. Waiting made me feel unproductive and stagnant. I felt my will power was all that it would take to straighten out my life. I was wrong. I was soon to learn that this great shaking down of my life in 1996 was a remaking of my outer self, the losing of the will and the awakening of my spiritual presence that knows all of the answers and makes things happen.

Throughout the years of struggling with Devon I studied different religions and meditation techniques. We attended, as a family, numerous churches. I had also tried practicing the spiritual lessons that we learned in the ministry, but I found that in the wake of problems, they were simply intellectual lessons. What I really needed was to feel God's presence. I knew that I had been separated from my Higher Self but I didn't know how to get back home. My Kauai trip helped me touch my Higher Self, but I needed now to find it from within and tap into that powerful energy each of us has inside.

I could read and study spiritual lessons all I wanted, but until I felt my Higher Power, everything else was a lesson in futility. Lessons would be in my mind but not embodied in the heart. Our heart is where we find God. Our hearts are God.

When I finally realized my biggest problem was that I was blocking my blessings, I was on the way to connecting with my spiritual self that was already whole, perfect and complete.

I kept trying to be in control, but how could any spiritual help come through if I kept blocking my good despite my acknowledging that my way didn't work? I needed to step aside; I didn't know how to step aside. I felt that if I did, everything would fall to pieces in my life. Looking around in 1996, it already had.

What led me back to Spirit was the practice of mindfulness. I remember when I was first introduced to the concept the last day I worked at ABC. After leaving a small farewell party, I stopped at a bookstore in the upscale Century Plaza shopping center, hoping for direction for the new life I was about to embark upon. I was standing before the spiritual section when a book literally fell off the shelf as I reached for another. This was no accident. It was a sign. I put the first book back and picked the other one off the floor. "The Miracle of Mindfulness" by Thich Nhat Hahn. This book saved my life.

I hadn't resonated with any particular teacher or church since the death of Dr. William H. Hornaday, the minister of Founder's Church of Religious Science, who had married Walt and me. I just couldn't seem to connect with any of the churches that we visited. Often I conducted Sunday School for the kids at home. Meanwhile, I stayed in bookstores, looking for spiritual material and studying the religions of the world, hoping for a connection and a way back to Spirit.

In my studies of Jesus Christ and Buddha, I remembered thinking they could have been brothers.

Jesus and Siddhartha Gautama, the Buddha, both taught a moral and ethical code. The basic theme they both taught was love, morality, and justice. They both said we have already been given the gifts for which we search. And both teachers gave me comfort.

I often reflected that I have everything that I need from my Higher Power. My problem was that I didn't recognize my gifts. We don't realize that everything we are looking for, we already have. The challenge I faced was realizing this truth.

Mindfulness taught me how to do just that. The living-in-the-moment approach to life dates back to the Buddha's discoveries 2,500 years ago. The practice today is often used in Western hospitals without religious or Buddhism connotations.

I bought nearly all of Hahn's books and forced myself to practice mindfulness – being aware. It's a study of how to pay attention in the moment without judgment. Being in the present is observing your thoughts, your feelings, your actions, your breath, and the sights and sounds around you. It's being here now without opinion. It's observing whatever experience we are going through without attaching opinions, judgments. This is so freeing.

Living in the moment helped me to tame what Easterners call our monkey mind, which jumps around constantly, never giving us rest. I learned how to simply observe my thoughts and how absolutely enter-taining they can be. I was amazed the first time I did this how many negative thoughts ran over and over again in my head. These were my thoughts that were giving me grief. I learned that it's not what happens in life, it's what we think about what happens that causes the pain.

I then became aware of my feelings, which I ran from and tried to suppress with food. I didn't want to feel, especially the uncomfortable feelings. These were the first I had to work on.

Through the practice of mindfulness I learned how to be aware of my feelings that I ran from, how to be aware of my thoughts that plagued me, and how to focus on whatever action I was doing to find peace. I found that my mind calmed and I wasn't as scattered or fearful.

During the time at BIY, I found that living in the moment was powerful. It was not religious, but a practice also used in some hospitals to help patients calm their minds to heal. When the mind is at peace, a connection to God can happen.

I taught mindfulness to the BIY volunteers and students. I was vigilant with them with the practice because they say if you want to learn something, go teach it. You then have to learn and embody what you teach. I made up games to help our children with mindfulness. They were like little ducklings as they opened to mindfulness prac-tice, which helped them to calm. It was like magic to see them fly into the program after school, unruly and hyper. But when we did mindfulness practice, it seemed the room turned into one large, peaceful, and silent heart.

Everyone seemed to adapt to the practice except Devon, who constantly disrupted the class, angering the other children. He was sending me into a rigorous mindfulness boot camp. This forced me to go deeper into the practice in order to cope with his behavior without getting upset. At first it was extremely hard because I wanted to see Devon change. But I learned that the practice of mindfulness is not about getting others to change. It's about living in the present so that whatever happens in life will not throw you into suffering. Buddha says its about equanimity -- living a balanced life, never getting too high or too low.

I practiced living in the moment off and on, but it wasn't until the pilgrimage to Hawaii that I felt that I needed more intensive study to be more disciplined with the practice.

I went in search of a teacher who taught mindfulness meditations.

I didn't realize that I once had the perfect teachers, Shinzen Young and Eiko Michi, when Walt and I were in the ministry. Eiko, a beautiful Japanese mystic who was one of our teachers in the early '80s, first introduced me to meditation. Looking back, her teachings were Mindfulness. I just wasn't as open to the practice then. After she stopped teaching, I searched for her for years but without luck

I'll never forget the first time that Walt and I came into Eiko's class when we were in the ministry. We both came from our jobs, met for a bite to eat and rushed through bumper-to-bumper traffic to be in class on time. When we entered the room I saw this small, gorgeous, chic Japanese woman with such grace and poise seated at the front of the class, looking pensively out of the window. Eiko had on knee-length black high-heel boots and a beautiful teal, hand-knitted sweater with a black knee-length skirt. I remember thinking that you can be fashionable and still be very spiritual.

The class quickly filled, and the other students were like us, anxious for Eiko to start her lessons. But Eiko seemed oblivious to us as she continued staring out the window while the evening shadows took over the classroom and the sun slowly went down.

"The sunset is so beautiful," she said in her soft, hypnotic voice, her eyes still glued to the sky. Soon all of us turned to look out the window.

"Watch how the sky dances with different colors. The orange, yellow…" Her voice faded away. Suddenly I found myself in awe of the sunset as if I had never seen one before. Looking back, I probably had never looked at one like that with deep intensity and mindfulness.

"Just be in the moment and see," said Eiko in a soft gentle voice that I had to lean into to hear.

This was the first of many spiritual lessons that I would learn from Eiko, not just from her teachings but also by the example of how she lived.

I remember one day in the middle of class a car alarm went off. We all looked out of the window since it was blaring loudly just below our room. It turned out that it was Eiko's alarm. She politely excused herself from class, and out the window I could see her gracefully strolling toward a few other people from the ministry who were already gathered around her car. She turned off the alarm and chatted with the people. Moments later Eiko returned to our classroom.

"It was my car. Someone broke into it," she said calmly, as if she was floating on a cloud. Eiko then snickered to herself, "Oh, well, that's the yin and yang of life, isn't it? Just another of life's little occurrences."

We all sat there amazed at how peacefully Eiko accepted the break-in. I would have gone through the roof, but Eiko simply told us to turn to a page in the Bhagavad Gita, and she resumed the lesson as if nothing out of the ordinary had occurred. I was learning. Keep your balance on life's roller coaster ride.

During those days I tried to get into any class Eiko was teaching. One time she held a weekend journaling workshop at a ranch bordering on three Indian reservations near San Diego. We ate vegetarian meals and learned how to give parts of our bodies voices through Progloff's journaling techniques that she once taught as a professor at the University of California, Los Angeles. Ira Progoff, a psychologist who studied under Carl Jung and D.T. Suzuki, developed a method of structured journal writing that enables the writer to access the deeper layers of his or her consciousness.

At night Eiko took us on walks on paths lit softly by the silvery moon, and taught us how to feel and be sensitive to Earth's energies.

When Eiko did body balancing on those who asked, I was anxious to get my session with her. Anything to get close to the inner peace she possessed. Under her soft healing touch I found myself peacefully floating out-of-body and hovering over both of us at the ceiling. When Eiko finished the session I was ecstatic, blurting out that I had had an out-of body experience with disbelief.

"I know," she said softly, "I looked at your body, and you weren't there. Just a soft white light."

I was magnetized by the incredible peace and calm that Eiko possessed and that I wanted. But the only way that I would attain that peace was to find it inside of me.

After my mother's place sold in the summer of 1996, I prayed for the right teacher to come forth to help me since I couldn't find Eiko. No one at the ministry seemed to have a forwarding address on her.

One day I was at the Bohdi Tree bookstore, the largest metaphysical bookstore in Western America. I was in line to pay for a book when my eyes drifted to the bookshelf above the cashier's head. I couldn't believe it. Eiko's eyes were looking down on me. Her picture was on the cover of a tape series that was being sold at the bookstore. I bought the tapes and listened to them repeatedly. I was reliving her lessons and feeling her energies. After playing the tapes for about the fifth time I realized that I was leaning on Eiko's inner peace, her inner wisdom, and I needed to find my own.

After I returned from Kauai, Walt and I decided to facilitate our workshops full time on effective communications. In the meantime I needed to find a new mindfulness teacher. I don't remember how I was led to the Thai Wat of Los Angeles but I found it. Surprisingly it was just minutes away from where we lived. The Thai Wat of Los Angeles is also known as the Theravada Buddhist Center, the largest Thai Theravada Buddhist Temple in the United States, which serves an estimated 40,000 people.

The first day that I arrived at the Wat, I was fascinated by the structure. The temple was the first in the United States constructed according to Thai architecture. It was like stepping into the Far East, looking at the collection of buildings, shrines, and monuments that surrounded me. Walking on the octagon red-bricked courtyard that was enclosed by a wall, just like the temples of Thailand, I felt such peace.

The main temple with the red tile roof and chofahs -- bird-like gold decorations placed at the end of the roof -- was breathtaking. Around the temple doors and the staircases were carved nagas, a mystical serpent that according to the holy scripts sheltered the Buddha while he was meditating.

I hesitated before entering the temple, looking up at two huge, frightening, 25-foot Yaksha statues with spears in their hands. Yaksha is a demi-god/demon, the guardian of wealth and symbolic of fertility and abundance. Quickly I took off my shoes and placed them with dozens of others on the long racks.

I entered the huge temple and was awestruck, seeing a huge, shimmering gold, 30- foot Buddha seated on the altar. Gifts from devotees and what seemed like a small truckload of food and flowers lined the red-carpeted floor leading to the Buddha. The monks I saw praying in bright orange robes were members of the Theravada section of Buddhism, which adheres closely to the pure teachings of Buddha. I saw men, women, and children, all of whom sat on the floor repeating decrees and chants.

I remember how people first stared at me, after the service, which made me feel slightly uncomfortable. I was the only non-Thai there. But after the initial stares they seemed used to me. After the service, which I didn't understand since it was in Thai, I visited the large food court where the men and women gave me welcome smiles and stuck out samples of food on toothpicks for me to try. My favorite was the fried banana.

I asked an elderly woman with a warm smile if there was someone who taught meditation. I hoped whoever it was could teach me more about mindfulness meditation. I needed mindfulness to live in the moment as a busy mother. I needed to find peace when Devon was acting out. Peace when the kids squabbled at home. I read from Thich Nhat Hahn if just one person in the house practices mindfulness that peace spreads to others in the family.

The woman introduced me to a young monk. The monk led me across the courtyard and through black gates to a small white house.

"That's where you go," he said and left me.

Moments later I was in front of the house taking off my shoes at the door. I placed them on a shoe rack next to two other pairs of sandals.

Quietly I opened the door to a large blue-carpeted empty room. At the far end, opposite the door, was an altar with a six-foot-high Buddha. A table with a white cloth was before the altar, where incense burned and flowers decorated.

I was told by one of the meditators in the room that a teacher would be there. A couple of more people came and left while I waited, but no teacher. I watched the people sit with closed eyes in silence, so I did the same. I had meditated for years so this was easy, but just being in that room filled me with peace. Finally I left, thinking the teacher was not going to show.

I returned the next day in search of the teacher and found the meditation room empty -- or so I thought. I sat cross-legged on the floor, hoping a teacher would come. I closed my eyes and then I heard a rustling coming from underneath the altar table. My eyes popped open and I saw a small Thai man, about 70-years old, crawling to his feet. He had been lying on a mat behind the large table.

The man, dressed in a white shirt and off-white pants, smiled warmly at me. "I was just taking my nap," he said with a heavy Thai accent.

"Do you teach meditation here?" I asked, still sitting cross-legged on the floor.

He came over to me.

"Yes, I do," he said softly as he nodded. Suddenly I felt the same peace and centeredness that I felt being in Eiko's presence. A calm. His eyes were filled with love and compassion, and his copper skin glowed. I felt like a lost child who had finally found her way home. We bowed to one another and he told me his name was Pisit as he sat down before me on the floor with the agility of a teenager.

For the next 10 minutes I began to retell my story of 1996 and about Devon. I poured out my heart, saying I desperately needed to learn mindfulness to help my family, especially Devon and me. As tears streamed down my face, Pisit nodded and took my hand in his soft hands as if to say, "I understand. Everything is going to be alright." But he didn't say a thing. He didn't have to. His peaceful energy spoke volumes. I knew instantly my new teacher was going to help me find my Higher Power.

Pisit put his finger to his lips as if to quiet me from spilling out all my problems. He sat directly in front of me and moved closer to me with his knees a couple of inches from mine. He then closed his eyes, with his palms upward resting on his thighs, and disappeared into a meditative state. Not knowing what to do, I closed my eyes, too. Within seconds, I found myself lifting into a cloud of peace and serenity.

Whenever I came to see Pisit, he would sit with me like this without saying a word. Finally I realized what was happening. He was helping me to just surrender to the moment. Just to be in that moment. Tons of stress seemed to roll off my back just by being quiet and sitting. I realized that in my busy state I needed to just sit and find a few minutes away from the turmoil. If I have to do this in the bathtub when the kids have gone to bed, I just have to do it. Find a few minutes of quiet just for Janet.

When we weren't in sitting meditation he would walk the length of the floor with me, teaching me how to concentrate on my breath in a walking meditation. Slowly I followed Pisit, lifting each foot off the floor and placing it down before the other. I would walk along side of him mimicking his moves. I felt like I was floating as our heels and then our toes touched the ground with our hands hanging to our sides, and breath flowing. For the first time I was aware of my toes sinking into the carpet, the muscles of my hands, my skin, and most importantly my breath. All of this mindfulness awareness gave my mind such peace.

During the following days that I practiced with Pisit we had talks of my journey with Devon and the deaths. As I spoke, Pisit looked at me with such compassion and sat so still that I felt like I was the only person in his world. Listening, I learned, is one of the highest forms of loving others.

It wasn't easy for me to understand Pisit with his heavy accent, but as I leaned into him, I got the most important teachings. I needed more mindfulness in my life to not be so angry with Devon.

"I know that Devon can't help his actions," I said, "but I get so mad at him and at myself for how I respond to him."

"Anger and sadness are the same thing," he said, his eyes penetrating mine. When I thought about it, he was right. I was angry with myself because I felt sad that I couldn't help Devon. I was sad that Devon couldn't enjoy life more, and that made me angry, thinking of his drug parents and the foster care system that emotionally damaged him.

"You can accept anything," said Pisit, "if you just pay attention to your feelings and thoughts without judgment, and then let them go." Again, he was right. The events in 1996 had come and gone. But my suffering was because I kept holding on to the past. I was reliving the events again and again in my mind.

"Thoughts and feelings are connected."

I didn't really understand what he meant by that until years later. The mind has a thought. The emotions and feelings follow that thought. If I have a happy thought, my body feels happy and free. If I have a bad thought, my stomach feels upset.

"Stay present and just observe the feelings in your body. Don't analyze," said Pisit. When I put my attention on the feelings in my body, the uncomfortable sensations went away like fading smoke. It was my attachment, my grip on what I was feeling that created the pain. Buddha taught that attachment was the reason we suffer.

"Accept," said Pisit nearly whispering. "Don't hold on, just accept life."

Our lessons would continue. But the hardest lesson that I would learn in the years to come was surrendering.

"You need to practice bowing down," said Pisit. I had seen monks and the congregants come into the meditation room and get on their knees and then move flat on their stomachs in front of the Buddha, but I thought this was like worshiping a false idol, and like some of the other teachings in Buddhism, I simply ignored it. I would learn later that the meaning of bowing was to become humble, to surrender, to let the Buddha, Jesus, or whomever was your higher power take over. When I finally practiced bowing, I found it was a way of moving my bloated nothingness out of the way and letting my Higher Self take over my life.

I was honored to be in Pisit's presence and to have him as my private teacher with all of his wisdom. He reminded me of my talks with the late "Roots" Pulitzer-prize winning author, Alex Haley, who had become my mentor. When Alex and I traveled together on a publicity tour, he told me, "Every time a senior citizen dies, it's like a museum burning down." Pisit was many museums to me.

Six months passed when one day I felt my museum was burning down before my eyes. I came to see Pisit, and I saw an excitement in his eyes that I hadn't seen before.

"I am leaving to take my last vows. I will become a monk."

I thought he was already one even though he didn't wear the traditional orange robe, but apparently he was still in training.

"You are? How wonderful!" It fascinated me that at his age he was ready for the next new adventure in his life. How many people half his age have stopped growing?

"Yes," he said enthusiastically, "I am going to Thailand."

"Thailand?"

I stopped breathing. My mind raced. Pisit, what about me? You can't leave me. But all I said was, "I'm so happy for you," and asked why he was going so far.

"The great temple is in Thailand. I will be teaching there."

"When are you going?" I cringed, fearing his answer. The same old abandonment feeling welled up inside of me. But then I stopped and gave my full attention to the feeling as Pisit had taught me. Steadily and slowly, the feeling dissolved.

"I leave tomorrow."

"Tomorrow? How long will you stay?" I said, mentally hysterical but outwardly calm.

"I don't know. Maybe I stay months. Maybe I stay years." He was going to be inducted to be a monk in the great temple in Thailand. They would give him his orders. Pisit had finished the tests, the initiation, and now he was going to be formally accepted into the brotherhood.

Excited, Pisit led me to the altar where he had his black duffle bag stashed underneath the table. A rolled-up mat was tied up neatly. After our second meeting I realized that, as the resident meditation teacher he actually lived in that room. It was his home. Teaching people like me was his life's work.

Opening his neatly-packed bag, Pisit proudly showed me his orange robe, identical to that worn by the monks I saw walking around the Wat. As I touched it with sadness, he told me that he couldn't wear it until he took the last of his vows in Thailand. My heart dropped. I had grown dependent on Pisit as I had on Eiko, and I told him so.

"You can come visit and stay at the temple anytime you want."

I lit up. "I can? People can do that?"

"Yes." He went on to explain that those on their spiritual quests do it all the time. I wouldn't have to worry about food or boarding. Just get there. I desperately wanted to, but knew that at this stage in our life, recuperating from economic losses, I couldn't go.

I couldn't leave the kids, and besides, who would take care of Devon while Walt was at work?

Still I turned the offer over and over in my mind. I had read books about people's spiritual quests and how they had life-changing experiences staying in the temples in the East. I desperately needed that type of spiritual journey to Thailand.

"I have something for you," he said, rummaging through his bag.

"Really?" I smiled, honored by his thoughtfulness. He brought out a Buddha pendant that he said was only available in the Great Temple in Thailand.

"You have Buddha inside of you." He tapped his heart. "You will teach people where the Buddha is inside of them, too."

"Absolutely, Pisit, I will," I said softly. My throat was closing up and my eyes brimmed with tears. "I will -- I will. I will teach them the lessons you have taught me."

"I know you will," he said smiling. "That is why I give this to you." Then without another word, he led me on our mindfulness practice walk in silence around the meditation room. It was to be our last walk together.

Eiko and Pisit came into my life when I needed them most and both would disappear, but I would carry them both in my heart forever. I was going to need everything they taught me in the hard days ahead with Devon.

CHAPTER TWENTY-TWO

The hurricane of 1996 was now behind us and I could see our lives coming back into balance. By surrendering through mindfulness, I found peace in the eye of the storm. But now I had to live mindfully daily. The big challenge would be to stay aware of my thoughts as I faced new opposition.

Initially I didn't know why being aware of thoughts was so important, but I learned that poisonous thoughts turn into emotions, and, if unchecked, they actually make us sick. The wonderful thing about mindfulness is that I didn't have to analyze my thoughts or figure them out. Just by being aware, my attention, like a laser beam, cuts through the thoughts and emotions, and they dissolved. The thoughts and the emotions didn't stop coming, but they didn't control me like before.

The universe was about to give me a new test to see if I embodied these lessons.

Ryan was now in middle school, and we decided to place Jada and Devon in the newly renovated elementary school in a neighborhood where homes were selling for at least a half-million dollars. The school reopened after the devastating Northridge 1994 earthquake, the first quake to strike directly under an urban area of the United States since 1933.

I particularly wanted Devon to finish his last semester in the new school because he had such a bad reputation at his previous school. I didn't mind the 40-minute, round-trip commute over two freeways, to help him start fresh. It seemed that teachers and students in his old school had begun to blame Devon for all of the problems, and he had become their scapegoat. Despite Devon's antics, Walt and I loved him deeply, and we weren't going to let anyone pick on him.

Devon started his new classes in the predominantly white school on the "right-foot," charming his new teachers, Ms. Rait and Ms. Holmes, who teamed to teach his fifth grade class.

"You're getting a new start," I told him as we drove to school. "They don't know about your past problems."

"I know, Mommy," he said, grinning. "I'm happy." My heart melted. Even though life was difficult with Devon, he had an irresistible charm. I loved our one-on-one time. With Walt and me, Devon was wonderful, but add other children to the mix and we had big-time trouble.

It would take only a month before the new elementary school was hit by another earthquake. Earthquake Devon.

His old behavioral patterns quickly emerged. There were so many ways he was disruptive in classes that I can't even count. He cursed, had temper tantrums, aggravated other kids, threw their food down on the cafeteria floor, and was constantly sent to the principal's office.

In the evenings I sat at my meditation stand, observed my thoughts, and stayed with the emotions I wanted to run away from. I knew if I just became aware it would help, and it also brought me insight. Mindfulness brings clarity. It dawned on me that I was carrying shame and embarrassment over Devon's behavior. They were the same feelings I experienced when my alcoholic stepfather drank.

I now knew that I had to stay vigilant of these feelings, and when I did I realized that I allowed Devon's teachers to bring out the shame and embarrassment in me.

Ms. Rait, who taught Devon's science and math classes in the morning, and Mrs. Holmes, who taught him English and social studies in the afternoon, had excellent reputations. The best in the school. These ladies were proud that their lessons were more complex than classes in other elementary schools and even the nearby middle school.

They were excellent teachers, although some of their "busy work" and nitpicking about assignments drove me and other parents up the wall, not to mention their students. They were the first to admit they were extremely controlling.

Needless to say this kind of strict structure set Devon off. He quickly rebelled and practiced triangulation, dividing me and his teachers against one another. It didn't work with Walt and me. Fortunately we have always stayed united on how to raise our children. But because the new teachers didn't know me and I didn't know them, Devon spun lies that kept us suspicious of one another.

It wasn't long before I found myself sucked into being at odds with these women. One time, as I was explaining Devon's background to Ms. Rait, she interrupted.

"I don't feel his background is a factor in his behavior." She pointed out that he had high test scores, "He can do the work, but he just refuses."

I could not get her to understand that he had emotional problems. This was a foreign concept. Over the years I found that people readily understand mental problems but not emotional problems. When I felt myself getting puffed up with anger, I observed my thoughts and my body sensations. I was surprised at my own inner rage and the thoughts that I fortunately didn't speak. Even a dummy knows that someone who was physically and sexually abused, put in three homes by the time he was three, and born with alcohol and cocaine and PCP in him, had to have issues.

I had explained to Ms. Rait that Devon had been diagnosed with ADHD -- which later turned out to be wrong -- but it was the only explanation for some of his behaviors.

"I don't believe in ADHD," she snapped. "That's just an excuse."

I had so many frustrating thoughts in my head that they shocked me. Immediately I knew that I was being tested by the universe. I needed to observe my thoughts and feelings and use my breath to calm myself if I didn't want to be manipulated by this woman. I was refusing to give my power away.

Devon's new teachers insisted that behavioral modification was the key to helping Devon, even though it hadn't worked with him in his prior school or with his well-trained therapists.

What I wanted them to realize was that Devon had issues beyond the average student. I wasn't asking that he be treated special; I just wanted them to take this into consideration. It was also important to me because I wanted them to know that I wasn't a bad parent. I took great pride in that my other two children were always called extremely polite by adults. I wanted these teachers to know that I had raised my children right. But even my wanting them to know this proved that I was being manipulated and trying to please them.

Mindfulness is letting go of these types of thoughts. People will think what they may. You can't try to change them, just yourself.

One evening at Open House I walked into Ms. Rait's room while she was talking to a small group of parents. When she saw me she looked up and shook her head, "Devon has really been acting out this week." The other parents turned to look at me, and I wanted to drop through the floor with embarrassment. Was she trying to humiliate me in front of these people on purpose?

The last thing conscientious African-American parents want, or any parents want, is to be stereotyped. I felt that the other parents in the room expected my son to be the one that "acted out" because that's the type of young black men they saw on the evening news.

In those days pride and humiliation were huge issues for me. I needed to be aware of them along with my anger. When I did observe these feelings without judgment, I was surprised how easily they moved out of my mind. I then found that no matter what the teachers wrongfully said or did, I was able to calmly be assertive. I no longer wanted to strangle these women.

My tendency before was to try to ignore people's hurtful remarks and to suppress my angry thoughts about them. Now, when I observed both, I found myself feeling not only more peaceful but strong. I felt I knew myself better, and that alone helped me to stand tall and be peacefully assertive about my feelings.

I often heard Pisit's voice telling me to just watch the thoughts come and go and accept them without resistance. This doesn't mean you have to be a doormat.

"You will have to lead the mind like an unruly child back to observe your thoughts," he said. "Sometimes you have to take the mind back many times. Be gentle with yourself. Have compassion. Remember, what people say or do is not important, it's your reaction to them. That should be your only focus."

When I followed Pisit's voice in my head I realized those parent-teacher conferences were now different. Suddenly I felt a deep compassion for the ladies and their work. Slowly my defenses dropped, and my heart was opening. In turn I realized that I was communicating with them easier, without the anger and frustration. They were still the same diligent although narrow-minded teachers, but I was no longer upset by them. Now I just had to master this technique with Devon.

One day I got a call from Ms. Rait.

"Devon pushed a second grader down and injured him. The family thinks the child may need stitches."

Immediately I raced to the school. Devon, as always, had an excuse. "He took my sweater," Devon pouted, "so I snatched it back, and he fell down."

As always Devon felt his actions were justified, and he refused to admit that he was wrong for being in the little kids' area, which was off limits to his class. He also didn't think he did anything wrong after Ms. Rait benched him for the incident, and he refused to stay seated. Needles to say, she was furious with him.

This was another opportunity, as Pisit would have said, for me to practice mindfulness of my thoughts. I needed to because my head was filled with fears. "My God, is the kid okay? Is he scarred? The parents must be livid. I would be. He's just a second grader, a baby, and Devon is huge compared to this child. They must think my son is terrible. They must think I'm terrible."

Magically, the more I observed these rampant thoughts the less terrified I became. I found my breath slowing down, my body relaxing, and I found clarity. I was no longer operating from everyone's fears, including my own, but from a deep inner wisdom. I called the parents to apologize and made Devon apologize to the child. Fortunately, the boy didn't need stitches.

Mindfulness doesn't stop life from happening, I would still have problems, especially with Devon, but I was determined to deal with these problems without my raw emotions running me ragged.

With every Devon incident it seemed I was running to the library, researching everything I could on difficult children, trying to find answers that professionals could not provide. In the meantime I managed to keep in control and to be calm when the teachers still sent furious notes home that ordinarily would unnerve me.

What was especially perplexing to Devon's teachers was that they were logical, linear-thinking ladies, and they felt confident they could find a reason for his actions. But Devon operated in the gray area. Trying to figure him out was like trying to catch smoke. This was particularly infuriating for Ms. Rait and Mrs. Holmes, who were known as problem solvers and peer counselors to new teachers. Devon, they found out, could not be counseled and definitely not controlled.

I can look back now and laugh, but then it wasn't funny. One day Mrs. Holmes told me through gritted teeth that I should do more behavioral modification with Devon.

"Praise him constantly for doing things right."

"We do that, Mrs. Holmes," I said. "We do it constantly with our other children, but it doesn't work with Devon. In fact, it makes things worse."

Mrs. Holmes looked at me strangely, and I couldn't figure out if it was with disgust or pity. Either way I knew she thought I needed parenting classes. She didn't understand that Devon sabotaged himself despite my warning her. Years later I would find out from a therapist that maintaining good behavior was a lot of pressure for Devon so he simply acted out. In his mind he figured that sooner or later he would mess up, so he chose to do it sooner. It was a low self-esteem issue stemming from his abuse.

One day Mrs. Holmes experienced this first hand. I felt vindicated, although Pisit would have disapproved and told me I was being pulled off my balance by this woman. But I did feel smug when Devon proved me right. He had been behaving beautifully in class for several days, and both teachers kept constantly praising him. The very next day Devon went on a rampage in school, driving everyone in the class crazy.

He came home with a note from Mrs. Holmes that read: "Devon wants the world to operate HIS WAY. He is not to be left alone for he is not to be trusted. This is really too bad after going through a day of pretty good behavior. I am very upset with him right now."

It was not what Mrs. Holmes wrote, it was the tone of the notes she sent home and her attitude of disgust that kept me on guard of my thoughts and feelings. Neither of Devon's teachers could control him, and they were deeply frustrated. But this was my opportunity to keep working on me, to live in the moment and not be sucked in by their frustrations.

During my constant research to find answers to Devon's behaviors, I became convinced that he had a split personality. He was sweet, helpful, and loving to Walt and me, but he simply couldn't get along with anyone else. He seemed to take great pride in provoking people. It was almost a sport to him. Several times when I talked to him about this he smiled, which gave me an eerie feeling.

What was especially aggravating was that whenever he got off punishment for behaviors such as stealing, before the day was over he would steal again. On top of that he would start a new behavior -- like the time he fed our dog hot cayenne pepper because he didn't want to do his chores, which included his turn to give the dog food.

During this time I received a call to facilitate workshops for drug and alcohol addicted women from a parent who had been in my meditation class when we ran Believe In Yourself. I decided to give mindfulness classes to keep me disciplined in the practice. Every week I hurried eagerly to that class because it forced me to live in the moment while teaching these ladies from the streets and jails how to do the same.

I was so touched because the ladies in my group were anxious to get on the right track and start a new life. They were hungry for information and grasped onto the concept of mindfulness to find inner peace and strength.

The class helped me to understand and have compassion not only for Devon's teachers but the women in my class who were like Devon's birth mother. They had addictions and previously operated irresponsibly because of them, but they weren't bad people, simply unaware. I remember my conversation with a stranger who told me, "If people knew better, they would do better."

I began my classes with the phrase that would become the title of this book, "Have you ever been in such pain and darkness, without direction? I have. It's a cry for light. We can shine the light on our dark moments when we become awake and live in the moment. Our awareness is like a laser breaking up the pain we carry inside of ourselves."

About half-way through Devon's semester, Walt and I wondered if we had made a mistake putting Devon in a predominately Caucasian school. I knew these teachers didn't know the struggles a child coming from an inner city experienced. On the other hand, Jada was now attending the same school and was on the honor roll. Her big challenge was her embarrassment upon her schoolmates learning she was related to Devon, the kid they couldn't stand.

Before I could go into an anxiety attack over Devon being in the wrong school, I simply put my attention on these thoughts and my body sensations that were tensed with stress. Suddenly I felt myself relaxing. I found clarity and answers, as well. How could these women who grew up in the suburbs and taught in an upper class neighborhood know of the misery, poverty and drug addiction many inner city children were exposed to?

It was clear. I needed to stop power struggles with Devon and the teachers and find him another school.

I remembered hearing about MacLay Middle School, which was located not far from our house. I didn't send the kids there before because it was, at that time, ranked at the bottom of the school performance index list. I decided to enroll Devon because they had an outstanding psychological team that worked closely with Hathaway Family Services to support students' mental health issues. They would understand Devon's behavior, and I didn't have to be embarrassed because Devon refused to behave. Most of them were Caucasian, too, but they were used to working with children like Devon who had come from the system.

Still, Maclay's teachers, like most of Devon's teachers, were about to be challenged.

CHAPTER TWENTY-THREE

Living in the moment helped me to transcend the deep emotional pain of raising Devon, which kept me debilitated. Now I had the tools and the power to separate this agony from myself.

Before, I would ball up in a fetal position overwrought with depression. Fortunately that was now behind me. Instead of running from my hurtful feelings, I opened to them and rode the wave. At first I was resistant to the thought of opening and surrendering. But I learned that surrendering was not about giving up. It was simply accepting what came to me in life, including the pain. The suffering occurred when I denied or ran away from these feelings, which persisted and grew stronger. The only way I would get over the emotional hurt was to go through it. When I did, I had new energy to put on solving the problem that initially caused the pain.

Mindfulness practice is exactly that -- a practice. Many times, I had to keep disciplining my mind to stay in the moment with the feelings and thoughts that crippled me in the past. My mind was like the small unruly child who strayed. Constantly I had to lead my attention back to the practice at hand. Eventually it became easier, and soon it became a habit.

Sometimes I would focus on my uncomfortable bodily sensations and talk lovingly to them as if they were small children.

"Hello, pain. You've come back. You don't have to be afraid." It was a way of integrating and loving the good and the negative sides of myself.

The great thing was that I didn't have to sit on a mountain and be isolated from everyone when doing mindfulness practice. I could do it while standing in a grocery store line, in a meeting, or driving my car.

When the painful feelings were too difficult to handle, I would back off from them and simply observe the inhalation and exhalation of my breath. Other times I would just observe whatever my body was doing. If I was in the car, I focused on my hands turning the wheel, or the muscles of my legs contracting as I pressed my foot on the brake pedal. Since our minds can only really have one thought at a time, it was this kind of single-mindfulness that allowed the stress to roll off me. I now understood how my frantic racing mind was what really caused my stress.

It was incredible to discover that even mundane housework gave me opportunities to practice mindfulness as I went through the drudgery of cleaning toilets or washing clothes. I was learning to find peace in every moment, such as listening to the dish water run or watching the glistening white suds on my hands. The housework that I once dreaded now became my temple of mindfulness and the grist of this moving meditation.

Through all of this I found myself growing closer to my spiritual self. Suddenly the lessons I studied from my meditation teachers were clear. "Everything in life has two sides," Pisit once told me. "On the other side of pain is joy." Mindfulness helped me to go through the pain to find the joy of my spiritual self.

Through this practice I found self-love. I use to hear people say over and over, "Love yourself." Before, I didn't know how to love myself. However, through mindfulness, I was doing just that. I was paying attention to my feelings, my thoughts, and my bodily sensations instead of turning away from them. Suddenly everything Janet thought and felt was important.

When we love someone, especially in a new love relationship, we want to be with that person and hang on every word they say. We want to be with their feelings to be closer to them. Now I was doing the same thing for me. I wasn't running from Janet's feelings or from Janet's thoughts. I was opening to them. I was giving myself the same kind loving compassion and attention that I wanted from others. But now I didn't have to look outside of myself for that validation. I found it within.

Wayne Dyer, one of the most profound and prolific spiritual and motivational teachers, says, "Every day we have about 60,000 thoughts. Most of them are the same negative thoughts that we recycle repeatedly." I became a witness to this first hand when I started tuning into my thoughts.

I was surprised what went on in my head, especially since I had gone through spiritual training in the ministry. I was even called Guru Janet by my friends and some colleagues in the entertainment industry. But when I really tuned in to the negativity in my mind, I was shocked.

The great thing was that I didn't have to change these thoughts. I merely had to observe them. When I did, I was putting space between fears and me that had previously turned into uncomfortable feelings in my body. I realized that I didn't have to suffer like that anymore. My attention became like a laser beam, cutting through the unwanted drama. Of course, many of the same thoughts came back, but without the same force and magnetic pull that threw me into depression. I could now see them before I embodied them and they became emotional pain.

I began to see the similarities in Devon and myself. The unruly side of Janet didn't want to practice mindfulness, but instead wanted to keep suffering. But even that was good mindfulness practice because I was now awake to the undisciplined side of myself that sometimes preferred to sulk, rather than transcend the pain. That was a rude but invaluable awakening.

Life with Devon was now becoming less stressful, even though he continued to have the old problems at his new school. That's life. Things don't stop happening to us. We simply learn to cope better.

Over time he seemed to become more stable. I didn't want to admit it, but my angst of wanting so badly for him to do well had in some way affected him. It created a lot of the pressure we both were under. Even the best parenting can sometimes be restrictive and suppressive because we are clinging so tightly to the thought, "My child must do well." This is stressful not only for a parent but for the child.

Mindfulness allowed me to release not only the pressure stemming from myself, but from Devon, and when he continued to do wrong things, they didn't pierce me like a knife.

Walt and I decided to put Devon back into Hathaway treatment since the psychologist at his new middle school worked closely with that mental health facility. I was even asked to become a member of the new parent advisory board at Hathaway, which I eagerly joined.

The waiting list for Hathaway extended for months, but we finally got back in and Devon was assigned to a beautiful, young, blonde therapist, Linda McCarthy. I had always been skeptical when Devon was assigned to a young, female therapist. I found that those who saw Devon automatically assumed that his problems were related to his family until they got to know Walt and me. Perhaps it was how they were trained coming out of therapy schools.

However, Linda was like the African-American therapists and the older white ones, male and female, who saw through Devon's angelic behavior in therapy. They not only perceived his game but confronted him with it, as well. Unfortunately, we weren't able to continue therapy with those others because either they left the clinics or they were too far away.

Maclay Middle School gave Devon another fresh start because his skin color or behavior didn't stick out. The students were mainly from Pacoima, a suburb of Los Angeles, which was then known for gangs and crime. Ninety percent of his school was Latino and the rest were black. Many kids came from broken homes and some were wards of the court. Therefore, Devon's teachers, who were exposed to a variety of behavioral problems, weren't shocked by his antics.

Although Ryan and Jada would have rather died than go to Maclay, Devon easily adapted, making friends with siblings of gang members and loving them. Still I worried. If he crossed one of these kids, his same new friends could get their gang member-brothers to retaliate not only against Devon but also our entire family. On the other hand, Devon had always flirted with disaster. Amazingly, he knew just how far to go with people to keep from being physically hurt.

Two of Devon's sixth-grade teachers were newly credentialed, and because they were new in their jobs I found them incredibly supportive and patient with Devon. I often wondered how they would have reacted to his drama after being in their jobs for a few years.

I was thrilled to discover that the Maclay teachers, the school's full-time psychologist, and counselors, were very much like the CASA volunteers I loved so much. They understood children from Devon's background. They weren't shocked and dumbfounded like the teachers at his other schools. Devon seemed to feed off people being shocked and awed by his behavior. He got some type of internal glee from controlling people and smiled when I confronted him on this. Fortunately, Devon couldn't yank chains so easily at Maclay like he did at the other schools.

During this time I was still volunteering with CASA as a court-appointed child advocate. One day I went to hear one of the many speakers who trained CASA volunteers to handle our court cases. A petite, pretty, brown-skinned woman named Evelyn spoke, and when she did I felt the heavens open up. Evelyn represented UCLA's Ties for Adoption, a University of California at Los Angeles program founded by Susan Edelstein. Ties promoted the successful adoptions and healthy growth of children who were prenatally exposed to alcohol and other drugs. Ties had also been successful in securing placements for children who had experienced one or more adoption disruptions in the past and may have been labeled "unadoptable." Depending on children's ages and identified problems, the Ties child development coordinators provided individualized consultation to help parents better understand and deal with difficult behaviors.

As Evelyn spoke I heard for the first time someone describing some of the symptoms of children born with substances in their bodies. She was describing Devon. In my years of searching for the reasons behind Devon's behaviors, I had never heard of anyone coming so close to why Devon acted as he did. Usually the mental health experts were as perplexed as I was.

Tears streamed down my face as Evelyn continued speaking. I had not met anyone with my mother's name before, and I immediately took this as a sign. She was an angel coming forth with information especially for me. When I failed to suppress my tears so I wouldn't make a spectacle of myself, I ended up mindfully focusing on the sensations inside of my body. Waves of sadness and joy battled for my attention. Finally I had met someone who understood the pain and problems parents and guardians experienced raising this type of child.

After Evelyn spoke I bolted to the front of the room to talk to her. I was desperate to get information that would help Devon, even though he had a therapist. I was fidgety awaiting my turn as Evelyn spoke to other people before me. Immediately I transformed into publicist mode from my television life, refusing to let her get away from me. During my publicity days I had to hound certain stars to take photographs and do interviews to promote their network shows when they didn't want to, although it was part of their contracts.

I took the same stance with Evelyn, who was rushing out the door to another meeting. But I refused to let her leave the room without talking to me, so I planted myself in front of the door. My persistence paid off. After we spoke she connected me with support from her office, and later was instrumental in guiding me through the process.

Devon was 11-years-old then, at the cut-off age to enter the Ties program. Nevertheless, Evelyn still referred me to an educational advocate who often worked for the program.

Lori Waldinger, a sharp, no-nonsense woman with short brown hair, was known around Los Angeles as a guardian angel, not only for special needs children but also for their parents. Lori was fierce in getting them the proper services.

This petite woman had a reputation for making school personnel quiver because she knew the law to a "T" and made sure the schools abided. Some schools hated when she was the educational advocate for a student. If the school was budget conscious, that was too bad if Lori was on the case. She didn't care about budgets; she cared about children getting the services that were due them. Fortunately, Lori took our case pro bono, knowing our financial situation and sensing my desperation.

Immediately Lori and Linda teamed and got the school psychiatrists, counselors, and teachers to sit down and map out a plan to help Devon get control of himself in school. The wagons were circling.

Hallelujah. Our prayers were being answered. I can't explain how much stress rolled off Walt and me after finally having the perfect team for solutions to Devon's behavior. It had been well over half a decade that we fought many battles with teachers and administrators on Devon's behalf. I haven't written about all of them in this book because they are too numerous and painful to describe. Most parents with special needs children understand. Raising these types of children often means battles to get your child services. In addition, since Devon was mentally sharp and seemed perfectly fine outside of his behaviors, it was extra hard because no one seemed to understand that he was emotionally damaged and was handicapped by the conflict raging constantly inside of him.

Now we no longer had to battle this alone. No longer did Walt and I feel isolated and stressed having to convince and continually fight for Devon's rights by ourselves. This new super team not only understood him, but they made it their personal mission to help him.

Immediately Devon got a new IEP and a 504 plan attached to his school file. The IEP is an Individualized Educational Program (IEP), which describes the special education and related services specifically designed to meet the unique educational needs of a student with a disability. The 504 prohibits discrimination against individuals with disabilities and ensures that the child with a disability has equal access to an education by receiving accommodations and modifications. In other words, by law teachers now had to recognize Devon's disability and make efforts to help him. No longer did I have to argue with teachers who insisted that he only needed more discipline at home.

With these two things in place Devon got "corrals" in each classroom. These were cardboard partitions that sat on his desks, blocking off his view of other children. It helped him to focus on his work without disturbing others. Devon still found ways to be distracted and bother his classmates, but the corrals definitely cut down on his mischief.

The team also came up with special codes for Devon. Whenever he found himself getting out of control in class, he simply went up to his teacher and inconspicuously slipped a colored card on her desk. A red card signaled to the teacher that he was on the verge of going off. In turn the teacher excused Devon to go to the counselor's office, where he could take deep breaths, calm down, and then return when he was collected.

With these plans in place, together with medications, there was remarkable change in my son. He still continued some of his behaviors, but they were nowhere as frequent as before. Surprisingly, for the first time in his entire life, he was making real friends. Nobody before wanted to be his friend.

As always with Devon, he was still full of surprises. Although he didn't have nearly as many behavioral problems, when he did have them they were serious. One reason? He was now older.

It was 1998 when the televised world of wrestling was taking over the teenagers in the country, and even girls were avid viewers. Devon was fascinated by the wrestling world and often talked of his dream to become a wrestler like many young boys of his age.

We didn't permit Devon to see wrestling except once in a blue moon as a reward for good behavior. The way they talked and mistreated women on those shows was most disturbing to me. But even though Devon wasn't permitted to watch, he got detailed reports from other children in his school of the latest wrestling title match.

We permitted Devon to see wrestling periodically against our better judgment because it was the only thing we found that made him want to cooperate in school. It was our bargaining chip. I was amazed at how compliant he was at school when he knew a wrestling match was at stake.

We also worried that since it was all the rage with young people, especially in our children's three schools, Devon might rebel further if he couldn't watch, too.

But one day the world of wrestling would knock Walt and I to the ground. According to the Maclay principal, Devon and his friends were walking down the hall together, talking about wrestling and emulating moves he saw on television. Suddenly Devon grabbed a girl he knew who was walking in the opposite direction. He put her in a headlock and pushed the girl's head toward his penis.

Devon may have been the pain in everyone's side, but he had never been violent like that toward anyone, especially girls. He loved to irritate people, but he had never been physically aggressive.

When I was called to school after Devon was suspended, I was told that the school had to file a report with the police. I had so many feelings rushing through my body; I didn't know what to focus on first. I was crazed with anger over Devon doing such a thing to anyone, especially a girl. I was afraid of this becoming a new behavior for him, and I was guilty for letting him watch wrestling against my better judgment.

Walt and I had brought both of our boys up to be gentlemen and to respect girls so this incident horrified me. I was especially worried about the girl and if she was all right. Maybe her big brother was in a gang. I also felt betrayed because I had let my guard down, thinking Devon was growing out of his mischievous behaviors and had improved.

Looking back, Devon was in the crucial pre-teen years with raging hormones and at a time when he wanted to impress his new friends, especially since he never had any before. But not in my wildest nightmare did I dream he would be so aggressive.

There was another school incident that surfaced during this time. One of his teachers caught him twirling a condom around on a pencil in the class. The teacher was too embarrassed to contact me directly because he thought I gave Devon the condom, which, of course, I did not. Eventually, in a parent conference, I found out everything along with Devon's explanation that he found it in the schoolyard.

At home, Devon's regular arguments with Jada escalated, taking on a frightening tone. One day he told Jada to suck his private parts, using a wrestling gesture he had seen on television. Another time, when he and Jada were in one of their fierce arguments, Devon went up to the television during a commercial and pointed below a woman's waist.

"I'm going to put a knife down there on you, Jada!"

During this time Jada noticed that one of her dolls had its clothes on backwards. When she took the dress off to put it on correctly she made a horrifying discovery. Devon had used matches to burn the doll's breasts and pubic area.

Jada had not told me about the television incident until she showed me the doll. Immediately I put in an emergency call to Linda. Air raid sirens went off in my head. After that Walt and I refused to leave Devon alone with our daughter. The level of behavior problems was now growing scary, and we needed a higher level of mental health services than Hathaway could offer us.

Linda immediately found a pre-teen sexual offenders group sponsored by another mental health agency. For over a year Devon attended those therapy classes while still in therapy with Linda, to whom I was growing so attached. She had a comforting way of not only dealing with Devon but listening to my parent problems. The therapists before her usually ignored my opinions and focused on Devon. How could you heal a child by ignoring the parent?

I attended the parent component of the sexual therapy group alone because the sessions were held during Walt's work hours. Sadly, I found that the parents acted like victims, refusing to take even minimal responsibility for their child's behaviors. What was worse, the therapists heading the parent group didn't call them on it, and they continued to bleed out their "woe is me" reactions. I kept thinking, what did I have to learn from this experience?

Even though we were devastated by Devon's new, devious, sexual preoccupation, his behaviors were nothing compared to the crimes other children in that group had committed. It was shocking. Most had spent time in juvenile hall. In fact, Dr. Levin, the psychologist in charge of the group, felt Devon did not belong with the other children. He had verbally threatened Jada and roughhoused the girl at school, but like everyone who knew Devon, we thought he was trying to get attention. He had plenty of opportunities to act on his threats to Jada, but mainly he ran off at the mouth to scare her. Still, Walt, Linda, and I were very concerned, and we wanted to take precautions and put out the embers before they turned into flames.

After our pleading with the psychologist, who reminded me a lot of the actor Robin Williams, Dr. Levin allowed Devon into the group. His concern, which became my concern, was that Devon would pick up new ideas or act on his words just to impress his peers. We took that chance because we had no other recourse.

During those days my salvation was prayer, mindfulness, and the terrific new team God had sent to support us. I found so much relief just talking to Linda before her sessions with Devon. I was able to vent my anger and frustration of raising such a difficult child.

Fortunately, Devon got a strong message while attending the sexual perpetrators group for over a year. The meeting site was about a 45 minute drive from our house, and during the long rides home we talked about the things that we had both heard in our respective groups that shocked us. I was relieved to see that he was genuinely upset and could not understand how some kids could be so cruel to others. He admitted that he never wanted to hurt Jada, only to scare her because she was making fun of him, and also that he felt bad about assaulting the girl in the hallway. He had apologized to the girl several times, and they became friends.

It was during these times, our quiet talks, when I felt most close to Devon. We had always gotten along, except when he could not handle being around other children and had problems in school. However, I could look deep into his soul when we were alone and see that the shenanigans were simply a smoke screen for the pain he had suffered as a baby. I could feel our deep, loving connection and his yearning for wanting to do right. He simply could not seem to control himself and break out of his self-sabotaging role that pushed others away.

Another redeeming feature was that he was remorseful for his sexual comments. Thankfully, Devon never mistreated or spoke to a girl like he did before Dr. Levin's group. It was clear that he was scared straight.

During those days I was emotionally and physically exhausted from plodding all over town, picking up kids from three different schools and racing between Devon's two therapy sessions each week. Walt wanted to split the duties when he wasn't working, but the pick-up and drop-off times were always during his work hours. Since he was the main breadwinner, I was the kids' taxi service.

I remember thinking: This adult thing is just too hard. I want my Mommy.

I truly did miss my deceased mother. I wished that I could have talked to her, especially when Devon went bonkers. She had always been his greatest supporter.

"He'll be all right, Jan."

Her words gave me comfort, and when she told me to "keep on pushing when times get rough," I was able to breathe deeply and move on. After she died I had to find new strength from inside of myself.

Enter mindfulness. There were times when I found myself sucked back into feeling sorry for myself, especially when I saw friends with one or two children thoroughly enjoying motherhood. When I didn't want to practice mindfulness the universe sent me a message. Get back on track!

One day I was looking outside when I saw a hummingbird making her nest on a rose bush inches from our living room window. I love nature, and I made sure that the kids watched her progress with me. I even had them look up hummingbird habits on the Internet. But I was the one most fascinated by her. Every day I watched the tiny creature diligently attend to her mothering duties of nesting.

When the harsh Santa Ana winds came and tilted her nest almost 45 degrees, she still sat on her eggs, leaning dangerously. I thought the hummingbird and her eggs would slide to the ground, but she sat stoically, refusing to abandon her mission or her eggs. This was the first lesson that I learned from her. Despite the windy turmoil that Devon kept the family in, I must continue to stand up to it and, like the hummer, not lose my balance.

When the babies were born, the hummingbird I had named Lady flew back and forth it seemed like a zillion times a day to get nectar to her newborn babes. She made so many trips to our backyard honeysuckle bush and back to our front yard where she nested that I became tired just from watching her.

It dawned on me that my few trips dropping off and picking up our kids at three different schools each day was nothing compared to her tasks. Even though we both often hit 50 miles per hour, she flying and I driving, Lady was expending far more energy than I flapping her tiny wings 200 times per second.

I was amazed at how one of nature's smallest birds had such endurance and fortitude to do her tasks while fighting the strong Santa Ana winds. I remember how she sat perfectly still on the eggs even though the winds whipped her and the nest back and forth. She refused to leave the nest. I guessed that Lady had to be meditating, practicing mindfulness.

Nature and animals are perfect examples of how we should approach life. Native Americans believe an animal or a bird will mysteriously come into our life and begin to haunt our consciousness. The image of that animal becomes associated with our sense of who we are and where our values come from. Different yoga positions are named after certain animals so that we can practice how they move to improve our health and well-being. Like the American Indians, I believe animals are some of our greatest teachers.

Hummingbird Lady taught me another big lesson. It dawned on me that all of the complaining I was doing about being a taxi cab driver for my children was draining my energy. I was doing more complaining than driving. If I stopped complaining I would have more energy to do what had to be done. I needed to follow Lady's example -- shut up, get up, and just do it. It was a profound lesson.

It wasn't long before Lady's babies matured and I saw her urge them out of the nest. I watched her stay close to her two babies as each hopped and then flew about two feet before resting in the bushes. Lady stayed nearby chirping, probably encouraging them to keep trying to fly. A few hours later I saw one of her children fly away, and my heart soared. I felt like I was the mama.

I had reflected on the babies when I saw them break through their shells. What a blessing that Lady had built her nest so close to my window. I was convinced that it was a divine gift just for me since I could easily see out of my window and inside the nest.

One of the chicks had taken much longer than the other to break through the shell. I thought of Devon as also having some type of shell around him and forbidding others to get close. I just wondered if he would ever break out of his shell and fly.

I continued to watch Lady stay with her last baby, who seemed to have problems flying. I thought that was probably her Devon. He seemed to have the most problems. Another day had passed since the first bird flew away, and Lady continued to encourage the one remaining. I was riveted to the window when all of a sudden that baby took flight with Lady squawking. I watched it circle around a nearby tree, and eventually it finally flew away. Lady went in another direction.

I took this as another sign. Maybe eventually Devon will find his wings, too.

That afternoon I sat on the couch looking at Lady's empty nest. It was my last lesson. It seemed at times that the last baby just couldn't get it together. However, Lady stuck with him until he got it together and flew away.

In the days ahead, like Lady, I would find myself kicking my son Devon out of the nest. Would he fly?

CHAPTER TWENTY-FOUR

After watching Lady, the mother hummingbird, fly away, I had a revelation. She was detaching from worrying about her children. Somewhere deep inside she must have felt that they would be all right, so she released them.

It was another profound nature lesson. I, too, needed to have more faith and detach from worrying constantly about Devon. I had been killing myself by doing everything that I could to assure his success. Often I got sick with painful fibroid tumors that were aggravated by stress and turmoil when he didn't do well. I had been plagued with guilt, having sacrificed precious time from my other two children, not giving them my full attention they deserved. It exhausted all of my energy to be locked in power struggles with Devon.

Now I didn't need to be so vested because not only was I practicing living in the moment, I finally had the perfect team in place. I had high hopes that these education and mental health experts could help me find solutions to Devon's problems. I could now step back and concentrate on giving Devon love and support since the burden wasn't all on Walt and me to find answers. I hadn't been able to just love this child like I wanted because I was too busy playing policewoman, trying to make him stay on course. I was drained emotionally as well as physically.

Devon now had great compassionate but firm teachers who easily worked with me along with Linda and Lori. All I had to do was continue backing them as I had always done with teachers and mental health experts. The only difference was that I felt these people knew what they were doing. That alone helped me to stop struggling with Devon and detach not from him, but from his behaviors.

When I stepped back what I suspected all along became clear. Devon derived great glee from knowing that people were spending countless hours trying to help him. He loved this kind of attention. I remember his smug look when he walked into the first IEP meeting at Maclay, and saw twelve people sitting around the table just for him. After that I suggested that Devon not attend because as usual, the next day he went bonkers.

Detachment is a byproduct of practicing mindfulness, and it would help me regain inner peace in the rocky days ahead. Also after years of searching and pondering, I was soon going to discover that detachment would unveil the mystery behind Devon's erratic behaviors.

Reflecting back on my life, I have always gone after what I wanted with a vengeance. My Mid-West upbringing taught me to work hard and keep focused on the goal. So I went after my Hollywood publicity career refusing to accept less than my dreams, which eventually came true.

But when Devon entered middle school, I finally realized that the same level of intensity and attachment to results that I exhibited promoting television shows wouldn't work in raising a special needs child. I couldn't will him to correct his behaviors. It only created a deeper conflict between us. The more I was vested in wanting him to cooperate, the more he seemed to go the other way.

That alone causes tremendous amount of stress.

Ryan and Jada were shining stars in their schools, and I was attached to the idea that Devon could be the same. It took a while to retreat from that idea and realize that Devon's successes would be quite different from those of his siblings.

I didn't see it that way at this time. When he would fail my attitude was to push harder to find more services, better therapists, and better educational support. It's a whirlwind life that parents of special needs children constantly live. I can see now that I needed a balance to finding him services in order not to lose parts of myself. Every time he had a setback -- -if a mental health agency tested him and said he didn't qualify for their program -- -I lost a piece of myself.

I wished Devon's teachers in his previous schools had resigned from the job of making him get good grades. I know this sounds horrible, especially because many parents don't think teachers care enough. But I needed low grades on Devon's part because that was the only way the school system would recognize his emotional problems. Failing grades would get him proper classification and services he needed.

Fortunately I developed a good relationship with the teachers at Maclay, and in our conferences I explained why his grades should be reflective of his efforts. He was never permitted to fail in at his other schools, so teachers gave him passing grades, probably just so they wouldn't have to see him again in their classes the following years. Could you blame them?

When this happened, Devon felt he could act out, not do the class work, not turn in assignments, and still get passing grades. The Maclay teachers agreed with me. Devon's grades must reflect the work he put in to them.

So for the first time in his life Devon began to see the consequences of his actions in school, and he was shocked. It was a time when he had became interested in team sports at school, but he couldn't join a team with failing grades.

Soon we saw a shift in Devon. With Linda's good therapy, great teachers, medication, and Lori riding herd over the IEP Devon again began to get along with other children in his classes, and he started completing his work. When he did, he was able to join teams. It was great news, but also perplexing. Could he not be as emotionally handi-capped as we had all imagined?

Devon's eighth grade was his best. He was maturing, and I felt comfortable enough to put my focus now on my career. Walt and I had facilitated team-building workshops on and off for many years, but now, with Devon improving, I had the time to build our business, Self Awareness Trainings, full time.

We landed contracts with organizations and companies, using the DISC, a powerful self-assessment tool used in Fortune 500 companies and by other companies around the world to help people understand their behavioral styles and others. We taught people how they could adapt to get along with even the most difficult person.

I had personally relied on these techniques over the years to interact with the small army of Devon's professionals and in my television career, working with difficult actors. It was invaluable in understanding my family members. It helped me to separate a person from their actions and understand why their needs made them act a certain way. Even though I had conflicts with the teachers in Devon's last school, they were minimal because I knew the teachers' behavioral styles. This was powerful, and it even helped me to separate Devon's natural behavioral style from his antics that still were a mystery to our special team.

September 13, 1999 was a proud day for Devon. He had improved so much that after he graduated from Maclay we enrolled him in Granada Hills High School, which where Ryan attended. Today it's the largest charter high school in the nation.

Still we all held our breath, especially Ryan, hoping Devon would continue his progress in this new environment. I was somewhat leary, but I was determined to remember the hummingbird lessons and to have more faith and detach. Besides, where else would he go?

Granada Hills High School had the reputation of being the crown jewel in the Los Angeles Unified School District. It was a big, well-organized and disciplined school, with nearly 4,000 students. The faculty approached their work believing every student was college material. The level of teaching was on a par with, or better than, many private schools. A number of parents whose children had always attended private schools in the lower grades, put their children in Granada. Other parents who lived out of the school's district as I did, entered their child in the school's lottery system, hoping and praying their student's number would be called to enroll.

When Ryan's number was selected, you would have thought we won the lottery. This made way for Devon to attend the next year on the sibling admission policy they had in place back then.

Since I had always been active in my children's schools throughout the years, I was volunteering at Granada when I heard of a part-time community-parent representative position opened there. I applied and landed the job.

The largest part of my work at Granada was reaching out to alumni, and I was having a ball exercising my old public relations skills. The three hours I spent at the school each day in the mornings fit perfectly with working on Self Awareness Trainings later in the day.

Devon was doing well the first months at Granada. He was still attending weekly therapy sessions and taking medications for compulsive and depressive behaviors. We had a diagnosis different from the ADHD, as some of the therapists thought who had seen him throughout the years. Now, the psychiatrist working with Linda said he was bipolar, and treated him for the disorder.

During this time I had a full plate. Each morning I drove two freeways dropping Jada off at her new middle school, and continuing to Granada Hills High School a few miles away with the boys. During this time I was also on the CASA fundraising board, Friends of Child Advocates.

I loved the CASA work, but with my schedule I was forced to let it go. When I left I realized that I needed time off from always thinking about so many abused and neglected children who needed CASA volunteers. The volunteers could only serve one percent of the children who needed them because there simply weren't enough.

In contrast, at Granada, I was surrounded by young people who appeared to come from loving homes. It seemed to me that their worries were limited to getting into colleges and prom dates. I was dead wrong.

On December 1, 2000 I was dropping the boys off at school when we saw a flurry of police and ambulance activity up ahead. News helicopters circled above, and reporters walked the campus interviewing students. The next few hours was so unnerving that I was compelled to share the experience through an email.

"Hello, Family and Friends:

"I'm writing to you to balance myself. I needed some stability in my life right now to help me make sense of this morning. Thinking of you grounds me.

As you know, I've taken this great part-time job at Granada Hills High School as their community-parent representative. It's been a relief getting away from the children's court where I helped with their publicity and sat on their board. My brain needed a rest from hearing about yet another abused child.

I was relieved to come to one of the top public schools in Los Angeles county where kids didn't seem to have all of the problems unlike the kids I advocated for at the children's court. Many here come from middle class homes and others live in million dollar estates. Quite a few have their own cars, and everyone seems so happy. They're a great group of kids, open, and polite. My two boys love it here. They have made some wonderful friends. There was a lot of angst trying to get them into a good public school where there were few problems with gangs, drugs, etc. Granada has an outstanding reputation, except for one thing. Lately kids here seem to be killing themselves.

The boys and I drove up to school this morning and saw yellow police tape everywhere. Circling news helicopters made it impossible to hear the person next to you.

An Asian male senior had set up a video camera in the parking lot, and turned up his radio loud in his car parked several feet away. He asked a few people he knew coming on the campus to be in his video. They were giggling and joking, happy to help him out with what they thought was a school project. When they were all in place in front of the camera, the young man stepped in front of them as if to give an introduction. Then, in front of dozens, maybe hundreds of students walking to class, he shot himself in the head."

In the email I went on to say that the senior's death comes on the heels of another suicide victim who was attending the school. Just a month earlier a young lady tied weights to her legs and jumped into the family pool.

When I dropped the boys off and parked, the campus was in sheer choas. There was an immediate lockdown, and teachers were told over the loud speaker to keep everyone in their classes.

While a crisis team raced from downtown Los Angeles, all of the school's counselors and available special needs faculty were busy taking care of hysterical students. I heard another announcement for all available staff to go to Highlander Hall. Supervision was needed for students who couldn't handle sitting in class. They weren't allowed to leave campus, but they could sit in Highlander.

When I stepped into the hall I was engulfed in a wave of sorrow. Approximately fifty of the suicide victim's classmates were consoling one another or walking around in shock. I was the only adult in the hall and all I could do was jump from one crying, shaking teenager to another, hoping another crisis didn't break out. Thankfully, about ten minutes later, Orna Nathan, a mother who headed the volunteers, came through the door. For the next hour we continued to talk to the students, watching for which ones needed the most attention as the Los Angeles Unified School District crisis team fought rush hour, coming through traffic thirty miles away.

It amazed me how many students told me through their tears that the suicide may have been their fault.

"How could I have missed the signs?" "I just talked to him last night." "He seemed all right then." "If only I could have known." And then the most surprising comment that was uttered by a number of students, "Why does this keep happening to me?"

It's not uncommon for young people to feel tragedy, even in a group situation, was directly related to them somehow, especially in this case, where some students knew both suicide victims well.

I bent down in front of huge football players seated on a bench who were sniffling and bouncing their legs vigorously or shaking. I don't remember what I told them, but I do remember being silent. I knew that there is usually nothing you can say in those situations, but just holding a person in love and compassion is the comfort they needed which I did. My shoulder was soaked from a mix of tears from all sizes of students. I fought back my own.

The student I was most concerned about that morning was the victim's girlfriend. The petite, dark-haired girl came into the hall holding her books tightly in front of her as if she were clinging on to her own life. She walked as if she were a zombie with glazed eyes. Students rushed to hug her, but she didn't embrace them.

Seeing the flurry of activity, I walked over to her and introduced myself then asked if she was okay. She nodded without looking at me. I stayed by her side, fearing her state of mind. I wished that the crisis team was already there because she was the one I wanted to alert them to first.

What bothered me most, was that she was stone-faced while others were breaking down crying. "You can cry honey. It's okay."

"I can't and I won't," she said, shaking her head slowly.

"Why sweetie? You can just let go."

"If I cry," she said, "I won't ever stop."

Finally the crisis team burst through the doors. I rushed over to tell them that they should attend to the girlfriend first. As I left the auditorium to return to my office, my mind was flooded with concern for Devon. The energy on campus was eerily strange and extremely heavy. Devon was always hyper sensitive to, and reacted to, his environment.

Would he commit suicide, too? I remembered a television movie that I worked on for CBS, "The Silent Heart," about teen suicide, and learning that about half of all suicides could be attributed to bipolar disorder.

When my boss told me to put together a publicity campaign for the movie, teenage suicide was rampant. For months I talked to numerous suicide prevention organizations around the country. I learned that many of teen car crashes were thought to be suicides and that most suicides occur when there is a pre-existing mood disorder, depression, or substance abuse. The cocktail for many teenagers.

Months before the Granada suicides statistics showed that approximately 4,200 US teens and young adults died by suicide annually between 1992-2001, with an additional 124,000 making an attempt serious enough to land them in the ER.

A Suicide Prevention Symposium held recently announced that new studies show the incidence of 'copycat' and clusters of suicides -- which occur most often with adolescents -- increases after extensive newspaper or television coverage. In the days ahead, there were plenty of media on the Granada Hills High School campus.

I cannot say enough about how the new principal, Brian Bauer, who was only on his second day at the school when the incident occurred, fashioned a protective net around the school, bringing in top mental health people to work with the students and staff, who were reeling from the suicides. The shock had a wave effect. Initially I wasn't too upset, but as the weeks went on, as with many people, the effects set in on me.

I kept vigilant watch over my boys during this time, tuning into their feelings even though they said they didn't know the kid and were not affected. On the way home that day neither could understand how anyone could take his life.

"Don't worry, Mom," said Devon, smiling, "I'm not going to kill myself."

Still I was watching for depressive signs in both him and Ryan. How could they not be affected when so many students were obviously shaken up? Walking onto that campus for weeks after felt like entering a morgue. It was extremely quiet, and subdued.

In the days ahead there were times when I clearly understood why people get so depressed that they commit suicide. They must feel like their world is coming down on them, just like what was about to happen to me.

CHAPTER TWENTY-FIVE

I've worked on hundreds of dramatic television episodes for the CBS and ABC Television Networks, and now it seemed I was re-living them all at once.

Devon had done so well his first months at his new high school, but all of his progress began unraveling. By the end of January, 2001, he had received twenty-three citations for behavioral problems at school. Several teachers reported that he smelled like marijuana, and even though he knew I was on campus in the mornings, he didn't go to class.

I went into policewoman mode and started staking out Devon's classrooms to see if he showed up. I had made many surprise visits to his classes when he was younger, and I warned Devon that I would do it again when he got to high school.

He did not believe me. Therefore, when he refused to serve detention time for his citations, I took drastic action. During his last period I posted myself outside of his classroom door. After the bell rang he came out of class joking with his friends, but when he saw me his face went ashen. He tried not to show any emotion as I escorted him to detention, but I smiled to myself, knowing he was furious.

During this time Ryan felt he was losing his identity to Devon. Classmates, and even a couple of people he didn't know, told him, "Your brother is an ass-hole." Ryan was filled with embarrassment, which is the worst feeling a teen can have during his development years. I knew how he felt. As an employee of the school I found myself constantly explaining Devon's background to other staff members because they knew this unruly child was mine.

By this time oppositional defiant had been added to Devon's mental health chart at Hathaway, and the medications he was taking everyday were no longer working. Devon sank into major depressions, with mood swings ranging from excessively high to irritability, sadness, hopeless, and then to high again. I never knew what to expect when I woke him up to go to school. Who was he today?

I couldn't believe how fast Devon was spiraling downward, and I was even more baffled over why. He was suspended from school for throwing a pencil at a boy in class hitting his face. His hygiene, or should I say continuing lack of hygiene, was every mother's nightmare. He put on wrinkled or dirty clothes and refused to comb his hair, which was more perplexing. High school is the place where young people start dating, and he was definitely interested in girls. Obviously, Devon was self-sabotaging again.

The worst was when he had periods of enuresis, or involuntary urination during his depressed days. He refused to take showers or wash up unless his father or I hounded him. I would later find out this was his rebellion to keep people away and to be in control.

I remember one day driving the kids to school with this overwhelming odor coming from Devon. Ryan and Jada were hanging their heads out of the window to breathe when finally I stopped the car a few blocks from school.

"Get out," I said, turning to Devon glaring at him.

"Why?"

"Because you refuse to shower, and I refuse to smell you. You are punishing the whole family with your odor. If you want kids to laugh at you in school, then fine. That's your business. But you're not going to punish us, so get out and walk the rest of the way."

Devon threw open the car door, nearly tearing it off its hinges, and stormed his way to school. But he got the message. We didn't have that problem again.

Then there were the gentle times between us. I would come in his room and sit on his bed beside him and talk. I didn't want to fight this kid. I loved him so much.

"Honey, I know something is bothering you. I know you don't want to act the way that you've been doing. How can Dad and I help you? What do you need from us? You've got to help us help you."

Devon shrugged his shoulders and hung his head. He was in pain, and despite his tough front I knew that deep down he wanted help. But he didn't know what to ask for, and I didn't know what to give him.

"You need to tell me what's wrong, what's going on inside?"

"Nothing, Mom. I'm ok."

"All right, then. If you think of it will you come and tell me?" He nodded, and we hugged. I sat with him as we listened to a couple of his favorite CDs. Music and love calmed us that night.

Walt and I concluded that Granada was simply too big for Devon to handle. He needed a more intimate environment. Talking to Lori and Linda, we all agreed that a non-public school would be the answer. Unfortunately, the ones we applied to turned Devon down. Not one ruled he was eligible even with Linda's letters recommending him for this type of structured environment. There were accommodations for students with mental illnesses but not for emotional problems like Devon had, which were growing worse.

After school Devon was now refusing to be at the pick-up location I designated for him and Ryan. It became an afternoon ritual. I returned to school after working our business always worried if Devon would be waiting with Ryan.

At first I would wait for a half an hour for Devon to show up before circling the school looking for him. I would send Ryan in one direction to scour the campus, and I would go the other way. Finally we realized that he was simply being rebellious even after promising he would be at the pick-up place.

If Devon wasn't there we wouldn't hear from him until 10:00 or 11:00 PM on those nights. He would refuse to tell us where he had been. He said only that he walked home from school through gang territory, which amazed us since it took me twenty minutes traveling on two freeways to drive the kids to school.

Devon's shenanigans landed me in the Foothill Division police station to file missing persons reports several times a week. Walt came the first few times, but since we were there for hours, and I worked from our home office and he didn't, I went alone to the rest of the visits.

This same police station, which became infamous after Rodney King was stopped, was now becoming part of my routine. To keep from exploding, I counted silently the inhalations of my breath as I filled out the same long forms each time. It got to a point where the desk sergeant seeing me coming in knew instantly why I was there.

"Devon missing again?" she asked. Sheepishly I nodded my head now with a sadness replacing my anger. He was crying out for help, and I was crying out for light. What could we do to help him?

Since Devon was on three medications the police would immediately send cruisers to find him, but they never did. I desperately wanted them to locate him, but at the same time I clung to the fear that if they did the neighbors would see him getting out of the police car. What would they think of Devon? What would they think of Walt and me as parents? What would the neighborhood kids say to Ryan and Jada, who were already filled with embarrassment over Devon? Pisit's voice rang in my ears. "If you are concerned about what others think, you are not living in the moment. Be concerned only with what's going on inside of you."

Blood throbbed in my neck and my heart pounded as I waited on the hard, gray chair in the police station. I concentrated my awareness on the heaviness in my chest and the voice in my head. "We have reached rock bottom."

It was a relief to be able to focus on what was going on inside of me. Just being aware banished the fearful voices and the heavy chest from me. This gave me distance from those painful feelings that took all of my strength. I needed all of my energy to stay vigilant over Devon.

These brief meditations relaxed my mind, which I needed because I found myself waking up throughout the nights. Something inside of me must have known that I would soon be visiting the police station again for Devon, and it wouldn't be because he was missing.

On one sleepless night I wrote in my journal, "I can imagine what abused women must feel like. I feel Devon is emotionally abusing me. He has lied to me, stolen from me, done everything possible to hurt me. He says he is sorry, and things are all right for a few weeks, but then he turns around and does something even worse. Lately he doesn't even show remorse."

Not only did I feel that Devon's fury was directed at me since I was with him more than anyone else, I felt his anger was definitely directed at himself. He grew more self-destructive as the days passed.

It helped that at least now he was diagnosed oppositional defiant and bipolar. For so long Walt and I tried explaining to educators and mental health experts his problems, but they weren't listening. It was like having some dreadful disease but no one knew what it was. But now, even with Devon's diagnosis, I kept thinking there was something else wrong. Something more. So with this thought nagging me, I stayed on the Internet searching for what, I don't know. Looking back today, I think I was spiritually guided.

Then one evening it seemed the heavens opened up. Angels must have been singing. It was about 10:00 p.m. when I was surfing the Internet and found myself clicking onto the Evergreen Consultants website. Chills went through my body.

"This is it!" I whispered to myself as my eyes rapidly scanned the screen. I heard myself hysterically yelling, "Walt, come here quick! This is it! This is it! Come here and look."

"Wha…"

I didn't give him chance to finish as he sleepily padded into our home office. "Look here" I said, tapping the monitor. "This is Devon!" My knees were bouncing up and down with excitement as I read the symptoms of Reactive Attachment Disorder. "Devon has RAD."

Walt leaned over my shoulder as we both read the list of identifying RAD symptoms in children. They included frequent tantrums or rage, often over trivial issues; a severe need to control everything and everyone; trouble understanding cause and effect; poor impulse control; often an undeveloped conscience; argumentative, often over silly or insignificant things; lying for no apparent reason; indiscriminate affection, often to strangers, but not affectionate to parents; hyperactive, yet lazy in performing tasks; lacks of morals, values, and spiritual faith; cruelty to animals; destructiveness to property or self; stealing, sneaking of things without permission even if he could have them by asking; fascination with fire, blood and gore, with weapons, with evil; usually the making of bad choices; concern with details while ignoring the main issues; triangulation of adults, pitting one against the other.

"That is definitely him," said Walt, nodding his head.

I then continued reading aloud, "A RAD child keeps himself moving in and out of closeness, both as a conscious decision and as an unconscious manipulation. He puts physical barriers between himself and the adult. He also tries to get the adult to move away and distance by acting obnoxious. He insulates himself, has frequent tantrums or rage, often over trivial issues; thickens his internal defenses and makes them stronger so no one can get in."

I sat back. I felt like I had discovered the cancer cure. RAD was the cancer that was eating our family alive.

Just knowing about RAD helped me to replace some of the anger behind Devon's defiant behavior with a deep empathy for him. I learned that kids who suffer early childhood trauma develop the disorder as a defensive mechanism to survive. When a young child's needs are not met, they put up a protective shell thinking the world is hostile and filled with betrayal, rejection, abandonment, neglect, and abuse. Naturally they don't think in those terms as children, but these are the reasons they develop RAD symptoms.

I stayed up nearly all night studying more RAD websites on the Net and was fascinated at what I found. There are many children who develop RAD who are not adopted. They include children who were taken away from their birth parents, premature birth children, children who experienced hospitalization, those with parents dying or whose mothers had postpartum depression. Other children who develop RAD may have had multiple caretakers, traumatic experiences, insensitive parenting. Then there are those children who had painful or invasive medical procedures or were born to young mothers without parenting skills

In the days ahead I shared my discovery with Linda and Devon's psychiatrist. They agreed. The RAD symptoms fit Devon. I knew it was him. This was my son. Now I understood why Devon had been diagnosed as bipolar and ADHD. RAD is often misdiagnosed as these disorders.

Devon was a typical RAD child who grew up trying not to show a need or vulnerability that he cannot take care of himself. As an older child he will tend to become aggressive and defiant toward authority. RAD children are also unable to understand other people's pain or difficulties, primarily because they are unable to feel or understand their own.

Anxious to talk to anyone I could about RAD, I went to the CASA office at the Children's Court where I volunteered, and spoke to one of my favorite supervisors. She of course knew about RAD, and to my surprise I would find out later, so did many people associated with children's social services. It's a known disorder to those working with high risk children, even though it's an alien term to the general public.

I cried in the CASA supervisor's office as we talked about the disorder. For so long it was mind-boggling to me. After giving Devon everything he could ask for, and everything I had in my soul and the love in my heart, he continuously did things to push us away, even though teachers and mental health workers often told me how much he said he loved his family. Why then did he push us away? Finally I had the answer.

Discovering the reasons behind Devon's actions was liberating, but it didn't help his problems.   At home he continued to play mind games with all of us, continuing to steal anything in his reach. We often joked that thank goodness, something in Devon wanted him to get caught, because if he didn't he could be dangerous.

I remember the time when Devon said he had not seen my missing cell phone. Later that afternoon, when I dropped him off for group therapy, he called asking permission to play basketball with a few friends afterward. When Jada answered the phone she saw that my cell phone number showed up on caller ID. Still Devon denied having the phone. It wasn't until the next day that he dropped the lie and returned my phone. Usually after three days he would finally confess to lying.

I wrote furiously in my journal to vent about these types of occurrences. It helped to take the steam off when I didn't feel like practicing mindfulness. Walt and I talked a lot about Devon, but I did not want to keep bogging down our marriage with something so frustrating to both of us. I would have never survived Devon without Walt's strength, but I had learned my devastating lesson in 1996. Women especially should be careful of always using their partner to constantly complain about the same problems that have no immediate solutions. Men's normal psyche is to fix things when there is a problem, and women's psyche is to talk about their emotional reactions. And when men can't fix something immediately, like Devon's behavior, then they experience a deep frustration that can hurt the relationship.

Our heavy hearts can be lightened by talking to understanding friends and relatives, but with RAD no one seems to understand unless they observe the disorder themselves. It is incomprehensible that a child would have such symptoms. I found that outside of Walt, Linda would be the only one I could confide in. Unfortunately people are not going to always be there for us, so we have to find other resources like talking to our Higher Power, and journaling.

Just when we needed Linda the most another bombshell dropped.

"You're leaving?"

I sat there trying to wrap my mind around what she was saying. Linda had been promoted at Hathaway, to a director. I was happy for her, but, needless to say, sad for our family. I kept thinking, "Why is everyone always leaving me?" They're always the good people in my life who either die or move away. How could she be leaving us? And what are we going to do now?

"I'm sorry," said Linda as we hugged. It didn't take a psychology degree for her to see that I was devastated.

Devon sat motionless on her tan sofa. He was growing increasingly hard to read lately, retreating further into a shell. When he asked to leave Linda's office after the news, we watched him amble heavily into the waiting room and slouch into a chair. He sank deep into thought, oblivious to the room filled with kids who were watching videos and playing board games as they waited to see their therapists. Parents sat quietly with crossed arms and blank or pained expressions on their faces. They must have felt like I did, ragged, and exhausted.

The next Wednesday -- May 23, 2001 -- I took Devon to one of our last therapy sessions with Linda. I drove home to pick up Jada. When Devon's group ended I then took both children on a twenty-minute ride to Wednesday youth service. I went to a nearby Starbucks to read and write until they were ready to go home.

After Jada bounded for the car around 9:00 p.m., we waited for Devon, who was in a different group. When the very last child filed out of the church, terror took over my body. I went racing through the halls to find Devon. None of the church leaders had seen him.

Did he slip past me and get a ride home? I was about to call Walt when I saw that I had a message on my cell phone that I forgotten to turn on.

"Mrs. Jackson, this is Sergeant Pavli at the Devonshire police station. We are holding your son Devon. Would you please come down to the station?"

I raced Jada home and, together with Walt, traveled to the station with my heart pounding. Devon had been arrested for stealing at Wal-Mart, which was across the street from church. He was with a few of his white friends from church who had dared him to steal. The police let his friends go but took Devon into custody.

On the way down to the station, Walt called a police officer friend of his to ask if there was anything we could do to get them to hold Devon over night to teach him a lesson. There wasn't. We had to go claim him.

I'll never forget walking into that police station. I felt that Devon was playing out all of the stereotypes whites have about blacks, and I was livid at this happening in our family. I sat, watching my breath to keep calm, as we waited for him to be released. Of all of the embarrassing situations Devon had gotten into, this was the worst.

When we saw Devon in a back room where we signed release papers, I thought he would be saddened and just as embarrassed as I was. But he walked out smugly and had this unforgettable thuggish attitude. He appeared not to be intimidated by the police. His whole aura was foreign to me. This kid before me didn't seem like the poor child with an emotional problem that I had known. Instead he had a hardened-criminal attitude that frightened me.

This was the turning point for Walt and me. Despite Devon's smug attitude, we knew he was crying out for help, but we weren't going to tolerate a life of crime coming from any of our kids. As parents of a special needs child we had gone through hell to help Devon, but we absolutely refused continuously to bail any of our children out of jail. This is where we said, "enough is enough."

That night, after we returned home, Walt told Devon to sit on the couch. He plopped down with the same "So what? attitude." Walt then went into Devon's room, and within minutes things went flying into the hallway, knocking up against the walls. Devon's CDs the television, his play station, everything was now crowding the hallway. When he was done, Walt stormed through the house, taking all of it, throwing it in the backyard.

"Tomorrow Devon, it's all gone. I'm giving it away to charity, to children who can appreciate it. The law says we only have to feed you, keep you safe, give you a place to sleep and send you to school. You want to break the law then that's it. That's what you get. Things like the play station and television are privileges, luxuries. You have to earn those gifts."

By the time Walt was finished with Devon's room there was nothing left but his clothes hanging in the closet and the mattress.

That night Walt and I talked.

"We can't keep going through this," Walt said. His anger was gone, and now it was survival. "He has crossed the line."

"I know. What's scary is he is not even sorry," I said. "It's a matter of time before he thinks he can get away with something worse."

We discussed for hours that we didn't have any more resources for Devon, and now we had to look for a placement for him. We had nothing else to give. We had to think of the well-being of Ryan and Jada, who were suffering under this constant turmoil in our house. Often I didn't have the energy to give them the attention they deserved because it was used up on Devon. This wasn't fair to two kids who did everything we asked of them at home and at school. It was their turn now to live.

Before we did not want to look for placement for Devon. We kept ignoring it, hoping that Devon would get better. We both dragged our feet about calling DCFS. We knew they wouldn't take him back. It was long past the adoption probation period. Neither one of us wanted to put him back in the system. I especially had seen what multiple place-ments did to teens who lived in sometimes thirty different foster homes. The thought ripped through me like a knife.

We didn't know where else to turn for help. There was no place to get Devon the intensive help he needed. No one knew who could help this RAD child. We just knew that after all of agony our entire family suffered, we had to stop the cancer from spreading. Devon would have to go.

CHAPTER TWENTY-SIX

Throughout the years I have learned many lessons from Devon. The hardest was how to detach. Ironically, he was detached from people. Devon was my mirror. Other people reflect what we need to learn about ourselves.

One of the Four Noble Truths of Buddha's teachings that fascinates me is that our suffering comes from attachment. Attachment is a desire, a lust, a grasping, a craving, or clinging out of our failure to recognize that all things are imperfect and impermanent. The ancient teachings say that we try to hold on to moments of happiness when all things in life are changing. Instead of going with life's flow and seeing and accepting each moment as it is, we fight it, fearing a return of our past pain and frustration. So this is what creates suffering.

I kept attaching to the idea that Devon could be a well-behaved student who followed the rules at school and at home, but due to the injustices done to him as a toddler he simply could not control himself. Like a typical parent I desired only the best for this son of mine, and I clung to the notion that with good parenting, I could make him behave.

My lesson included recognizing that what I thought were my compassion and unconditional love for Devon were delusions. Desperately searching for light upon why I was in power struggles with Devon, I faced myself with hard-hitting questions.

Was the reason that I wanted Devon free of his problems ego driven? Did I simply want this son to be like my other children so that I could impress people with this wonderful, model family? Was I raising him according to my expectations instead of looking at Devon as an individual? And the hardest question of all, "Doesn't Devon need more help than we could possibly give him?" Looking at the truth can be painful. The answers to all of those questions were yes.

I remember once reading a profound passage on parenthood. It said that many mothers think they are being good parents, but some parenting is influenced by our own selfish egos. When we pacify a crying child, are we comforting him out of pure compassion or are we doing it just because we want the noise to stop? When we tell our children that they can't do things independent of us, is it because we want to keep them tied to us out of our own selfishness? And when our children are ill or depressed, do we wish them to recover quickly because we really want their company again or so we don't have to witness their pain?

With Devon's increasingly scary behavior I was forced to detach from my fantasies and accept him on his level, even though this was extremely difficult. I had spent well over 10 hard years trying to help him go down the straight and narrow path when he seemed to prefer the crooked one. Now I was forced to let go.

In order to change my suffering I had to change my vision. I had to see life with Devon as it was and concede that Devon needed much more help than Walt and I could give him.

Over the years we thought that Devon might need a live-in treatment facility, but neither Walt or I really wanted him to go. We kept hoping that with his next therapist, his next change of medication, or his next birthday he would get better. Instead, when Devon entered high school his mood swings intensified, and, as he grew taller and matured, his angry outbursts became more serious.

One morning the boys were tending to their chores before school. Ryan's job was to back the car out of the garage and warm it up for me. Devon's job, since our electric opener was broken, was to take the iron bars out of the slot that locked the garage door and lift it up for Ryan. But before that could happen the boys got into their usual morning bickering, which escalated into an unimaginable crisis.

From my bedroom, as I slipped on my heels, I could hear them shouting in the garage, which is attached to the house.

"I'm going to kick your butt," said Ryan. He was boiling over from Devon's constant threats.

"I'm going to kick your ass. I'm gonna get my friend's brother to get you, too," barked Devon. "He's in a gang."

According to the boys, this is what happened next. Ryan grabbed a hammer. "Okay here." He threw it to the ground and it slid to a stop at Devon's feet. "Take it, if you're so damn bad," he screamed. "Do something! Do something!" Devon shook his head, turning away and smiling to himself.

"I didn't think so, punk," said Ryan, also turning away. Suddenly out the corner of his eye, Ryan saw Devon lunging at him with one of the iron bars raised above his head. Ryan turned in time to grab the bar coming toward him.

Just as I was thinking about stopping the argument I heard a guttural scream. I sprinted into the garage, where I saw Ryan fighting to keep Devon from hitting him with the bar. I grabbed Devon from behind while trying to keep my balance. Suddenly I slipped, and we all tumbled to the floor.

Ryan managed to grab the bar from Devon and threw it out of the way. I then clambered to my feet and, seeing my ripped stockings and scuffed heels, I screamed at them both.

"He started it," said Ryan, huffing and sweating as he recounted what had happened, "and he tried to hit me in the head with that bar."

"Is that true, Devon?"

"Yeah, he kept daring me, so I was going to," said Devon, glaring with folded arms. "I'll kick your ass again, too," he said.

"Yeah, well, do it. Do it now," said Ryan, leaping toward Devon. I jumped in between them.

"Don't go to sleep," Devon warned.

My heart pounded spastically as I yelled at both of them to stop arguing. In all of our years together there had never been a physical fight between the kids. Walt and I simply didn't allow them to put their hands on one another. But this morning, not only were they fighting over a dangerous weapon, but someone could have been killed. My family was falling apart before my eyes.

Tearing up and seething with anger, I called Walt at work, telling him what happened. I hated mornings, which were always a battle. Walt, trying to find a solution, had even put the kids on separate schedules so they could get dressed without conflict. That worked, but they still had to ride to school together. Fire and gasoline.

"Okay," said Walt, "I'm coming back home to be with Devon. You take Jada and Ryan to school."

I sat with the kids, seething as we waited for Walt. A while back we had stopped leaving Devon home alone, and on this particular morning we knew that if he went to school angry it wouldn't take much to set him off there.

After dropping Jada off at her school, Ryan and I rode to Granada Hills High still unnerved by the morning. When we arrived I went straight into the temporary office of Sylvia, a visiting psychologist. She was stationed at Granada Hills High to assist the school's regular psychologist. They were continuing to see any student or teacher who had trouble coping with the campus suicide that had occurred a month earlier.

I had become friends with Sylvia, who had large compassionate brown eyes and a warm smile. She was easy to talk to, and I took advantage of that as I unloaded my morning drama. I told her that I had never seen Devon actually violent with anyone up until that morning.

"What scares me, Sylvia, is that wild look he gets in his eyes. I'm also afraid of Ryan and Jada hurting him. They're so mad at his constantly provoking them. No telling what they will do. They could hurt him out of rage or self-defense." I was shaking my head in disgust. "Children's Services could take them away and leave Devon in our home. Wouldn't that be something?"

"Since he knows you're looking for placement, he probably thinks he has nothing to lose," said Sylvia.

"Yeah, I know. Lately I've been sleeping with one eye open."

"It's getting that bad?"

"Walt's not worried about him hurting us, but I am. I don't know who this kid is anymore. He has fits of rage, and you never know what's going to set him off," I said as tears began flowing.

"You know, if you're this afraid of his being violent you can call in a PET team."

"A PET team? For animals?"

"No, PET stands for Psychiatric Emergency Team. They'll go to your house, pick up Devon, and take him to a psychiatric ward to observe him for a couple of days. They can't keep him long, though."

I called Walt and told him about the PET team. It consists of mental health workers who are empowered by the Lanterman-Petris-Short Act (LPS), a mental health law to place people in involuntary holding if they are a danger to themselves or to others. They can be held up to 72 hours while they are under evaluation. The PET team generally is called for in emergency situations.

"We've been talking. He's calm now. I got him under control," said Walt. "They don't need to come, but get their number just in case."

The PET Team was a frightening solution. We didn't want to admit that our son had spiraled so far down. I hung up the phone, hearing the sadness in Walt's voice. He has this tough veneer, but underneath he's a sensitive man who deeply loves his kids. In the last few months I knew that he was hurt and deeply disappointed that Devon's great progress in middle school was now spiraling downward fast. Walt always talked to Devon about his great potential, and what faith he had in him. It was Walt who had spotted Devon at the adoption party. He always believed that Devon could reach the sky and told him so. It was Walt's heart that Devon touched first.

Just after I finished writing about Devon's and Ryan's fight for this book, I took a break to watch the television news. Coincidentally there was a story about a 13-year-old and a 15 year-old-boy, nearly the same ages of my boys when the incident above happened. In Palmdale, California, at a Pony League baseball game not far from us, the 13-year-old had been detained for allegedly hitting the older teen in the head with a baseball bat. The 15-year-old died.

The iron bar fight propelled us with lighting speed to find Devon a placement. We were afraid that this was just the beginning of a violent wave with Devon. It also seemed that every day he tested us, daring us to send him away. As I look back now I see it was more a cry for help.

After looking into different residential mental health programs, again we had the problem that no one thought his behavior was that extreme. He didn't have a history of crime or violence that they thought warranted ongoing treatment. They didn't see that Devon was a walking disaster, waiting to happen.

Frustrated like Walt and I, Linda suggested that we place Devon in Hathaway's youth residential treatment program. When we agreed, she went to work trying to convince the executive director to take Devon into the program. At that time they were almost up to capacity with young men with backgrounds similar to Devon's. Finally, after my pleading that we had nowhere else to turn, the director agreed.

With Linda's strong letters and calls we got his school staff psychologist to do an emergency evaluation of Devon to get him into placement. It almost didn't happen since she was overwhelmed with work because my friend, the temporary psychologist, had been pulled from the school, and there were many cases before Devon's that had to be wrapped up before summer vacation.

At that time Devon still tested academically. He was a 9th grader reading at 12th grade level. Intellectually he was three grades ahead, but emotionally, like many children coming from the system, he was three years behind.

I often wrote to my Higher Power during those days, trying to make sense of what was happening. Journaling not only bought me clarity, it was my spiritual sanctuary.

"Dear God, we can no longer help Devon. I signed on to be his mother, but I have become his jailer. I just want to love him. We are way beyond being able to help him. I don't want Devon to go into placement, but it's not fair that he is now living in a house with everyone always angry at him. He does things constantly to provoke, and we're all constantly losing our temper with him. Devon needs to be accepted to boost his self-esteem and not be put down. For years we tried to accept him, but we don't have the strength anymore. It must be tough for him. He never shows his emotions, but I know he must be lonely inside. I would be. We have all tried so hard to work with Devon, but he pushes everyone away. He just can't seem to accept our love. Poor baby. I wonder which is the real Devon -- the sweet charmer or the demon? I know that underneath everyone's negative mask is good. Devon has that, too. God, please bless him. Please help us to help him. Help him to find his way."

~

While waiting for Devon to go into placement, I sometimes lied to myself, thinking things were not so bad with him. Maybe he was merely going though a bad phase. But no sooner would I convince myself of this then Devon would do something else outlandish. It was as if he sensed I was backpedaling and he was going to make sure that I followed through with our plan.

It was these moments that made me flash back on the workshops Walt and I facilitated at prisons. Our company had trained 80 prison educators and 60 lieutenants at the California State Prison, Los Angeles County, and Ironwood State Prison in Blythe, California, on team-building and effective communication. I thought of my first tour of the high-level prison yard at the California State Prison. Hundreds of young men, many of them extremely handsome, watched Walt and me being escorted by the assistant warden and correctional officers.

As I looked into the inmates' eyes I remembered statistics that I had read. Eighty percent of the inmates at a Chicago prison were former foster children. How many of these were past foster children who were detached from society because of RAD and never got help? How many were Devons? I know from my research that a large percentage of children who are in juvenile facilities have mental health issues. It takes a lot to help a child like Devon. Most people just give up on them. Thinking of the inmates fueled my mission to get Devon placed before he ended up in one of those prisons. Throughout the years, people warned us that could happen with him.

~

It always seems like our family gets crises in double doses. Walt's mother suddenly fell ill, and she was taken to a hospital. Walt, her only resource, rushed up north to Stockton, California to be by her side and get her affairs in order.

At the same time, Devon was about to move into Hathaway's residential treatment facility in the mountains, not far from our home. Thank God Linda was able to take care of this before we said goodbye to her on June 13, 2001. She was more than a therapist to us, she had become our friend.

As I journaled about our last meeting, her voice came into focus in my memory.

"I'm leaving for another position at Hathaway, Devon," said Linda. She was sitting a few feet across from Devon, who was slouched on her office couch, looking distant. "You remember that I told you I won't be your therapist anymore?" Devon looked down and shifted uncomfortably, refusing to look at her. He nodded slightly.

"How do you feel about going into placement?"

Devon's jaw muscles twitched. Lately it was the only sign that showed us he registered any type of feelings. Most of the time he acted as if he didn't care. He took his time before speaking.

"Well, Dad says it will be good because therapy hasn't helped," he said sarcastically.

"I really feel scared for you, Devon, although I think for right now residential is the best place for you," she said tenderly. "You'll learn to make better decisions. You're not going there because you're a bad person."

As she continued talking one tear streamed down Devon's somber face. It was a relief to see any type of emotion coming from him.

Linda reached over, placing her fingers on Devon's arm. "We don't know how to help you anymore, Devon. I feel sad that I won't be your therapist, but I will still be around. I hope in 10 years to get a card from you saying you went to college and you're getting married."

When they talked about his upcoming hearing for shoplifting, scheduled for the same day he would enter residential treatment, Devon slowly opened up. "I hope I can get in there so the judge won't put me in juvenile hall." Tears were now flowing from his eyes.

"You know, Devon, you are one of the few kids that I really feel close to." Devon began joking with her when she mentioned his tears.

"Those tears weren't real," he said, smiling. "I should go into acting."

"You're not that good of an actor," Linda replied.

We talked a little longer about arrangements, and then Devon and Linda hugged goodbye and he went into the waiting room. I stayed behind to talk to Linda.

"I'm curious, Linda," I said. "I always felt that Devon was teaching people about themselves. Did you learn anything from working with him?"

"I learned to be patient," said Linda. "I had a big agenda for him, but he has to go at his own pace. I learned that I was gullible at first. I was taken in by his charm. I also learned to be more candid with clients, because of you. I learned to respect trauma in adults, and how deeply wounded people like Devon can be. You know I did a case study on Devon. I talked in front of a class with my colleagues for about an hour about Devon. They told me that I was really getting emotional. I said yes. Devon grows on you."

"Doesn't it break your heart that it's come to this?" I asked.

Linda placed her hand over her heart. "Oh, yes," she said, her eyes filled with warmth and love. "Your family is really something special to me."

"You can't even begin to imagine how special you are to our family." We hugged for the last time.

Most of us go through life in a dream state while we're awake. We live in our past memories or fantasize about what's going to happen in the future. I certainly was living that way, fearing Walt's mother would die. I had been tossed in a whirlpool of anxiety over what Devon had done yesterday and afraid of what he might do next. Since both brought me terror I had no choice but to focus on the present. I focused not just on one day at a time but on one moment at a time. Living in the moment, taking in only my immediate tasks at hand, brought me peace. It was the only way I could find serenity since each day was a question mark.

It's funny how worlds collide. On the morning of July 3, 2001, Walt was in Stockton to place his mother temporarily in a rehab home, and I was on my way to take Devon to residential treatment.

Devon and I loaded the van with his bags in silence. I had taken the other kids to school earlier. I insisted that they tell Devon goodbye, which they didn't want to do. Before this day, Walt spent private time with Devon taking him shopping for new clothes and other items he needed. He said he told Devon how much he loved him and believed that he could turn his life around.

After loading the van, Devon and I headed for the probation appointment before checking into Hathaway residential treatment. We entered a county building in Pasadena filled with adults who were waiting to see their probation officers.

In a tiny office we met with a large, toned female probation officer who had a withering stare. Even Devon was unnerved by her.

After listening to me explain about Devon's history, therapy, and our appointment to check him into Hathaway, she looked through a report in a beige folder. She then turned and locked eyes with Devon, who was sitting a few feet away.

"You're a lucky young man that you are going into the facility today," she said icily. "I am going to drop the charges with Wal-Mart's permission. But let me tell you something. The next time you do anything like this, we don't care what your background is or what medication you're on, you're going to be locked up. Do you understand?"

Devon sat at quiet attention as she explained what it was like to live in juvenile hall. I could tell he was unnerved even though he tried to play it cool. When we got back in the car he told me that he was glad that he was going to Hathaway. This made the drive to Hathaway that much easier for me but not any less sad.

We turned off Little Tujunga Canyon Road to Gold Creek Road and followed the pavement at 10 miles per hour. Navigating this narrow passage that overlooked a thousand foot drop, doubts surfaced about the mission that I was on. But I was not going to turn back now. Not now. I couldn't.

It wasn't an easy decision to take this ride today. It ripped me apart like paper going through a shedder. I prayed that the end result would be wholeness for our family. I craved to find the part of me that I had left behind. Because of Devon, I had become an uptight bitch who had long ago lost her joy.

Today I was about to start a new chapter in my life. I was giving up trying to find my happiness through an ideal family. I was giving up trying to stay in control. I was giving up battling with Devon, who was even more controlling than I. I was giving it all up to God, who had the real control.

We passed a dry riverbed with another sign. FLOODING. Ten minutes later we had reached the mountaintop. Our destination. Suddenly my breath became shallow, and my palms sweaty. Perspiration poured down my back. I wished that Walter was with us.

I slid out of the front seat, inhaling the pine scents of Christmas on this hot summer day. Each year in these same mountains, our family cut down our Christmas tree. The air was thin, and still. It was exceptionally quiet, like the day after the holy day when everyone is exhausted from shopping and festivities. But this was no holiday.

Devon ambled out of the car and stood next to me as I looked around. He was nearly my height, handsome and slim in his oversized jeans and green plaid shirt. He flashed me his ever-present grin. I never could figure out if that expression meant he was in pain or happy. I always felt that it was really his mask.

I smiled at him and took a deep breath. A sudden gust of dry California wind ruffled my hair and the bushes surrounding us. I felt it was God's gentle hand pushing me forward with a whisper, "Don't turn back now."

I looked over toward the scattered, pastel, one-story structures that seemed oddly out of place. I pointed and led our way toward the two-tone green building with a sign. "Administration."

As we walked, I stole a glance at Devon out the corner of my eye. I wished that he would register some little bit of remorse or grief in his blank, brown eyes.

"How are you feeling?" I asked.

"Fine." I knew that he wasn't, but I had to ask. "Okay" and "fine" were his stock answers. Devon had taught himself long ago not to feel, not to trust.

I tried swallowing my sadness. My steps became more deliberate, pounding the pavement to suppress my anxiety. I had a mission to do.

When we reached the building, I pushed open the double glass doors, holding them for Devon. He walked slowly and solemnly past me into the residential treatment facility.

How could it have come to this? Why?

CHAPTER TWENTY-SEVEN

I drove back down that mountain without even a slip of paper proving that I admitted my son to a residential treatment program. When you take your dirty laundry to the cleaners, you at least get a receipt. I felt so empty driving home. Nothing to hold onto but the steering wheel.

Tears formed in my eyes as I reflected on what I had done with Devon. I filled out what seemed like hundreds of forms and answered a zillion questions about his history. I had answered them all before over the years with other mental health practitioners. But there was one question that I had never heard before, and I'll never forget it.

A tall, thin man fastened his eyes on mine and studied me closely when he asked, "Do you wish to relinquish your parenting rights?"

At first I was taken aback by the question, and then I quickly regrouped. "Oh, no," I shook my head vigorously. My voice rose an octave higher than normal. "No, I don't want to give up my rights!"

Sadly I would find out that this is the point where many parents give up their rights. I could never do that, and I knew Walt couldn't either, although we fantasized about it when Devon made us angry. Still we loved this child and we definitely weren't going to abandon him. That was his big problem. Devon's birth parents deserted him. Several social workers left him. He was moved from several foster care placements. His favorite therapist left for a job promotion. His grandmother, my mother, whom he loved so much died, and now his adoptive family was putting him in residential treatment.

I knew as a CASA volunteer that when a child enters the system, he especially needs someone to advocate for him. I was prepared to monitor every nuance of Devon's treatment at Hathaway the same way

I had stayed on top of his education and his outpatient treatments. To me, out of sight, didn't mean out of mind.

While I was driving down that mountain, the van and my heart seemed so empty. I had spent over a decade trying to work with Devon and his problems. Now, suddenly, he was gone. My mind was filled with a deep sadness wondering what he was facing, even though I also felt relief.

When I returned home, I walked into the living room and felt an incredible peaceful energy that I had never experienced before. Jada, who had been dropped off from school by a neighbor, came downstairs.

"Do you feel that peace in here, honey?" I asked. I couldn't believe the wave of serenity that engulfed the house, and I wanted someone else to witness it with me. Was I imagining this? It was as if I had been transported to a small chapel on the white beaches of the Bahamas. My body was unhinging for the first time in years, and I actually felt like I was levitating.

Jada nodded with a mega-watt smile and blurted, "Yeah, it's quiet now since Devon's gone." She then turned on her heels to leave the room with the exuberance of a slave suddenly freed from her oppressor. Devon had taunted Jada the most, probably because she was the youngest and petite.

I looked over at our family portrait hanging on the cream wall. Before Devon went into residential, I insisted that we take a family picture. I wanted him, and the entire family, to have a recent photo with all of us together. When the portrait was ready, I packed an 8 x10 copy in Devon's suitcase to take to Hathaway. It was important for him to remember that regardless of us living apart he was still part of our family. He would always have a home. Everyone was smiling or at least looked happy in the photo except Devon. He had a faraway expression of tentativeness in his eyes. Within days he would be leaving his home.

I looked out the window at the rose bush, remembering the day Lady Hummingbird cajoled her children to leave the nest. I had done the same for Devon. I stood there floating on a mystical wave of peace, thinking it was another spiritual sign. After weeks of anguish, worrying if Walt and I were doing the right thing for Devon, the energy in the living room that afternoon was my confirmation. We had made the right decision for him and for our family.

For the first few weeks at Hathaway, Devon followed his usual pattern in any new situation. He was angelic. When Walt and I went to see him at the end of his first week he seemed so content, but still I had to ask him if he wanted to come home.

"I'm okay, Mom," he said, smiling, putting his arm around my shoulders. "I'm fine." I was relieved that he was actually happy. Then I realized that this new experience was like camp to Devon.

He was living in a cottage with about 10 other guys of different ethnicities, and he was bonding with them. I had been prepared to see my son sad and angry for being locked away, but he wasn't. For the first time he was identifying with other kids who, like he, had been hated and ostracized because of their behaviors.

The facility, located in the mountains of the Angeles National Forest, was beautiful and only 10 minutes from our house.

Devon's room with a view, which he shared with another boy his age, was comfortable. It was filled with oak furniture, and looked better than his bedroom at home.

When Walt and I arrived, a few of Devon's housemates were laughing and joking with one another in the immaculate kitchen as they teamed to cook lunch. Others were gathered in the living room, watching a taped wrestling show, which I didn't approve of. Devon had just returned from swimming, which he loved. He didn't seem to be under any pressure, especially since the program was not a locked facility or strictly structured like Juvenile Hall, as we had expected.

The Hathaway residential program was the vacation Devon needed from the family. He had only been away a few times before. Once for a brief stay at a jointly financed UCLA and Jewish camp for special needs children. And then a few times when my friend Velvatine Sykes let Devon spend the night to play with her son. No one else was as brave.

Ryan and Jada would have been devastated to go to Hathaway, but since Devon had attachment issues, being detached from the family didn't seem to bother him so much. But that would soon change when the new experience got old. Furthermore, there were certain rules he would have to get use to.

A couple of weeks later, just when I had begun to settle into the thought that Devon would be in the treatment program for at least a year, we got an earth-shaking call. He had repeated the same vicious attack on a kid that he had made against Ryan. An argument had erupted between Devon and a 17-year-old in the gym, and in a fit of rage Devon picked up a free weight and went after the older boy. Fortunately staff members corralled him in time.

I thought immediately of the Hathaway director who had been reticent about allowing Devon into Hathaway. I knew he wasn't going to tolerate much of this type of behavior. If Devon didn't get a grip he would -- Lord forbid -- be sent home.

In the days to follow I received a string of phone calls from his therapist, a short young man about 30, whom I had no faith in. I wished that Linda could have continued counseling him because I knew she could see through his shenanigans. Unfortunately for us, she was so good that she was at that time settling into her new director job.

I knew Devon's new therapist had no idea what to do with him, especially when he told me that Devon would behave better with family time. Walt and I were already seeing Devon religiously each Sunday, but the therapist thought that wasn't enough. He reminded me of one middle school teacher who, trying to find ways to help Devon behave, suggested that I have a chat with him about his behavior over cookies and milk. Yeah, right!

The Hathaway therapist said that every week we should come get him and take him to a movie or on some other outing. First, what about our other kids? If we gave Devon special weekends we would have to do it equally with Ryan and Jada. How in the world could we do all three every weekend? Second, where were we going to get the time to spend a half day with Devon? Besides housework and yard work on the weekends, Walt and I were already running split errands, taking Ryan and Jada in different directions to their extracurricular activities.

I wanted to yell at him, "You dummy, do you think that if special time was all that it took for Devon to behave, that he would be where he is today?" Ironically, whenever we did give special time to Devon, like clockwork the next day he would go berserk. It was a natural response for a child with RAD to push people away when they got too close. Yes, Devon, like most children, needed special time, but he needed so much more.

Over the weeks ahead I was polite with his therapist, although I knew he knew I wasn't impressed with him or our family counseling sessions. I had become an expert on mental health experts since Devon had seen so many. And I made no bones about facing up to them when I thought they were not effective at treating Devon. I wasn't rude, just truthful. It wasn't their fault. They simply needed RAD training, which was difficult to find in a therapist. Conventional therapy just doesn't work with these types of children.

During this time I joined the newly formed Hathaway Parent Advisory Board, which met monthly. I got Lori Waldinger to be the featured speaker at our first event to teach parents how to get services for their children at school. It was a good little group. We came up with improvement suggestions for Hathaway, and they were quickly implemented. We felt that Hathaway's outpatient side really cared about perfecting its service. I wasn't so sure that the residential side wanted that kind of involvement.

Soon phone calls from Hathaway became more frequent because Devon was becoming increasingly difficult. Obviously his honeymoon stage was over, and the real Devon was emerging. True to his pattern at new schools, Devon's behavior would quickly change when he learned the lay of the land. At Hathaway, it didn't take him long.

One day we got a call that was about to blow the lid off of his treatment. Devon's therapist said he was trying to help Devon stay in the program, and did I have any ideas to make him behave? I thought, "if I knew the answer to that one he would still be at home."

In the days ahead I was filled with anxiety, worried that any day Devon would boomerang back home because they couldn't control him. The calm I first felt when Devon went to Hathaway had now left my body.

The latest call I got from his therapist was about Devon constantly breaking the rules by passing notes to a girl when they were in the dining room. The therapist had intercepted Devon's note requesting to have sex with the girl. She was 12 and Devon had just turned 15. Emotionally, according to his psychiatrist at Hathaway, he was 2 years old, being stuck at the stage when he was abused in foster care.

I explained to the therapist how Devon's mind worked, and how this defiance of authority was a typical RAD symptom. But I knew he secretly snickered at me. I was just a mother, a lay person, diagnosing Devon. After all, he was the expert. I respected that, but I still told him what I thought.

"You have to look deeper than the proposition he made to the girl," I told him. "Devon continuously does these things because he knows it's a way to push your buttons and get kicked out of Hathaway."

When I got off the phone I was extremely nervous over the therapist being anxious about Devon. I feared that the therapist was going to need therapy himself over my child. He had admitted that Devon was the toughest case he had ever encountered. I wanted to tell him to fasten his seat belt because it probably was going to get worse before it got better. I had been in, and witnessed, these power struggles with Devon before. Linda used to show Devon how stubborn he could be by drawing a parallel with a mule.

In the meantime the therapist was attempting to go into deep treatment with him by delving into the sexual and physical abuse of his past in foster care. This had never been addressed before. The deeper the therapist probed with Devon, the more Devon acted out, refusing to follow the rules.

Since I had signed the authorization for Hathaway to inform me about Devon's discipline problems, I was called constantly. One day his therapist said that because Devon kept insisting on propositioning the young girl, they had called the sheriff's office. A deputy came to talk to Devon about his behavior because the girl was so young. In no way did I condone Devon's actions, but it seemed that his desires were normal, given that teens had raging hormones at that age. The Alan Guttmacher Institute (AGI), a nonprofit organization focusing on sexual and reproductive health research, as well as policy analysis and public education, released a study in 1999 when Devon was at Hathaway. It said 7 out of 10 boys are sexually experienced at age 15.

I figured that having a sheriff visit Devon on campus was more about Devon's defiance of authority than just sexual propositioning, as I was told. His behavior got so bad that one time he had to be physically restrained by staff.

Devon continued propositioning girls for sex, which the Hathaway officials said threatened their license. But I knew for Devon it wasn't just about having sex. It was his way of manipulating the staff, who were frustrated over his refusal to follow rules. He knew that he had struck a nerve and challenged the one thing that the Hathaway staff wouldn't tolerate.

I'll never forget a remark from his therapist.

"Don't worry. We'll get everything under control. He won't be kicked out. We want to try to work with him." Somehow I wasn't comforted.

Less than a week later we received another call from his therapist, asking if Walt and I would come up to Hathaway. He wanted to brainstorm ways to keep Devon in the program since he was growing worse.

When we walked into the meeting room, immediately I knew we were in trouble. I was shocked to see so many people in what I thought was going to be an intimate little brainstorming session. Present were his therapist, the house unit manager, the head of psychiatry, a doctor who supervises the nurses, one of Devon's teachers, a supervisor who supervises the supervisors, and the Department of Mental Health social worker assigned to Devon's case. This meeting was going to be more serious than we were led to believe.

I don't remember who said what because I felt myself go into a panic attack complete with heart palpitations. But I remember specifically what was said.

"Mr. and Mrs. Jackson," someone began, "we had thought that we should meet with you to discuss ways to keep Devon in the program, but now we think it's best that Devon leaves. He needs a higher level of structure than we can give him." I darted my eyes to the therapist. He was looking down, and when he did look up, he avoided eye contact with me.

I couldn't speak. I felt so betrayed and devastated. Walt took over and asked the questions that flooded my mind. All I could think about was that I was lied to. How could they do this? I heard them reiterate that Devon's propositioning could get their license taken away. And then the bomb dropped.

"He will have to leave Hathaway in 14 days."

"But we don't have any place to put him," I said weakly. Walt then explained our fears. Now that they had begun deep therapy, delving into Devon's abuse from his foster care days, he was a raw nerve. Putting him out of the program was like operating on a patient and then throwing him out of the hospital without closing the wound.

Waves of acid welled up in my stomach. How could they ask for a brainstorming meeting and then kick Devon out of the program? They knew we were willing to work with them. Walt and I were even told by Devon's teacher at the open house that he wished all of his parents cared as much. We were surprised that, despite there being six cottages filled with kids in residential treatment, we were among the few parents who had attended that night. Why didn't the parents come?

In the meeting, though we were desperate, I got a sense that, unlike with Linda, there wasn't the deep concern for Devon's well-being. I could have been wrong, but I got that impression from one of the ladies in charge of that meeting, who was crocheting a sweater as we discussed Devon leaving. Right away I knew what she thought of us and Devon.

"Mr. and Mrs. Jackson, you do not have to claim Devon," a voice wafted in the air, bringing the room to dead silence.

"What do you mean?" asked Walt.

"You can leave him here," said the voice, "and we can call the Department of Children and Family Services to come get him. They'll take him into custody."

Another voice spoke up, "If you do that, charges could be brought against you."

"We don't want to abandon him," said Walt abruptly.

"Well," replied the voice, "you'll have to find another placement."

After the meeting I walked out of the room like a zombie. I had never felt so helpless. The only good result was meeting Amida, a dark-haired, Jewish caseworker from the Department of Mental Health who was assigned to Devon's case.

Amida quickly became our new best friend. "I'll find Devon another placement." I heard angels singing.

During the following days Amida and I were on the phone constantly as I combed the telephone books and surfed the Internet, trying to help her find another program. I also called lawyers to see if our dismissal from Hathaway was legal. It seemed to be.

I wondered how many kids have been kicked out of programs like this? How many parents were forced to abandon them because they were to scared to bring them home? When you live for years in turmoil like we did, and then find peace, you definitely don't want to go back into hell.

Even though I had worked hard with mindfulness meditations on my anger, I had to practice even harder because I kept thinking that we had been ambushed in that meeting. Here we were, thinking that we were going to brainstorm to help Devon stay there, and instead we're told he's getting the boot.

I thought later maybe it was because we were the type of parents who questioned everything, and that irritated the staff. It was natural for us to stay involved and ask questions. Over the years I learned that many parents don't question authority figures as we have always done. Walt and I wanted to know Devon's Hathaway agenda and even requested a copy although it wasn't standard procedure to give it out to parents.

As I searched for residential programs I called Amida to tell her what I found. She was already steps ahead of me. The problem in getting Devon placed was that even though he had been sexually propositioning girls, he wasn't classified as a sexual predator. Facilities that had those types of kids were afraid he would be preyed upon. Those that didn't feared that because he kept making propositions, he could act on them. That wasn't my fear. I knew he was simply pushing buttons to get out of Hathaway, but they were right to be protective of their other clients.

There was no doubt that Devon needed a higher level of structure, but since he hadn't been convicted of a crime, there were no locked facilities he was eligible to enter that just treated emotional problems. Our son, as always, was falling in between the cracks. However I would be damned if I let him slip through.

Two days before Hathaway's deadline I was home alone, crying in front of our altar with burning candles. The tabletop fountain was running, but I was pouring out the most water as I prayed.

"God, please help us. You know we do not want to abandon Devon, but we can't bring him back here. Not now. They've started deep therapy. I know that's the reason he's even more defiant than before. If he feels he can beat the system I know we'll pay hell if he comes back here without being treated. Ryan and Jada have been through so much with Devon. They deserve the peace we've had since he's been gone. What should we do, God? Please, please help us... Point the way."

Suddenly a deep calm engulfed me, and I had an idea.

I grabbed a pen and paper and began drafting an e-mail that I was going to send to family and friends. I explained exactly what had happened about Devon and that I was going to send out a press release. The press release would say that we are being forced to abandon Devon since we cannot bring him back in the house to endanger our other kids with his rage. I wanted them to know that we could not abandon Devon, but we couldn't bring him home either. Maybe press attention would bring some solution. Perhaps someone would come forth with a program for him. But I especially wanted the world to know what parents of special needs children went through.

I sent the e-mail to a few people, but before writing the press release I called Amida to tell her what I was going to do. She didn't answer her phone, but I left a message.

Immediately my phone rang. "Ms. Jackson, aren't you pleased with the services?"

"Amida, this is no reflection on you or the Department of Mental Health, but I want people to know, after all of the years of struggling to find Devon help, it has come to this. My husband and I are good parents. We are put in a corner. We have no choice."

"Well can you wait just a little longer Ms. Jackson? I've still got a couple of facilities that haven't called me back. Don't do anything drastic. Just wait, please."

"Okay Amida, but only for you. I know you're really trying to help us."

When I got off the phone with the social worker, I got another call immediately from Julie, a friend who had received my e-mail. She was once a mental health worker for the State of California.

"Listen, you can get a stay-put order to the facility to give you more time."

"A stay-put order? What's that?"

"A stay-put rule, or a stay-put order. It's 'due process.' That's when you can request a pre-hearing conference or a hearing. Until things get settled, Devon's placement is considered to be pending. So that means as far as the facility goes, they have to abide by the law and keep him there. That's what's meant by a stay-put order."

"Oh, my God! Thank you, thank you, Julie. Why don't parents know about this?"

"Maybe because parents would get them and the facilities would be controlled by parents."

"Yep, that's right, and I'm certainly going to get one. Thanks so much. It sure helps having friends in high places."

We both laughed, and when we hung up I jumped on the Internet and found the state department in Sacramento that issues stay-put orders. I was so grateful for my journalist training that had led me to some very helpful people. I stayed up all night downloading and filling out the stay-put forms. This was better than the press release I was going to put out. I would get immediate results.

Amazingly, the next afternoon I got a "friendly" call from Devon's therapist. That morning I had formerly applied for the order, and I wondered if Hathaway had received the order so fast. I wasn't going to bring up what I had been doing all night long. I wanted the therapist to be caught off guard. I wanted revenge. I itched to say, "Surprise, Devon is staying with you." Instead I just politely said, "No, we haven't found placement."

"Well, I hope you do," he said. "I wouldn't want the Department of Children and Family Services to file charges against you."

I was livid when I got off the phone at his comment, but at the same time I had a huge Cheshire cat grin pasted on my face. My ego and my aggressive television industry competitive spirit was fired up, and I intended to win. Sadly, Devon was going to lose either way.

I never found out how effective the stay-put order was because something else more important happened.

On the 13th day before Hathaway's deadline for us to move Devon, I was pumping gas into our green van when my cell phone rang.

"Ms. Jackson, guess what?" It was Amida. Her voice was electric. She could barely contain her excitement. "Devereux will take Devon!"

"Devereux?" I hadn't heard of them even though I thought I knew of every facility in California. "Where's Devereux?"

"It's the only place that will take him, Ms. Jackson. It's in Texas."

I worried for a moment that it was so far away, but we didn't have a choice.

"Tha -- that's okay, Amida, we'll have to take him there." When I snapped my cell phone closed, my legs began to buckle. I didn't have to fight another battle as I was prepared to do with the stay-put order. I managed to hang the gas nozzle back on the pump. I then crawled back into the van, threw my head back against the headrest, and collapsed, bawling with sheer relief.

I pleaded with Walt to let me be the one to take Devon to Texas even though he wanted to go since he had been out of town when Devon entered Hathaway. I wanted him to stay home with Ryan and Jada because I had been so involved with every detail of Devon's history. I had two huge binders filled with every conversation, every detail that I had recorded. I needed to follow through on this placement. I had to see where he would be staying.

It was just a few weeks after the fateful September 11th attack on our country when I was on my way with Devon to Texas. This was not a sad trip for me, like going to Hathaway, probably because, like everyone else, I was filled with so much anxiety over terrorist warnings. At that time the country thought they would strike again at any moment.

The Los Angeles International Airport was tense. Reports on the news said that L.A. was one of the terrorist targets. Everyone seemed nervous about flying, but I was more concerned about the terror I was traveling with. Devon's eyes were smoldering with rage, and he now seemed to have a permanent scowl. He was constantly searched because his airline ticket was specially tagged, alerting authorities that he was from a mental health facility. I don't think I exhaled once during that trip. I felt that the bomb that airport security was watching for was hidden inside of my son's soul.

Adding to the tension was the silence between Devon and me. He probably said all of 20 words to me on our trip. And those were only "Nope" and "Yeah" responses to my questions. He was more distant than I had ever known him to be, but he had reasons to be. Devon had to be feeling abandoned by his family again, going into another facility. He had been abandoned by his favorite therapist, Linda, and abandoned by the Hathaway residential treatment team. He was going to live halfway across the country not knowing a soul. Who wouldn't be angry and scared?

The Devereux Treatment Network in League City, Texas, is just minutes from downtown Houston. The red brick buildings with huge white pillars, sitting on acres of rich green land, were absolutely beautiful. We spotted one glaring feature as we entered unit four which Devon would soon call home. Locked doors.

We rang a bell, and Annie, a smiling, pretty lady with a Jamaican accent, came to the door jingling a set of jailer's keys as she opened it for us. As soon as we stepped inside she greeted us like long-lost relatives with such warmth. I took it as a sign Devon was in the right place. She locked the door behind us and then unlocked another door that opened into the main hallway of the unit.

We followed her, walking into the reception area where a line of curious teenage boys watched us intently. They were waiting to be escorted to dinner across campus. Devon refused to look at them. Playing to his audience, he sprawled out on the sofa dramatically with his CD earphones on his head, patting his loud, baby blue suede shoes. He was putting on a show for the teens, who soon began whispering among themselves about the new kid from California.

A tall, male staff member began leading the orderly line out the door to the cafeteria across campus when a large man, who could have been a football player with a shaven head, came to me, introducing himself as Sam. He then turned to Devon.

"Hello, Devon. I'm Sam. Welcome to Devereux." After Devon shook hands limply with no eye contact, Sam said, "You'll have to give me your CD player, young man."

Devon looked up at him as if he would spit in his face, but instead he rolled his eyes and slowly handed over the player.

"You have to earn music privileges around here," Sam told him. I could barely contain my glee. Now this is what I hoped for. Strict discipline.

After touring the facility with Devon and staff members I had a few moments with Devon alone. I reminded him how much Walt and I loved him. I told him that he could be out of the program and back home real soon if he followed their rules and worked the program. He nodded, barely saying a word. We hugged, and again I got teary-eyed, wanting to hold him longer.

I was taken back to the airport by a staff member who spoke like most of the staff, warmly in a heavy southern accent. She explained the program, how much they care about kids at Devereux, and how the clients had strict rules to follow. I kept thinking why in the world did I have to take him all the way to Texas to get this help?

My body was numb as I walked to board my flight. Even though I was sad that Devon would be so far away I was comforted by the Devereux staff. They assured me that Devon wouldn't be playing any more games as he had done with his therapists. At Devereux they wouldn't participate in any power struggles that he had engaged people in the past, and he would have no more excuses. They had full faith that he would excel to his full potential and become the young man of whom everyone, including himself, could be proud.

As I passed a gift shop I was thinking Devon was finally going to get the help he needed, when I saw a sign. It was another spiritual confirmation:

"Don't mess with Texas."

CHAPTER TWENTY-EIGHT

Devon went through his usual honeymoon stage at Devereux. He was so perfectly well-mannered and so cooperative that his case worker told me he didn't see why Devon was in the program. Blood drained from my face as I pondered that Devon could be rejected from Devereux because he was too good. I knew my son. It was another tactic to get discharged.

"Don't worry, Jan," said Walt. "He won't be able to keep that front up long."

He was right. Within several months Devon was cursing and physically fighting staff and other young clients. He was like a wild animal, having to be restrained and placed in a quiet room numerous times to cool off. Never could I have dreamed that my son would have to be locked in a padded room to keep him from hurting himself or others.

Obviously Devon had met his match with the Devereux staff. Despite the program being highly structured, the clients could earn points to go on field trips to amusement parks, the beach, the mall, and a variety of other outings. Devon didn't earn one.

The Devereux psychiatrist diagnosed Devon as depressed and oppositionally defiant. But the main diagnosis was Reactive Attachment Disorder. Hallelujah! I knew it! I knew it. RAD is what I researched and believed Devon had all along, but no one seemed to know what that was. The Devereux people not only knew about RAD, but more importantly, how to treat the disorder. It was going to take 24 hour attention and some tough love.

Although there were young people from all over the nation in the program, Devon had been one of staff's biggest challenges. He tried everything to unnerve them but nothing worked. Fortunately, the staff was united and consistent with his treatment. No one gave in to him or gave up on his treatment, not even when he said he didn't want to live.

I'll never forget talking to one of the staff members one evening when I called to check on him. "Devon has been placed on suicide watch."

My world came to a screeching halt. I was frozen, barely able to mouth the word, "Suicide?" I had always thought of Devon as this super-tough kid. After the young man committed suicide at Granada Hills High School, I was vigilant with Devon, but deep in my heart I didn't think that he, too, would attempt suicide.

"Don't worry, Mrs. Jackson, he's watched every minute."

I had full faith in the Devereux staff. Something inside of me knew that they could handle him. I just had a hard time wrapping my mind around the thought that Devon didn't want to be in this world.

Eventually he moved out of that depression. The days and months passed, and even though girls were housed in the same unit, closer than at Hathaway, Devon didn't sexually proposition one of them. It was as I suspected. He had used sexual harassment to push the Hathaway staff buttons, but he couldn't find those buttons with the Devereux staff.

Though I had been furious over how Hathaway handled Devon's dismissal, I realized they simply didn't have the program to treat a RAD child. Few places did.

Would I recommend Hathaway to other parents today? Absolutely, in a heartbeat, especially the outpatient program. They have an excellent reputation, and they have helped many children and families throughout the years. To this day I am still on their parent advisory board. But I learned that even the best treatment programs simply may not be right for certain children.

Devon's new therapist at Devereux was Diane, a laser-sharp, middle-aged, sweet lady with a heavy Texas accent and plenty of homespun wisdom. She read Devon instantly and knew exactly what kind of treatment he needed, but administering it to him would challenge her like rest of the Devereux staff.

For a year, Devon refused to follow the rules and was so disruptive that he could go to school in only 15 minute intervals before staff had to take him out of class. He spent a lot of time doing assignments in his bedroom while others were in school.

People have asked me through the years how the abuse in Devon's pre-school years could still have adverse effects on him as a teen. That's one of the residuals of RAD, if untreated. It amazed the staff how Devon would sabotage himself. It didn't seem that he could even manage small privileges such as eating in the cafeteria with the other kids. He ate a lot of meals in his room because he refused to cooperate.

Despite Devon's being on several medications for depression and mood swings, and even being placed on a modified program to help him achieve some success, he still refused to accept the program. Still we supported him every way that we could.

Every two weeks Walt and I were in family therapy with Devon over the phone for an hour, and we talked to him at least every other day. We flew to see Devon every other month. For the first two years, our visits with him were confined to a visiting room on campus since Devon did not earn the privilege of going off campus, or spending nights in the hotel with us.

I remember being on the phone constantly, talking to the unit nurse, his therapist, the case coordinator, his teacher, and the night staff, trying to monitor Devon's behaviors. I was convinced that the Devereux team fell out of heaven. They managed Devon with tough love and refused to give into his antics. Their consistency worked. After the first year of sitting in his room, Devon finally made up his mind to start working the program.

It was hard for him, but he was developing trust and a respect for the staff, something RAD children find difficult to do. He still didn't follow the rules entirely, but now at least he was trying.

What could have been a six-month to one-year stay at Devereux for Devon turned into three years. It took this long a time to heal the compulsions of reactive attachment disorder that had become his survival mechanism.

At last we began seeing a wonderful change in Devon. The most obvious difference was that he began articulating his feelings, and caring for ours. For the first time we were able to have long, interactive conversations with him. He even sent me a white stuffed bear that he had won at a carnival held on campus. For my birthday, he made me a bracelet in his crafts class, and another time, Devon sent me a horse he had drawn. Before he entered Devereux, he either skipped giving me presents for my birthday, or gave me something that he half-way finished making. Now the gifts came just because he wanted me to have them.

It was now a pleasure talking to him about the Devereux program, the team, and about his having faith in God. The more he came out of his shell and expounded on what was going on inside of him, the less defiant he became. The acting-out incidents, which were mathematically tracked by the staff, decreased and were reported to Walt and me.

My son was being reborn. His treatment was going well, and he was proud of himself for working the program. We were thrilled at his continuing progress until I got a call that would rock my world a couple of days before Christmas.

"Mrs. Jackson," began his caseworker, "we found out this afternoon that Devon's blood count is abnormal. We're taking him to the Children's Texas Cancer Hospital in the morning for further testing."

Walt and I had just returned from Devereux, celebrating the holiday early with Devon so that we could be home for Christmas with Ryan and Jada. How could this be happening?

"Should I get on the next plane?"

"No, not at this time. Let's just wait and see what the tests show. You may need to come then and no telling for how long."

We all agreed, including Devon, that Walt and I would wait. It could take several weeks to get the results back. The holidays would cause lab delays.

"Are you worried, honey?" I asked Devon as I clutched the phone tightly.

"No, not really. I'll be alright, Mom." I wished that I could reach through the phone to hold him. Never had I felt so guilty about being so far away from him. He then went on to tell me about the activities Devereux had lined up for the kids. The staff and the board of directors were going all out with tons of gifts for the children. Some didn't have families or they were deserted by them when they came to Devereux.

"You know if you want us to, Dad and I would get on the next plane."

"No, Mom, I'll be fine. Annie is taking me there." Annie, the unit nurse with the beautiful Jamaican accent and electric smile, had become his surrogate mother, and she became like a sister to me. She, like the other nurse, Maggie, talked endlessly to Devon about getting his act together so he could go home and about how lucky he was to have parents who cared. When Annie was with him, which was nearly 24/7, I knew everything was okay. We had endless phone conversations about Devon.

My biggest fear now was that Devon's progress could unravel. If he had cancer that would be the only reason that Devereux would send him back home in the middle of his treatment. The staff, which refused to give up on him, surrounded Devon with love, and he was changing and healing under their care. I was afraid, after searching for help for years and finally finding Devereux, that his treatment would again be disrupted. If Devon had cancer, how would we take care of him and his RAD problems?

I don't ever remember praying for anything as hard as I prayed that Devon did not have cancer. When I wasn't praying, I disciplined myself to live in the moment, watching my breaths to keep myself calm. It was too painful to let my mind drift to "What ifs."

Finally, after the holidays, we got the test results. The medications Devon was taking had lowered his white cell count. By changing his prescriptions his blood count returned to normal.

Two and a half years passed and Devon, now 17, had finally earned the privilege of coming home for a visit. It would be a matter of months before his discharge. Would the family be ready?

Ryan was now a freshman at the University of Southern California, and Jada was a junior at Granada Hills High School.

For months we had been hearing from the Devereux staff how much Devon had changed. I heard it in our phone conversations with Devon, saw it in Devereux's monthly behavioral reports and on his report card, but still the thought of Devon returning home was frightening. We still didn't know what to expect. His change had occurred under the watchful eyes of a 24 hour staff. How would he do at home?

My mind raced through a variety of negative scenarios, and it seemed that every time I turned on the television or read a newspaper, I learned of somebody killing a family member. A father kills his wife and children. A son kills his parents. I felt like I was drowning.

My mind was pulled overboard, and I was wading through a sea of terrifying thoughts when I wasn't practicing living in the moment. Would Devon take revenge on us for sending him away? Would he hurt Ryan or Jada to hurt us? Was he jealous of them for staying at home and doing the right things?

It didn't help that one of my friends, who was the director of a youth facility for special needs, warned me: "Usually mentally and emotionally disturbed kids don't take their medications once they leave a facility. They do all kinds of things, mainly violent." Despite her trying to be helpful she wasn't aware that she was terrifying me.

The day Devon was scheduled to visit home seemed to roll around fast. Too fast. We had spent weeks psyching ourselves up, and I still wasn't ready.

That morning Walt and I were playing tag team as usual, taxiing the kids to different places. Even though Ryan was living on campus, he needed us to take him places since he didn't have a car. Our schedules conflicted, and I wanted to be the one to pick up Devon from the airport. I felt since it was I who had sent him away, I should be the one to bring him home.

Often I thought that it was my karma to be so close to Devon. Perhaps because of unfinished business with Larry, my late, alcoholic stepfather. I used to wonder if Devon was a reincarnation of Larry, who never made peace with his demons before dying. They both acted out. Devon because of his past in the foster system, and my stepfather because of the bottle.

I took Jada with me to the airport, not only for support but because I thought that Devon should have some kind of welcome home delegation to greet him. It would also be healing for her since he used to constantly provoke Jada. He used to play her like a pinball machine. She was the silver ball bouncing off the walls trying to get away from him.

"Leave me alone, Devon!" she would scream. There would be times when she would fall to the ground, shrieking like a wounded animal and kicking her feet, pounding the ground with her fists. During those times Jada, herself, seemed as dangerous as a wounded animal. Even though she was petite, much smaller than Devon, I was always afraid that she would attack him with something.

We sat at LAX airport in the seats closest to the glass doors the passengers would be passing through after coming off an escalator. Nearby were two tour guides -- a middle-aged man, and a young, blonde, girl -- both dressed in bright yellow shirts bearing their company emblems. They anxiously stood by the doors holding up signs, "Hawaii Tours," as they waited for their clients. I wished that I was going with them.

Next to them was a man in shorts, holding flowers and chatting with a teen and a pre-teen girl. When they spotted a woman coming off the escalator from an arriving flight, the girls jumped up and down and shrieked with excitement. Their mother had come home. We didn't feel that kind of excitement waiting for Devon.

As Jada and I watched people hug their loved ones and talk excitedly, I felt sick to my stomach. My whole body seemed to tremble from a mini-earthquake like those I had felt so many times living in California.

I felt like my emotional scars from struggling for so long with Devon were open wounds again.

"How do you feel?" I asked Jada.

"Strange," she said, lightly rubbing her stomach.

"Your tummy hurt?"

She nodded, wincing. Ever since she was adopted at age 4, she had stomach problems. Her foster mother sent a huge bottle of mineral oil with her when she came to live with us. After a battery of medical tests that found nothing wrong, I kept her under close observation. I surmised that her stomach got upset when she was stressed. Of course she would be queasy now. We were going back in time, and neither of us felt prepared. I had a different reaction. I felt like a slave on the auction block. My nerves were bare and raw, whipped by years of emotional slavery in Devon's bondage.

Suddenly I saw him. He reminded me of a floating ghost as he descended down the escalator in a crowd. My breath quickened as I watched him walking toward the glass doors that separated the passengers from us. Just before going through the door he stopped and looked behind him. He was waiting for someone. Moments later I saw a Devereux staff member walk up behind him with another client from the treatment facility who was clearly mentally disturbed and needed help.

Devon said something to the man, and they both looked over at us while other passengers poured past them. The staff member then shook hands with Devon, who walked through the doors and headed in our direction.

As I stood up I couldn't believe my eyes. He looked so mature dressed in a light gray suit and tie. I had never seen him look so formal except when he was little. Walt used to dress him and Ryan like little business men in suits for church services. But seeing him with this new image as a young adult was mind-boggling. Like his clothes, he appeared very reserved.

"Hey," said Devon, greeting me with a smile.

"Remember what I told you?" I said, playfully pinching his nose and smiling. "Hay is for horses."

"Oh yeah, right. Hi, Mom." We then reached to hug one another. I loved his hugs, especially when we hadn't seen one another for a while. They were now long and tight. It was if his arms said the words that his mouth couldn't form. But I felt them through his embrace. "Mom, hold me. I missed you."

Without eye contact, Jada and Devon embraced awkwardly for a quick, limp hug, and both turned away quickly. We then headed to the baggage area.

When Devon's huge, shapeless, brown suitcase arrived, I was reminded of when he first came to live with us. He came with a small, battered, yellow suitcase filled with faded clothes that were either too big or too small for him. None of them appeared to be his.

Devon struggled to lift his bag off the carousel and then flung his backpack over his shoulder. The suitcase was so old that it didn't have wheels.

"Let me help you carry that."

"No, Mom, I have it," he said politely. Gone was the defiance in his voice of the old Devon. He now exuded a gentler, kinder energy. I knew that he was trying to show me his independence and how much he had grown up.

When we arrived in the parking lot he admired our new, black SUV as he crawled into the front seat beside me. "This is nice."

As we headed out of the airport, Devon soaked up the sights like an amazed tourist landing in Hollywood.

"Wow, they sure have changed things!"

I thought of how a convict must feel tasting freedom for the first time in years. My heart sank at the thought of how long he had been away from home.

"Yeah, that's right." I fought a rising lump in my throat. "You haven't seen the airport since they've been adding on, huh?"

"No," he said with wide eyes, his head rotating from side to side.

My body was still tensed, wondering who was this person who had crawled into my car? Jada was silent in the back seat, but I knew she was thinking the same. Had he changed? Would he slink back to his old antics? How long would this new and improved Devon last?

I practiced mindfulness as we headed home, observing my frantic thoughts without judgment. They came like pouring rain. Relentless. Often they were more like thunderstorms.

As my mind calmed from the quick meditation, I thought about Devon's sleeping arrangements at home. He would sleep in the loft we used as a meditation room that overlooked our living room. It had squeaky floorboards which on this day I was glad that we didn't have fixed. I thought if he roamed the house at night I would wake up. For years Devon had problems sleeping, and I didn't want to be caught off guard. Jada and I half-heartedly joked that we would take shifts sleeping when he came home.

I thought of my aunt's son, Jack, a pre-med college student with top honors who became addicted to drugs. One night, when he was home on Christmas break, my aunt awakened to him standing over her bed with a knife. She was able to talk him into a rehabilitation facility, but he promptly left the program. A couple of months later he got into a fight and was stabbed and killed. The thought of Jack had always haunted me. I heard that story as a child, and it explains why people say adult conversations should be left between adults.

When I told Walt my fears about Devon, he brushed them off. He was never afraid of him or anyone else for that matter. His strength, as usual, gave me strength to conquer my fears.

I went back to practicing mindfulness as we sat on the 405 Freeway, stuck in traffic. Devon was content listening to the radio as his head continued pivoting, soaking in the sights. At times frantic thoughts invaded my mind like enemy soldiers. But the more I observed them, the less strength they had. Finally they laid down their swords and disappeared entirely.

When we arrived home Devon got out of the car, looking around as if seeing the neighborhood for the first time. He grabbed his bags and went up the walkway. The door opened and Walt greeted us. He smiled, looking Devon up and down. I knew that Walt was pleased and surprised, as I was, over how much our son had matured. When they hugged he patted Devon on the back.

We all stood there for an awkward moment. I was amazed at how tall Devon's 5'11" frame seemed in the entryway. We had seen him just two months earlier when he appeared so much shorter than Walt. Now he had only two inches to go to catch up to his dad.

"I told Ryan that you wouldn't be sleeping in his room, Dev, so you have to stay up there," I said, pointing to the loft. It was only fair since he used to steal Ryan's belongings. Even though Ryan was away at school and didn't use his room except during school vacations and holidays, he had plenty of personal items there that we thought Devon might steal.

"That's okay, Mom," he said, walking upstairs to the loft.

As I watched him trying to balance the awkward suitcase and backpack, I could see that he was thrilled be home. His fast-paced footsteps reminded me of what I used to call "happy feet" when he and Ryan used to race up the stairs when they were small.

Just as I was going into the kitchen, I heard a crash coming from the loft. I reminded myself to stay calm. Whatever he broke I could easily replace, or so I thought.

Devon came down a few minutes later with three figurines in his hands, two of them broken.

"Sorry," he said softly, dropping his head.

I took them from him and muttered, "That's okay." Inside, I wanted to scream, "Those were Aunt Eva's!" She had died about five years earlier, and I was so grateful to have something of hers as a remembrance. Fortunately I restrained and consoled myself thinking that even though auntie was dead, she still lived in my heart and not in those broken figurines.

"I'm sorry, Mom," he said again. Obviously when Devon was trying to balance his backpack and that big, clumsy suitcase, he knocked the figurines off the table. Anyone could have done that. Still my mind was propelled back into a time when he used to break so many things in our house, including his own toys, a RAD characteristic.

When Devon went back upstairs, I turned the set of figurines over in my hand and noticed for the first time that they had been signed on the bottom. They were collectors items that were 30 years old or more. I didn't know that before. They were different poses of the same Asian woman in a kimono playing with her child. The third figurine had not been broken. I quickly took it and walked upstairs to put it safely away in my bedroom.

I realized that Devon's accident was another sign which I felt was so important to observe. Signs are spiritual messages that can direct and interpret our state of affairs. I wondered what message was I being given that day. Then it occurred to me. I was Devon's mother, and he was my child. We were the figurines!

Had that relationship been broken too? Yes, long ago. But as I thought deeper about the figurines of a mother playing with the small child, I interpreted it as a message that our relationship had changed. Spirit was telling me to forget the old, small Devon who use to get into trouble. Like the figurines, he was no more. Before me now was the new and improved young man, all grown up. I would have to relate to him as a young adult and not the unruly child who left a few years ago.

I placed the unbroken figurine, a reminder of our past, on my dresser and then focused on the weekend ahead. I began planning our days as if

I was going to show Los Angeles to a visiting, long lost relative. He actually was that.

That night I had problems getting to sleep. Devon, exhausted from the travel and the excitement of being home, went to bed early. I was grateful because I was able to relax, too. The next morning I awoke surprised that I had rested easier than I anticipated, and actually slept the night through. In fact the whole family seemed more settled as we got to know the new Devon.

That weekend we did everything he wanted: went horseback riding, to the movies, and roamed the mall. With each passing hour I realized that my fears had been unjustified.

Next on the agenda was business. I took him to a transitional housing placement facility where I hoped he would be accepted when he came back to California to live. It was a house in a lovely neighborhood where six other clients about his age also were living. The foundation that ran the house taught the clients skills to be self-sufficient. Devon had expected to come back home, but we weren't comfortable with that notion quite yet and wanted him to ease back into our lives.

We toured the neat, clean, little yellow house with a lovely lady who was the director of the residential program. As she explained the house rules she exuded warmth, and I felt this was the right place for Devon. After we left Devon told me that even though he wanted to live at home, he could be happy with that placement. I was glad that he said that. Now my hope was that the facility would have a place for him once he was ready to come back in August.

The night before Devon was leaving to return to Devereux, I was fixing dinner when he came into the kitchen to talk to me.

"Mom, I have something to say," he said solemnly. I could tell this was serious. I stopped washing the lettuce, turned off the burner cooking the pot of vegetables, and turned toward him.

"Yes?" My body tensed.

"I just want to say that I'm sorry for all the problems that I've caused you and Dad." I was stunned. He had never expressed any type of remorse over his behaviors before, let alone tell me he was sorry.

Later, when I told Walt what he said, I was even more astonished to learn that Devon had told him the same. "When he said that he was sorry," said Walt, "it brought tears to my eyes." Tears were now streaming down my face.

Later, as we were about to sit down to Sunday dinner, Ryan called to check in on the family as usual.

"We're about to eat, Ryan. You know I told you that Devon's here, remember?" There was a long pause. After Devon went away to the facilities, I had repeatedly asked Ryan if he wanted to speak with Devon. The answer was always the same. "No."

I didn't push him. Ryan had not spoken to his brother since Devon tried to attack him with the iron bar. That was two and a half years ago.

"Let me speak to him," Ryan said. I couldn't believe what I was hearing. I nearly fell over a dining room chair scrambling to give Devon the phone before Ryan changed his mind and hung up.

I watched Devon's face light up as he heard his brother's voice for the first time in years. Usually Devon had an emotionless expression or an ever-present grin, but now his eyes danced and sparkled with sheer joy. He had a huge smile that I hadn't seen since he was a little kid. I was smiling watching an animated Devon walk around in circles chattering away to Ryan. The energy flowed from him like a fountain as he asked Ryan about school and told him of his experiences in Texas.

Hearing Devon talking, I was delighted that for the first time in their lives my guys were having a real conversation. They weren't throwing insults at one another but actually communicating, catching up on one another's lives. They stayed on the phone for at least five minutes, but it was a lifetime for two brothers who had finally reunited.

Our house was now vibrating with love. It was the most beautiful, healing experience we had since Devon went away. I could see a sense of relief and peace that glowed from Devon's eyes like two candle flames. He had completed unfinished business with Ryan.

Devon hung up the phone nearly jumping up and down, and bounced over to the dinner table. His energy was electric. Devon had written Ryan apology letters that Ryan never opened. But his big brother had obviously forgiven him on this day.

"You're so happy, huh?" I said to Devon, who was brimming with joy.

"Yep, I'm on top of the world," he said beaming. Throughout dinner Devon laughed and shared his thoughts and feelings about different subjects. It was Ryan's call that made him totally open up. He, too, had been scared about coming home and how we would receive him. Devon wondered if we would forgive him.

"Ryan doesn't know it, but he taught you a great lesson when he didn't talk to you for all of that time, even though we've taught you both to forgive people."

"Yeah?" said Devon nodding slowly, his lips curling.

"The world is like Ryan. Most don't forgive when you do them wrong. They won't forget things just because you want to make up with them. Some people never talk to those who hurt them for the rest of their lives. You're blessed Ryan is not that way."

"Yup," he nodded, rubbing his forehead in deep thought.

Then came another big healing.

"Devon, you're really doing well," said Walt, who then looked over at Jada. "What do you think about your brother's change?"

She giggled nervously, stole a glimpse at Devon, and then darted her eyes to her plate, moving her vegetables around with her fork. "I thought you were going to mess up again when you came home."

It was the first time that I had heard Jada give Devon any type of compliment. For years, like Ryan, she had lived with the weight of her brother on her shoulders. Other kids kept identifying her as Devon's sister. It was a cross she hated bearing.

As I sat watching my family talking, I saw the years of resentment and anger dissolving before my eyes. I thought of the dinners with the old Devon that used to always turn into angry battles. Inevitably he would say something to upset someone at the table. Dinners then usually ended abruptly with someone storming away from the table.

Tonight it was different. We were digesting love, peace and harmony with our food. The Prodigal Son had returned home.

CHAPTER TWENTY-NINE

The next day Jada and Ryan were back in school and Walt was at work. This left me to take Devon to the airport alone for his return to Texas.

It was 9:00 a.m. when we stopped to get breakfast before heading to the airport. As we sat waiting for our pancakes we reflected on the good weekend.

"I've got to hurry up and get back here," said Devon, who had been telling me how much he missed home.

"You'll be back here before you know it. Just keep doing as good as you can." The words came out of my mouth, but the thought of his being 18 in a couple of months and returning to Los Angeles with no more mental health experts to monitor his progress, or to give Walt and me support, made me shudder. I was still going through post-traumatic stress syndrome, and I wasn't ready to be abandoned by those who could help us, and I was worried because Devon had been taken off his medication for mood swings and depression at his request. Since he was so insistent and felt he didn't need the meds anymore, I asked Dr. Berno, the psychiatrist at Devereux, to wean him off them while Devon was still living at the facility so that he could be monitored. So far there had been no repercussions.

We finished eating, and were sitting in bumper-to-bumper traffic on the infamous 405 Freeway. Even though we had left home several hours early, I was worried about the long security lines we had to navigate that might cause us to miss Devon's flight.

"Lord," I prayed silently, "Please don't let this boy miss his plane." Everything had worked out so well, but I wouldn't exhale until he was in the air.

"Listen, Dev," I said as we pulled into the airport. "I don't think I'm going to have time to park and get you to the gate on time. You're going to have to go by yourself." This was not the way I wanted to leave him, but the traffic had put us on a tight schedule. The security line extended out the door and down the sidewalk.

"Okay, Mom," he said with a nod as I pulled up to the Southwest Airlines curb. We hugged one another goodbye, and a sadness suddenly engulfed me. I felt a lump growing in my throat as I watched him again struggle with his huge brown suitcase. Even though I was relieved to see him leave, at the same time I wanted him to stay.

I was about to pull away from the curb when I noticed that the parking garage up ahead was closer than I had realized. The recent remodeling of the airport had made everything more convenient than before.

Instantly I swooped into traffic, making a car brake and screech behind me as I pulled to the far left lane and into the garage entrance. It was surprisingly empty. I couldn't believe my luck. My heart raced as I turned into a parking space close to the exit door. I could still see Devon off if I hurried.

Just as in some sappy love story, I heard music as I raced out of the parking structure and over a skywalk to the terminal, nearly tripping down two flights of stairs.

Ahead I could see the baggage line. Was he still there? Did he go inside?

As I approached the line at the curb, I saw Devon's blue shirt. He was standing by a skycap who was busy tagging another traveler's bags.

"Devon," I called, thrilled that I hadn't missed him.

He turned around with his black backpack slung over his shoulder and a confused look in his eyes. He was holding his ticket with the baggage claim check toward the skycap, who had his back to him, expecting the man to do something else.

"Did you check your bags?"

"Yeah, but I don't know what I'm suppose to do now," he said softly. "I've never done this before."

My heart melted as I shepherded my confused son out of the baggage line. He didn't know the airport procedure that I took for granted.

"If he took your bags you can now go through security," I said, pointing to a line nearly a fourth of a block long.

"Oh," he said, looking rigid. I knew he hadn't boarded a plane alone before, but somehow I thought that he knew what to do from traveling with me to Texas and from his trip back home to visit. As the bustling crowd of travelers hurried past us, I realized that he was also frightened.

As we walked to the security line, I saw the clock. Twenty minutes were left for Devon to reach the departure gate that seemed at least two blocks away. I was wishing that I could go with him when suddenly I saw a customer service booth and got a bright idea.

"Devon, come with me," I said, pulling his arm to get him out of the security line. Five minutes later I had a special gate pass in my hands and we were back in the security line together this time. I knew that he would be definitely getting on that plane.

When we reached the inspection point, we both had to take off our shoes and coats. Why did I fear that Devon would have something in his pockets that could get us yanked out of line? It was conditioning from years of when he used to steal things.   "You have your ticket, Dev?"

We were halfway to the gate when Devon stopped cold, nearly tripping a lady behind him. He searched himself frantically. I stopped breathing. "Oh, no!" he said.

"The security check point," I blurted out, "Did you leave it there?" I locked on to his puzzled eyes.

"Yeah, I think so. When I was putting my shoes back on… I put it on the table."

We tore back to the security counter. I was thinking that this was the yin and yang of life. When things are going so good there's always something to screw it up, although it's these little upsets that help us to keep our balance.

I spotted the table next to the chair where he had slipped back his shoes back on. Amazingly, his ticket was still there even though droves of people had passed by it. Relieved, we raced back toward the gate, thinking this had been a miracle. Clearly God was watching out for us.

We finally arrived at the gate, where people were already lined up waiting to board the plane. I was now exhausted, mainly from nervous anxiety. The last thing I felt like was to continue standing.

"Dev," I said, eyeing an empty chair. "I'm going to go sit down."
He nodded and his eyes followed me.

I watched little kids behind him fidgeting as they waited to board and adults swaying back and forth and chattering to their traveling companions in line. Everyone seemed animated except my son, who stood motionless. I was amazed at how disciplined he was. The Devon I knew before would never be able to stand in line. Devereux had trained him well.

One of his big offenses at Devereux for the first couple of years was making contact in line and talking to others when he was supposed to be quiet. Now the young man before me stood straight and patiently still. Suddenly I realized that his discipline had developed from being institutionalized for nearly three years. The thought pierced my heart. I rationalized that at least he hadn't been in jail, where he was definitely headed. At Devereux he had the choice of having privileges or staying in his room until he decided to follow the program.

As I watched him, my heart ached for Devon. I knew that he didn't want to return to Texas even for the final few months. He wanted to be home with his family. But it would take us these extra few months to adjust to the idea of his coming home permanently. The dry run of his visit was good, but we still had to prepare ourselves.

My eyes were glued on him standing like a rigid soldier as I thought back to when Walt and I first met the little three-year-old Devon at that adoption party 14 years earlier as he stood quietly next to his social worker. I wondered what he was thinking now. How hard would he find it to do the remaining time at Devereux now that he had been home and tasted freedom again? Would he rebel once he returned to Texas? Would he cry in his pillow at night?

A voice came over the loud speaker.

"Flight 1351 to Phoenix is now ready for boarding. Please have your tickets and I.D. ready." I scanned the long line of passengers who were about to board the flight to Texas via Phoenix.

I got up and walked up to Devon to say my final goodbye.

"Ok, Dev," I said in a quivering voice. "I'll see you later." We hugged. "Call me when you get back to Devereux."

"Okay, Mom." He didn't look at me affectionately as he had that weekend. In fact he avoided any eye contact. Instead he looked toward the front of the line. I knew it was his tactic to keep from lingering in heavy farewell emotions that he couldn't handle, a survival skill that served him well over the years. He had said goodbye to far too many people in his young life. Too often he had seen the backs of people walking away from him. His mother, social workers, various therapists, and his family. I knew he didn't want to see me walk away so he kept his eyes straight ahead.

I watched him shuffle forward with the line. I hoped that he would look back at me as he did when I first saw him smile at me when he left the adoption party. He didn't. Instead Devon handed his boarding pass to the lady dressed in blue and disappeared through the door.

Finally I could exhale. I walked over to the huge bay window hoping to get one more glimpse of him through the airplane windows. I didn't. I sat down on the bright orange plastic chairs watching the last of the passengers board the plane before an attendant closed the door.

I sat there thinking about our relationship. I used to shrug off my suspicion that he was out to get me, until I researched RAD symptoms in children and realized I was right. This type of child needs to control his environment because he was hurt so early in life, so there was always a big power struggle between Devon and me. RAD children will quickly target the mother as the one who has to be broken. It's the mother who is the one who instills discipline daily, and makes sure chores are done. No wonder I felt constantly abused.

Experts also say that it was "a mother" who let a RAD child down in the past, so an adoptive mother like me is the target of payback.

I wondered how things could have been different for Devon, for our family. Life always seems easier when we look back on our struggles. Time and distance takes away the pain that seems so unbearable when we are living our nightmares.

The plane backed away from the gate. I watched it hesitate on the runway, waiting for clearance from the tower. I realized that this was the first time that I truly was sad to see Devon go. Whenever he went away before -- to spend the night with my girlfriend's son, the brief time he went to camp, and when he first went to a facility -- I was relieved to get a respite from his obnoxious behavior. Now that he had changed and he was a delight to be around, I was going to miss him even though I still had reservations about his coming home for good.

I pressed my hands against the window, straining to see the blue, red and gold plane roar down the runway carrying my son. Finally it took off, and I saw it lift into the air like an eagle soaring to great heights. A tear ran down my face as I wondered what Devon was thinking as he flew away from the place that was his home.

Was he crying on the inside like I was crying on the outside?

CHAPTER THIRTY

High school graduations are usually big events for families. When Ryan graduated I was crazy with excitement. It was as if I were graduating, too. But I didn't feel that initial excitement with Devon's graduation, maybe because he always had major school problems. Like typical RAD kids, Devon had major conflicts with his classmates, who are usually the first ones to bring to parents' attention that their child has a problem.

This was a more anxiety-filled than a joyful event. Graduation meant that Devon would soon be leaving Devereux. What would we do without the wonderful treatment team? What would Devon do with his life when he turned 18 in a few months?

When the graduation invitation from Devereux came in the mail, suddenly it all became a reality. He was going to walk across the stage, even though he had to stay at the facility through the summer to complete one more class to fulfill his graduation requirements.

Only a few weeks earlier we had been introduced to this new, matured, and disciplined individual. The treatment team told us that he went from being the most hated kid in the unit to being elected president of the unit. Other kids went to him now with their problems. Devon was also working a regular job in the school cafeteria.

I had thought earlier that if he could keep it together maybe he would go to a trade school when he got out of Devereux. But lately I could see him going to a community college rather than what I feared earlier: going to jail.

Another reality had also set in. I thought I could take a year off after the big, nerve-wracking scramble that it would take to get Ryan into college. Now I had to quickly shift into Super-Mom mode again. I would have to play catch up and help Devon plan his academic future.

In the meantime I was already working securing his living arrangement in a transitional housing program, hoping they would have room for him once he came back to California in August. It was my biggest worry. What if he couldn't get in? Despite all of his improvements, we weren't ready for Devon to come back home. He had turned his life around under 24-hour supervision, but what would he do with all of his newfound freedom?

Now that Devon was straightening up his act, I wanted to help him again. I had to. When he was at Devereux and not cooperating a year earlier, Walt and I were preparing to release him from our family once he turned 18 because we simply couldn't handle him. But we changed our minds because he changed. With this new revelation also came more fears. Now I would still have to worry about Devon after devoting so much of my life to him earlier, but if he was continuing to do good, then no way could I not help my child who was trying to make a new life for himself.

I felt like a swimmer on a diving board who is about to finally plunge into a beautiful, relaxing pool of tranquility when suddenly I'm called off the diving board to clean the pool again. When was it going to be my turn? But that's motherhood -- a maelstrom filled with sacrifices, details, and plans. And when you have a special needs child, it's double.

No matter how many times I have heard "Take care of yourself," it's nearly impossible. But thanks to Devon I did learn how to discipline myself and take mini vacation breaks through my meditations. Releasing stress that way was just as important to me as eating or drinking. I couldn't have lasted without any of them.

I meditated to connect with God and get strength and to tap into an inner wisdom. This was my way of putting myself first. I may not have been able to get massages, go on vacations, or even socialize with friends, but this was the way that I learned to love myself. Now nothing and no one could stop my morning ritual.

On May 27, 2004, Walt and I arrived at Hobby airport in Houston for Devon's graduation. It was only a half-hour drive to the Devereux facility from the airport. We had planned to see Devon at 3:30, a few hours before a big celebration dinner organized by the board members for the students.

When we arrived at the beautiful, sprawling complex set against a forest backdrop, the red brick structures, with huge white pillars, nestled among old oak trees reminded me of the South's beautiful plantations. Our beloved Annie greeted us. She's the nurse who had become Devon's mom away from home and my confidant. The beautiful Jamaican woman with flawless copper skin made me think about a Caribbean vacation every time I heard her accent. We were like old friends, greeting one another with warm hugs.

Devon was not in the unit. We told her that we would be back to pick him up so he could ride with us rather than with the other graduates.

Walking back to the car, I was so glad to have a little time to relax at the hotel before seeing Devon. Usually we had our first visit with him after arriving dead-tired from the trip. Most of these visits were spent in the facility meeting rooms because Devon had not earned points to go off the unit. Walt and I felt like we were in lockdown, spending hours trying to find things to say to Devon in these rooms.

Successful therapy with RAD clients needs to be confrontive and intrusive while yet being loving and supportive. The Devereux staff was just that. Devon had to earn the privilege of going off campus. Most of the time he didn't, so after a half-hour we were all bored stiff. We usually played cards to try to reconnect with Devon.

It was painful trying to make conversation with a teenager whose responses were limited to "uh huh", "yeah" and "no." Then there was the frustration of knowing that he had refused to cooperate with the staff and follow any of the rules. Often I felt angry and helpless during these visits. We were told not to chastise; disciplining would be left to the staff. The family visits were strictly for bonding.

It wasn't until Devon was at Devereux two and a half years that he finally earned enough points to go off the unit. Then we took him to as many places as we could cram into the short weekend, but nothing seemed to move him since all he wanted then was to return to California with us.

I remember one visit when Walt was thrilled to take Devon to the restaurant owned by former NBA All Star Clyde Drexel, since he and

Devon were both basketball fans. When we were seated Devon was indifferent. He sat mutely at the table, refusing to order food or engage in any conversation. This wasn't the slam-dunk that Walter had anticipated.

Still we kept returning to support Devon, refusing to be like some parents who, we were told, rarely visited their children. According to the staff, we were the parents that visited the most even though it was a grueling trip. We would get up at 3:30 AM to catch the first plane to Houston, and, after changing planes in Phoenix, we would fight traffic in our rental car and then try to cope with the hot, humid Texas weather. We had to struggle to reconnect with Devon, who at that time was still filled with rage.

Even when I worked with the television networks and chaperoned some self-centered celebrities on six-city publicity tours in five days, it wasn't as bad as making this one trip from L.A. to Texas. But looking back, that's probably because it was an emotional drain having to see the child I loved living in a mental health facility, sometimes with no hope for his future.

Just as we were pulling out of Devereux's parking lot, we spotted Devon in the distance walking with Diane, his therapist. My first reaction was dread. I needed to meditate to deal with the jet lag and the anxiety I was feeling over Devon about to return home. At the same time I was feeling joy over his completing the program and doing so well.

Devon, who saw us at the same time, loped across the sprawling lawn toward our car. He was wearing a blue jogging suit and didn't look like the rebellious, defiant kid we had dropped off a couple of years earlier. Instead he carried himself with poise, confidence, and the discipline of a young man who had undergone military training.

Devon came to a small bush separating our car from him and leaped over it with the fluid grace of a sleek tiger. He stooped, leaning into the passenger window and grinned in my face. Where was the hyper, scattered curmudgeon we once knew? This young man before me was now in control of himself and seemed so reserved.

After hugging Devon, I explained that we wanted to rest before the big dinner. Reluctantly he agreed to be picked up later, even though he wanted us to stay. But his new *modus operandus* was to be agreeable instead of obstinate as in the past. As we drove away I felt guilty for my initial reaction upon seeing him. I was dealing with post-traumatic stress, fearing he would once again misbehave.

I had to forgive myself. It was alright to have these fears, and it was okay to put my needs first. Experts advise RAD parents to take care of themselves to better deal with the child. The new Devon couldn't instantly erase years of painful memories in just a few visits with us, and he would have to earn our trust.

A few hours later we were back at Devereux in front of the administration office, meeting Devon and the rest of the graduates to caravan to the dinner.

Bubbly young ladies in long, rainbow-colored gowns flowed out of the building dressed as if they were going to the prom that they missed from being in residential treatment. Their hair was artfully coiffed, and a few teetered on high heels that they obviously weren't used to wearing. Next the guys came out of the building. It was easy to spot Devon. He and another young man were the only black male graduates.

Devon spotted us and strolled toward our gray rental car with confidence. He looked like a young business apprentice in his new, dark blue suit. I was amazed every time I saw him lately at how he was transformed. Despite the blazing heat he looked calm, cool and very happy.

"Nice suit, Devon," said Walt.

"Bought it myself," he smiled.

"From your paycheck?" I asked, surprised that he had earned enough working in the school's cafeteria.

"Yep."

Devon turned to talk to a friend who had ambled over from across the parking lot. Walt whispered to me, "I know he's burning up in that wool suit." He had to be. It was way over 95 degrees and extremely humid. Devon turned back and looked down at his sleeve, brushing off invisible lint.

"I got this on sale for $90."

I didn't tell him that it was on sale because those suits weren't suppose to be worn in the summer. It was his proud moment and mine, too.

"I bet you feel good about yourself, honey."

I smiled, patting his face. He nodded and then climbed into the back seat of the car.

"You know, Dev, I'm so proud of you not only because you look so handsome but because you took your own money and invested it in something practical."

He was beaming.

"Yeah, proud of you, man," added Walt. "You could have bought a new CD player or more CDs but you're thinking of your appearance."

It was a milestone. This was the same kid who made me want to jump off a cliff because he refused to comb his hair and often put on dirty clothes that smelled of urine to go to school when he was living at home. He simply hadn't cared.

"You know, you could have asked us for the money for a new graduation suit," Walt said. "That's our responsibility. But I bet it feels good using your own money, huh?" said Walt.

"I figured I was going to need it when I got out of Devereux," he said, smiling.

We joined the small caravan of cars carrying the graduates and their families, and I was reminded of the joy in my college days caravaning with friends to parties. I felt that same joy with Devon on this day. I was levitating, riding on a cloud, wrapped in the arms of God as we talked with Devon about graduation and his recent accomplishments at Devereux. My prayers had finally been answered. He was making something of himself.

Then I heard my mother's voice whispering softly in my ear.

"Devon is going to be all right, Jan," she told me. Before she died she told me this a number of times just when I was ready to kill him. No matter what he did horrible, Mom always stood up for him.

On this day Devon was now on the right train, headed to success even though he had gotten off at the wrong stops before. Next stop: graduation.

That evening, at the South Shore Harbor Resort, the Friends of Devereux, composed of board members, hosted an impressive buffet dinner in the conference center overlooking bobbing yachts. Most of Devon's support team was there -- Annie and Maggie, the unit nurses; Diane, his therapist; Mr. T, the unit director; Paul, his caseworker; his teacher, Mr. Randall. They were all raving to Walt and me about Devon's progress.

"He's a completely different kid," "Not the same person who came to Devereux," "We're so proud of him." These comments were drastically different from those I heard a year earlier -- "He refuses to cooperate," "He's fighting and cursing out the staff," "He's agitating the other kids," and the classic one I have heard from people all his life, which is classic RAD: "Devon wants things his way."

The evening could not have been more perfect. The graduates sat with their families, and one of the Devereux board members introduced each student to the entire room, telling of the teen's future dreams.

The excitement of the evening made me want to binge on the whole buffet, which was a feast way beyond the traditional banquet chicken dinners. The cheesecake and double fudge cake desserts alone made me want to cry they were so good.

All of the excitement that parents build up over months of preparing for their child to graduate was now compressed inside of me and about to explode. Life had revved up to full force. I was so proud of Devon. It was like trying to contain an entire July 4th fireworks show inside of my heart.

Waves of emotion swept through the room. Graduates were thrilled to have finally reached their big day and would soon be going home. The families seemed happy, but not exuberant like the parents at Ryan's graduation. I knew they must have felt like we did -- happy their child was graduating, but at the same time filled with worry. Where does our child go from here? Would he be able to handle the outside world with all of its pressures? Would she go back to her old ways?

I couldn't help staring at the Devereux staff and board members, who were like proud parents. There was no doubt in my mind: they had definitely raised Devon these last couple of years. They stuck with him when no one else would. Everyone in Los Angeles, except Linda McCarthy, his Hathaway therapist, and Lori Waldinger, his educational advocate, seemed to have given up on him.

But the Devereux people were determined to help him, and they did. It took all of them making their marks in his consciousness for him to change.

I watched Devon interact with the staff and board members, who congratulated him on his improvement and his graduation. Walt and I were proud and astounded at how he had magically transformed into the gentleman that I used to preach that he should be. Now when someone greeted Devon, he stood up, gave them steady eye contact, a strong handshake, and engaged in polite conversation with an open smile. The young, immature boy I had brought to Devereux, who looked away when adults talked to him, was now a man. He was reborn.

"But how," I asked God, "could I trust him to stay that way?"

CHAPTER THIRTY-ONE

The next morning I got up early to make sure that we left the hotel in time to arrive at the graduation comfortably. I have this habit of running late and then rushing like crazy to get to places on time. I think I'm addicted to the adrenaline rush.

Since the hotel bathroom was small, I had set my phone alarm to awaken me before Walt got up so we wouldn't have to crawl over one another trying to get dressed. Today I wanted to have plenty of time to put on my makeup before he rushed us out the door.

It didn't work.

Halfway through getting dressed I realized that I had lost my camera.

"We need to go buy a throwaway camera. I think I left ours at the banquet."

Walt simply nodded and continued to dress.

"We can stop at the Walgreens near Devereux," I said. I knew he didn't want to make any stops just by the way he muttered "Yeah" as he slapped cologne on his face. Even though we would have plenty of time, his mind was set on going straight to the graduation. No stops.

I could feel Walt's mounting tension as he continued dressing. I fought to suppress my rising anger, grumbling inside. I was the one expected to always remember every detail for our family events. Men depend on women to do that. But Lord forbid if we forget or lose something.

"No," I told myself. "Stay calm. Don't go there. Don't let him ruin the morning with his edgy attitude."

Walt had been stretched taut, like a rubber band, the whole trip. I knew he was tired from a hard week and jet lag. I was tired, too, but I was making every effort to be pleasant. He was dealing with his stuff in icy silence, which I hated.

When I drove up to Walgreens, Walt exploded, "Keep going! Just keep going, take me to Devereux," he barked. I looked at him as if he were an alien who had dropped into our car from another planet.

"What's wrong with you?" I shrieked.

"Just drive me to the place!"

I wanted to drive him to hell, where he obviously came from that morning, but I didn't say a word. Instead I puffed up inside, backed the car up, and burned rubber accelerating a half block to the Devereux parking lot.

When Walt got out of the car, he yelled back over his shoulder, "You're always late. You always do this!"

"Do what?" I snapped. It was over. I couldn't hold my tongue any longer.

"What's your damn problem?"

He slammed the car door and stormed away. Fortunately no one else was in the parking lot. If they had been, I knew they would think that is exactly why our kid was in Devereux, having to live with parents like us.

The early morning stifling humid heat in Texas had just gotten hotter.

When I returned to the Devereux ceremony with the camera from the store, I ran into Diane, Devon's therapist, walking toward the graduation.

"Walt's angry because he thought we were going to be late this morning."

"Oh, dear," she exclaimed in her southern drawl that always fascinated me.

Diane's energy and her voice were calming. Her mere expression made me think that our riff was stupid, which it was.

It was 10:05 when I spotted Walt sitting in a white, folding chair. I glanced over at the beautiful, weathered gazebo, decorated with flowers and serving as the graduation stage. Walt was one of the few people sitting in the empty family sections. When he saw me, he had a smirk on his face. I knew he was surprised that he was so early and not late. He is obsessed with being first, as I seem to be obsessed with running late.

I figured that somewhere in his childhood he must have been left behind because he's a maniac arriving first everywhere we go.

"So, I see we were on time," I said sarcastically as I climbed over him to sit down. The only action on stage was the technicians setting up the speakers.

"Well, you're always late," he said, refusing to give in. When he flashed me a toothy grin I was reminded that our willingness to let go of anger quickly with one another was one of the reasons why we had managed to stay together for so long.

"Walt, the ceremony doesn't start until 10:30. What were you so upset about?" I could tell he was surprised but he looked away.

"See," I said, shoving a graduation program in his face. It read 'Devereux Graduation 2004. May 28, 2004, 10:30 a.m.'

"I thought it started at 10:00 a.m." His voice was low and unapologetic.

"The problem is you don't listen to me, Walt," I whispered. A woman who sat in front of us pretended not to notice our breathy darts, but I knew she heard. Diane was chatting with another family seated in our section. She looked up at us and I rolled my eyes, indicating that my husband is nuts. She smiled and then continued talking to the other people probably feeling she was lucky to be a safe distance away.

Walt saw me and said under his breath, "That's the truth! You're always late. You need to deal with that!"

"Yeah, right," I whispered back sarcastically. "You deal with it!"

"See, look at you," he whispered. "You have us arguing in front of these people."

"Me?" I huffed. I knew he was feeling as embarrassed as I was. We always kept our business quiet.

We settled down, dropping our egos, and the seats around us began rapidly filling. Diane obviously sensed the danger was over and came over to chat.

I realize now that it was our tensions and rabid emotions that were swirling inside of us. We had been on an emotional roller coaster with Devon for so long, and now he was taking us to new heights with his incredible transformation. We had never been in a place with him where we were so optimistic about his future. Previously there was always conflict and animosity because of his actions, but on this day we couldn't have been happier. Still it didn't minimize our stress. We were like lovers on Valentine's Day. Our hopes that the day would come out perfect were overwhelming.

It was remarkably breezy under the huge oak trees that shaded us like circus tents. I was thankful to have protection from the blazing sun. I scanned the picturesque setting before us. It was a Thomas Kincaid painting. Dancing light bounced off the gazebo and its hanging baskets of rainbow-colored Impatiens flowers. Birds chirped happily as if they were the ones graduating. White, billowing clouds rolled rapidly across the blue sky. A red carpet dividing the sections of white folding chairs ended at the stage in front of a large vase of white flowers.

At 10:30 the music began. A color guard marched to the stage with the flag. After we said the Pledge of Allegiance the small crowd of family members and staff turned around to watch the graduates file from the administrative building behind us. My insides felt like fast moving white water. Suddenly I jumped, realizing that I had better get up close to the marching graduates because my little throwaway camera could focus up to only a 14 foot distance. By the time I also realized that I had to keep winding this new camera to take shots, Devon had passed me.

I could have kicked myself for losing our familiar camera. How could I have lost it? I had even made sure that I had packed plenty of film. What was that all about? I had never before lost a camera in my entire life. Why now? Was this a subconscious trick I was playing on myself?

The graduation ceremony was intimate and magical. Since there were only fourteen graduates, each one spoke of their experiences at Devereux, giving thanks to those who had helped with their transformations. Several graduates spoke before Devon.

Throughout the years, when our kids participated in their graduation ceremonies from pre-school to high school, I was always bored listening to other people's children speak at the ceremonies. But on this day I was enthralled when each Devereux graduate humbly spoke of their hard journey, their brushes with the law, their mental breakdowns, and how Devereux had saved their lives. I wanted to hug each one of them. They had overcome so much in their young lives, and now they were all trying to start over.

After each graduate spoke they each took two long-stemmed white carnations handed to them by Alicia, the principal. The graduate walked down the gazebo stairs and into the audience to find his or her parents. They handed their parents a carnation, and then walked through the crowd to give the other carnation to their therapists or whomever they felt closest to on the Devereux staff.

Finally, it was Devon's turn. I knew then what a parent must feel like when she sees her rescued child for the first time after a crucial accident. He was so beautiful, and I was so grateful that he had survived.

The crowd cheered wildly for him as he approached the stage. This was the opposite of what kids used to do when they heard his name. It seemed ironic that peer problems were his biggest issue when he first came to Devereux. All of his life kids hated him with a passion, especially his siblings. Now he was respected and the elected leader of his unit.

Devon approached the podium tall and straight like a soldier. I held my breath, remembering his concerns the night before.

"I hope I don't mess up on my speech," he told me at the graduation dinner.

"You'll be fine," I said, hugging him.

I was so impressed how strong he began.

"Good morning, ladies and gentlemen," his voice, projecting with authority, was much louder than the other graduates who spoke before him. We were impressed not only as parents but as professional speakers, having given our workshops for years to hundreds of participants.

As he spoke, I felt him move into "the zone." It's that magical point where a speaker hears his own voice and knows if he is in control or not during a speech. He was obviously in control. Words flowed, and so did the love in my heart for him.

"Let me start off by telling you a little bit of my history at Devereux. I was what you might call a problem child. My life was falling apart. My first year here was what I would call a dark period. I was in my room on refocus and restriction for months at a time. I was only in school for about half of each day. I was having suicidal thoughts and didn't share them with anyone. I didn't talk about my feelings. I basically didn't care about life. I would say it was caused by being away from home, relationships, and wanting things my way.

"This went on until I met one staff member. This man started working here in Devereux on unit 4 in late December of 2001. This person's name is Frank. For some reason I just connected with him the day he started working here. It was Frank who helped me to start opening up and talk about things that were going on with me. He helped me to talk about my feelings. I started to trust more people then than I had in a very long time. I started talking to Annie and Diane more, too. Annie is the charge nurse on unit 4. Diane is my therapist. After I started opening to these people I began to slowly stay in program and off refocus. I have made a great improvement and now I'm a level 4.

"I have been in Devereux for two years without going home on a visit. Until recently I hadn't talked to my older brother. It had been three years since we last spoke. We spoke when I went on a home pass last month. The way I see it is that basically the changes that I have made are slowly bringing my life back together. None of this would've happened if it weren't for Devereux and its staff and program.

"I thank you all for the efforts you put forth to help all of the teenagers here at Devereux. I would like to take a few moments to point out a few individuals who I feel are a big part of my success. First, I want to thank Ms. Diane Collins. Next, I would like to thank Ms. Annie. Last but not least I would like to thank Mr. Broderick Frank. I would also like to thank the whole treatment team which has been here for me since day one.

"I also want to thank my peers who have tested my strength and made me a stronger person. So if nothing else today, I want to say that Devereux changed my life. I went from a life-hating suicidal failure to a success all because of the time I spent Devereux. Thank you and have a nice day."

The white water that rushed through me was suddenly frozen. My whole body seemed numb. Was that it? I sat there in shock.

He didn't *thank his parents*!

Other kids before him thanked their parents. Why didn't he thank us?

As the crowd watched Devon in hushed silence, he walked off the stage and over to us. It took me a few seconds to remember to shoot his picture. I did it with resentment. We stood up as he approached. He gave Walt, who was standing on the aisle, the carnation. They locked in a long, extended hug. I then hugged Devon with tears in my eyes and tension in my jaw. I had mixed feelings. I was proud of how far he had come, but feared the psychological meaning of his not recognizing us in his speech. I didn't know at that time that a RAD symptom is the patient trying to stay in control of his caretakers. I didn't see this as being part of the disorder. I was simply hurt.

Still stunned, I watched Devon as he took the other carnation over to Diane and hugged her. I was happy that he did. She deserved that and so much more.

As he walked back to get his diploma, I mechanically and heartlessly climbed over Walt to take his picture. The question still echoed in my mind: How could he forget us? "He didn't thank us," I whispered to Walt.

"Some other kids didn't thank their parents," he said with a shrug.

I listened carefully to the remainder of the graduates, not with interest in their triumphs as before, but to see if they thanked their parents. Those who came behind Devon did, especially the girls, who often broke down in tears. There were a couple of failures from boys. His close friend "K," a handsome blond who reminded me of the rapper Eminem, didn't thank his parents, either. I was amazed that he didn't even give his mom a carnation. She had traveled all the way from California alone to support him. I felt hurt for her.

When the ceremony was over, Diane and Annie came back to us to congratulate us. When I saw them I broke down. "He didn't thank us," I cried in Diane's arms. She was much shorter than I, but I clutched her like a small child in pain. "Is there something there?" I sobbed to Diane. "Is he angry at us for placing him at Devereux?"

"No... no... I don't think so... ," she said, "but maybe there is." She was so honest, which is why Walt and I respected her so much. A straight shooter.

I knew at that moment that I needed therapy worse than Devon. Was this like the head games he used to run on me? I thought he was past that. I had worked so hard and sacrificed so much to help this kid. Still I couldn't believe that I had lost total control. That reserved, dignified persona Walt and I tried to project at the beginning of the ceremony crumbled with my heart. I cried harder. I was a blubbering mess.

This was Devon's milestone. His special day. I was embarrassed to be drowning in my self pity when I should have been celebrating with him. On the other hand, I was finally putting my feelings first for a change. It's important for RAD parents to take care of themselves.

Devon didn't see my breakdown. He was lost in the crowd, saying goodbye to his friends.

"He's just trying to be his own man," said Walt, reaching out to comfort me. I turned from Diane and then began crying in his arms. "He just doesn't want to show any kind of vulnerability in front of the crowd," Walt said. "He probably didn't want to get into the past by thanking us. He's dancing around that because if he really got into it, he may have showed emotions and cried." I rose up and looked him in the eyes. Walt continued, "You've got to remember, Jan, he's looked up to by other kids for the first time in his life. When thanking us, he would have broken down. Probably for the first time in his life he has a sense of himself and who he is as a person."

It was at times like this that I was thankful for the man I had married 24 years ago, the same one whom I had wanted to kill just an hour earlier. Walt has always turned my stormy waters into smooth sailing with his optimistic outlook on my problems. But this time I was still fighting the waves.

I looked around for Devon. Guilt had set in. I should have been taking pictures of him and his friends, but now he was nowhere to be found. Annie went with me to search for him in the classroom building. We couldn't find him. Finally she had to go back to work and I joined Walt under the big white tent where, again, the Devereux people had prepared an elaborate VIP feast for the graduates and their families.

Finally, I spotted Devon in the buffet line. It would take every muscle in my body to keep from asking him the question on his special day. I was glad when a smiling board member sat down at our table, introducing herself. She would bring out the self-control that I needed at that moment. The chic, mature lady with a warm aura carried herself like royalty and appeared to be financially well off.

I was still amazed at how much the South had changed. When Devon went to Texas, I reflected on the historical relations between blacks and whites that I had studied about when I was in school. I expected prejudices, but every trip I took to the Lone Star State to visit Devon was the opposite. Whites welcomed us with open arms, and the board member reflected the New South with her care and concern.

Devon finally landed at our table with his food. He couldn't eat. I barely could either, thinking how I had embarrassed myself in front of Diane and Annie. They probably thought that I was so self-centered, but deep down I knew they understood. They were special ladies who had the gift of honing in on people's feelings without judgment.

"Those are for you, Devon." The board member pointed to the presents at the center of our table.

Each graduate was given a watch at the dinner. Now there were more gifts? Devon opened a big purple gift bag, which held a blanket displaying the inscription, "2004 Graduate." Other gifts on the table for him included a "2004" necklace, a duffle bag, a framed class picture, and a photo album. The album was filled with pictures of him, posing in his graduation gown and in his suit on Devereux's picturesque grounds. That picture of Devon would make the Houston news paper the following week.

Thank God they had shot them. I knew that I didn't get a decent picture of him between the throwaway camera and my breakdown. These people were remarkable. The outpouring of gifts and love made me temporarily forget about my feelings as we chatted with the board member.

That afternoon Devon went to the movies with several of his fellow graduates. Then I took him shopping for a bunch of CDs, which was all he wanted from us for his graduation. Walt, a die hard Lakers basketball fan, stayed at the hotel to watch a playoff game.

When I pulled into the mall parking lot I knew this was the time that I had to do what I had told Devon he must always do, "Express your feelings and don't hold on to anger." The white waters roiled inside of me again.

"Devon," I turned off the engine and turned toward him, "you did a wonderful job with your speech today. You projected and delivered it like a pro. We were so proud of you."

He grinned.

"I was really nervous," he said, shaking his head, giggling.

I took a deep breath and let myself go. "I just have one thing to say about it."

"What?" he looked at me. His brown eyes widened.

"I felt so hurt because you didn't thank Dad and me." Large tears flowed from my eyes as he looked at me, deeply confused.

Devon turned away, dropped his shoulders and stared out of the front window. I had promised Walt and Diane that I wouldn't bring up the subject to him on his special day. I couldn't help it.

"I thought that we were just supposed to focus on the Devereux people," he said softly. The tension slowly oozed out of my body, seeing his sincerity. My body unhinged. He continued, "I also knew that I had already thanked you and Dad when I came out to visit last month." I reflected on that private moment between us when he told me that he was sorry for all the trouble he had caused me. My heart warmed.

"I know, Dev, but I just felt bad." He sighed. I knew that I had probably set him back into an old psychological place where he felt that he could never do anything right. But it was too late to call back my words.

Devon jerked and looked over at me remembering something. "I did think of you guys when I was writing it. But when I tried to add you to my speech after I finished, they told me it was too late to go back in the computer and change anything."

His explanation didn't soothe my pain. I didn't know if it was a lie. But what helped was thinking that this was the first time he was willing to empathize with my feelings. When he was at home he didn't seem to care about how he hurt people, especially me. He was on a mission to make everyone around him feel bad. This is typical behavior for someone with an attachment disorder, which was the reason Devon was living at Devereux. Don't let others close. Sabotage any close relationships.

I knew at that moment, from Devon's concern for my feelings

reflected in his eyes, that he was healing from his old self-destructive patterns. I felt better because I knew he was better.

"It's okay Dev."

I leaned over and kissed him gently on his cheek. He smiled. We then climbed out of the car and walked arm-in-arm to the mall in silence.

CHAPTER THIRTY-TWO

It's funny how our minds create a world of illusions. Fear especially can take us down dark roads that seem so real. Our terrors conflict with reality. We live in two separate worlds that intertwine and often we can't separate the truth from fiction.

I had lived with such dread of Devon's coming home that I had replayed out every horrifying scenario that haunted me for years. Only mindfulness and my connection with my Higher Power kept me sane and helped me to see my fears as runaway thoughts that, left unattended, made me paranoid. With the practice of living in the present, I saw these fears as separate from myself, unlike in the years before when I had simply acted on them.

The paranoid thoughts still came, but they weren't controlling my life. I watched them come and go without attachment. Would Devon be resentful of our placing him in those facilities? Would he try to harm us while we slept? Would I be able to sleep at night? Could he get sick, like he was before at Devereux, and something be seriously wrong where he would have to live with us forever? Would I be sentenced to taking care of him as a sick adult?

As I calmly looked at my thoughts, I found myself wondering, "Was there really a new Devon or was the shadowy, dark figure that I had conjured up in my mind real?"

On August 27th, Devon's 18th birthday, Walt, Jada and I stood in the Southwestern Airlines baggage claim area, waiting for him to arrive. I could feel their tension, and my mind was like the luggage I stared at on the carousel, going around in circles. Would the glowing reports Devon received during his last months at Devereux carry on into his new life out of the facility and without the 24-hour care watch?

About four months before he was scheduled to return home Devon asked to be taken off all medications. The staff, and especially Walt and I, were afraid, but Devon was adamant. At least while he was still at Devereux, his reactions could be monitored. To everyone's surprise he stayed stable, and as he contended, didn't appear to need medications anymore.

My plan for his transitional housing and independent living arrangement in California hadn't worked out. I had scrambled for months to get the right placement near home when he got out of Devereux. Nothing panned out. And now I stood in the airport, wondering how we would manage with him at home.

It had been three years since I battled the system trying to get Devon into placement, and in the coming weeks I would find myself once again fighting the system. A transitional housing facility that we investigated months before wouldn't return my calls, and when Devon phoned, they lied to him, telling him he had to be tested, which we found out wasn't true. Walt and I had met with the director of the transitional housing facility and his assistant. The place was highly recommended to us. During our meeting with the director, we found him rude, his attitude gruff. His assistant was the same. They were unlike the many people who work with special needs children, whom I found to be extraordinarily compassionate. But since this facility came so highly recommended by mental health experts, we overlooked the attitudes, thinking we had simply caught the administrators on a bad day.

After they persisted in not returning our phone calls, I filed a complaint with the Patient Rights Department of the State of California. According to them, the facility should have given us a notice of action, stating why they were refusing us service. The Department would follow up on our complaint. At the time of my writing these words, the case is still being investigated.

Meanwhile I learned that the director had been fired. I don't think it was due to our complaint; the truth simply caught up with the director. It is sad that special needs clients, like Devon, don't have any recourse against the system if someone is not standing up for them.

Many of these people cannot advocate for themselves, and some workers feel they can treat them anyway they please because of their mental disabilities, which hamper them from pursuing a case. They fall into the shadows of living on the streets or in prisons.

In the meantime, I put Devon's name on one other facility's waiting list.

My stomach was beginning to cramp as the passengers from Devon's flight poured into the baggage claim area. Suddenly I saw a striking image out of the corner of my eye. It was Devon in the loudest shirt and matching baggy shorts that I had ever seen. It reminded me of the outfits I saw growing up in the 1960s hippie era in San Francisco.

As he walked through the baggage claim looking for us, people turned and stared. He was a neon vision, strutting with the confidence of someone knowing he looked cool, completely unaware that he was in a time warp. I knew that Texas fashions were behind Los Angeles -- but not decades behind.

"Devon," I yelled out, chuckling to myself.

Devon saw us and broke into that ever-present grin. Walt and I chatted with him as we waited for his luggage that never came. I watched my thoughts and saw the patterns of my anxiety-ridden past surface when the luggage carousel came to a halt with a few pieces of luggage that were not his. Since there seemed to always be some difficult problems to solve concerning Devon, my mind quickly reverted to dread, "Oh, no. Not more drama."

An hour later, after filling out the missing-luggage forms, we were on the crowded 405 Freeway headed home. The Art Kelly birthday song, "Step in the Name of Love," came on the radio. We had heard it on the car radio the last time Walt and I had visited Devon in Texas. It was the beginning of Devon's change for the better then. Because he finally began to cooperate with the staff at Devereux he had earned the privilege for the first time in two years of going off the Devereux premises. I remember that when that song came on the radio, all three of us had sung it loudly as we traveled to a restaurant, thrilled that Devon was free for a few hours. That song was a brief but profound bonding experience for our family. For Devon, who suffered a reactive attachment disorder, any type of bonding was nothing short of a miracle.

"I know it's somebody's birthday tonight… somewhere," I sang the song's lyric to Devon as he grinned and sang softly along, too. "And I know somebody's gonna celebrate tonight... somewhere." Music had always been Devon's comforter and our connection. On this night it was expressing our joy, our celebration of Devon's birthday and his return home.

Our Higher Power has a way of giving us exactly what is right for us. Devon wouldn't be getting into transitional housing at that time. He was coming home to live with us. We were forced to bond with Devon.

Over the next days I saw the three-year-old we fell in love with 15 years ago. I saw the special person that we knew Devon would turn out to be and the reason why we had never stopped loving him throughout our most difficult years with him. I saw the reason why we called him our son. We had missed that bonding with Devon as a child, but now at 18, we knew we were finding that love.

"Mom, I want to show you something,"

Devon was unpacking, and I was standing in the doorway. He handed me a double picture frame. In it was the family portrait we had taken before he entered into residential treatment and a picture of each member of our family he had cut out and placed in the frame he had bought. "This was my motivation to get back home." An ocean of tears and emotions welled up inside of me.

"You know, Mom, I was wondering what you would think if I changed my name," he said. I looked up from the picture with surprise.

"Why? I love your name."

"Yeah, but Devon was the person who was always in trouble."

"You don't want to lose sight of that, Devon. He's who you are, and he's always a reminder of how far you've come and what an incredible accomplishment you achieved, turning your life around. You have gone through things that most people won't go through in a lifetime, and you changed. That's an inspiration for others." I was thinking how he had helped me to grow closer to my Higher Power, and I smiled at him. "That Devon did things out of survival from a difficult past. He wasn't bad, just different." Devon smiled back and nodded his head. The subject never came up again.

In the days following his return home, Devon did everything he could to please us. It was as if he tried to make up for all of the misery he had caused us in the past. When he was little and got in trouble, I had put him to work around the house, weeding the backyard, and mopping the floors. Now, he voluntarily started doing these things. He always had a knack for fixing things and he was happy to do so around the house. The battles with my pain and fears were slowly being relieved with a deepening love as I watched the new Devon in action.

On the last weekend of the Los Angeles County Fair, Devon and I attended alone, since no one else in the family wanted to go. I loved these County fairs as a child, and this one was the largest in the nation. True to his new behavior, Devon was more than happy to go with me.

We walked around the crowded fairgrounds, inhaling the aromas of fresh popcorn and grilled hotdogs, on that warm summer evening. Devon put his arm around my shoulders as he had done a few times in public since he had returned home. I knew that it was one of his ways of bonding. I wondered if he was embarrassed, seeing so many young people his age at the fair out with their dates. They obviously could see he was with his mother. He told me that he couldn't care less and continued walking with his arm around my shoulder, seemingly oblivious to everyone but me.

I remembered something about when we adopted him at age three; he did not want me to put him down. I realized that Devon's wanting to hold on to me at the fair was his way of reattaching. It was the lost connection he was deprived of as a child that caused reactive attachment disorder, and it was this touch he was deprived of during three years away from his family. It was the touch that was healing us both.

I convinced a leery Devon to ride the fair's main attraction, a giant Ferris wheel, one of the largest in the country. Against his wishes, wanting to please me, he agreed. It was the biggest Ferris wheel I had ever seen and the first time Devon had been on one. He had always opted for the fast rides when I took him to amusement parks.

I will never forget how smooth and quiet the ride was, in slow revolutions, steadily slicing through the warm summer night. It was indicative of how our relationship had become. Easy. Devon had his arm around my shoulder again, and we giggled, marveling at how high up we were. The view was spectacular. The noise from the thousands of people at the fair below us was muted. It was a mystical moment that I imagine astronauts feel in space. Everything seemed so far away.

When our ride came to the end, the Ferris wheel stopped, and we were suspended at the very top as the operator freed people from the seats below us. Playfully I rocked back and forth, shaking our bucket. "Mom!" Devon shrieked, his eyes wide, gripping the sides. "Please, Mom, please don't." He laughed nervously, looking anxiously below at the specks of people. I couldn't stop giggling, then he joined in merriment, too.

Then came surreal moments as he talked in hushed tones about how happy he was to be home and how residential treatment had saved his life. Sitting up there, gently swaying aloft, we both truly felt that we were on top of the world.

It was if we were transcending all of our worries, and our troubled past now seemed so far beneath us.

EPILOGUE

Devon hopes his story will bring awareness to Reactive Attachment Disorder.

There is no poster child, or telethon for RAD.

Janet and Walter, married 26 years, facilitate workshops for their company, Self Awareness Trainings and are strong child advocates.

Ryan attends the University of Southern California, and Jada, San Francisco State University.

Devon attends Los Angeles Valley College. He plans to become a mental health technician working in a residential treatment program for adolescents.

ABOUT THE AUTHOR

 Janet Alston Jackson, csl, facilitates "effective communications" and "stress management" workshops with her husband Walter Jackson (author of "Sporting the Right Attitude") for their company Self Awareness Trainings. Frequent guests on radio talk shows, the couple lectures to a variety of audiences; including corporate executives, parents, teachers, women in recovery, prison personnel, health care workers, and entertainment industry executives.

Communications has always been Janet's deep love. She was a publicist for CBS and ABC Television Networks, and a Court Appointed Special Advocate for children.

Janet lives in Los Angeles, CA. with her family.

For specific information on having Janet speak to your group, or for information on Janet and Walter's workshops, contact us at:

Self Awareness Trainings
P.O. Box 3414
Granada Hills, California 91394

www.selfawarenesstrainings
www.janetajackson.com

toll free (877) 796-8288
info@selfawarenesstrainings.com

~

WALTER H. JACKSON, csl, and **JANET ALSTON JACKSON, csl,** are a unique husband-and-wife training team. The couple is well known for their fun, high-energy motivating styles that have propelled even the most seasoned workshop veterans to discover new ways to capitalize on their strengths.

Their powerful and humorous personal stories, and proven techniques, create a safe forum for individuals to better relate their behaviors to their thoughts and feelings. The Jacksons have been a guest on radio talk shows around the country.

~

Workshops for groups and organizations

For Parents, Adoptive Parents, Foster Care Parents:
"How to Effectively Communicate to Advocate for Your Child"

For Child Welfare, Mental Health Professionals and Teachers
*"Effectively Communicating with
Children's Parents and Caretakers"*

Quick Order Form

Please send me _____ copies of "A Cry for Light: A Journey into Love" at $13.95 each, plus shipping and handling, as itemized below.

Name: _____
      (first name)   (last name)

Address _____
      (number)   (street name)   (apt/Suite No.)

_____
      (City)   (state/Province   (Zip/Postal Code)

Phone Number: _____

E-Mail: _____

Amount Due_____copies @ US $13.95 each _____

(California residents) sales tax 8.25% _____

+ shipping/handling   = _____

Shipping: 1 copy = $2.50, $2 = $4.00,
3 = $4.50, 4 = $5.00, 5 = $5.50, 6 = $5.75

TOTAL AMOUNT DUE = US $ _____

Payment: Check_____   Money Order_____

Send completed form to:
Self Awareness Trainings
P.O. Box 3414
Granada Hills, California 91394

For Quotes on Larger Quantities, phone or email:
info@selfawarenesstrainings.com
Toll free: (877) 796-8288